T0340336

The Second Bank of the United States

The year 2016 marks the 200th anniversary of the founding of the Second Bank of the United States (1816–1836). This book is an economic history of that early central bank. After US President Andrew Jackson vetoed the rechartering of the Bank in 1832, the United States would go without a central bank for the rest of the nineteenth century, unlike Europe and England. This book takes a fresh look at the role and legacy of the Second Bank.

The Second Bank of the United States shows how the Bank developed a business model that allowed it to make a competitive profit while providing integrating fiscal services to the national government for free. The model revolved around the strategic use of its unique ability to establish a nationwide system of branches. This book shows how the Bank used its branch network to establish dominance in select money markets: frontier money markets and markets for bills of exchange and specie. These lines of business created synergies with the Bank's fiscal duties, and profits that helped cover their costs. The Bank's branch in New Orleans, Louisiana, became its geographic center of gravity, in contrast with the state-chartered banking system, which was already, by the 1820s, centered around New York.

This book is of great interest to those who study banking and American history, as well as economics students who have a great interest in economic history.

Jane Ellen Knodell is Mark J. Zwynenburg Green and Gold Professor of Financial History at the University of Vermont, USA. Her research and teaching interests are in the fields of money and banking, macroeconomics, and economic history.

Routledge explorations in economic history
Edited by Lars Magnusson
Uppsala University, Sweden

For a full list of titles in this series, please visit www.routledge.com/series/SE0347.

70. **The History of Migration in Europe**
    Perspectives from economics, politics and sociology
    Edited by Francesca Fauri

71. **Famines in European Economic History**
    The last great European famines reconsidered
    Edited by Declan Curran, Lubomyr Luciuk and Andrew Newby

72. **Natural Resources and Economic Growth**
    Learning from History
    Edited by Marc Badia-Miró, Vicente Pinilla and Henry Willebald

73. **The Political Economy of Mercantilism**
    Lars Magnusson

74. **Innovation and Technological Diffusion**
    An Economic History of Early Steam Engines
    Harry Kitsikopoulos

75. **Regulating Competition**
    Cartel Registers in the Twentieth Century World
    Edited by Susanna Fellman and Martin Shanahan

76. **European Banks and the Rise of International Finance**
    The Post-Bretton Woods Era
    Carlo Edoardo Altamura

77. **The Second Bank of the United States**
    "Central" banker in an era of nation-building, 1816–1836
    Jane Ellen Knodell

The Second Bank of the United States

"Central" banker in an era of nation-building, 1816–1836

Jane Ellen Knodell

Routledge
Taylor & Francis Group

LONDON AND NEW YORK

First published 2017 by Routledge

2 Park Square, Milton Park, Abingdon, Oxfordshire OX14 4RN
52 Vanderbilt Avenue, New York, NY 10017

Routledge is an imprint of the Taylor & Francis Group, an informa business

First issued in paperback 2019

British Library Cataloguing in Publication Data
A catalogue record for this book is available from the British Library

Library of Congress Cataloging in Publication Data
    Names: Knodell, Jane Ellen, author.
    Title: The Second Bank of the United States / Jane Ellen Knodell.
    Description: 1 Edition. | New York : Routledge, 2017.
    Identifiers: LCCN 2016015490| ISBN 9781138786622 (hardback) |
    ISBN 9781315767215 (ebook)
    Subjects: LCSH: Bank of the United States (1816-1836) | Banks and
    banking--United States--History--19th century.
    Classification: LCC HG2525 .K656 2017 | DDC
    332.1/1097309034--dc23
    LC record available at https://lccn.loc.gov/2016015490

ISBN: 978-1-138-78662-2 (hbk)
ISBN: 978-0-367-87022-5 (pbk)

Typeset in Times New Roman
by Sunrise Setting Ltd, Brixham, UK

To my parents, Diet and Ellen, for stressing the importance of education, erudition, and emoluments.

Contents

List of figures viii
List of maps ix
List of tables x
Acknowledgments xii
Note on primary sources xiii

1 Introduction 1

2 Origin and purposes of the Second Bank 6

3 The Second Bank's branch network and the state banking system 28

4 The Second Bank and the "exchanges": conquering space 69

5 The "production" of monetary stability 99

6 The Second Bank's specie market operations 138

7 Conclusion 156

Appendices 161
References 181
Index 186

Figures

3.1	State bank density and Second Bank density across states, 1820	45
3.2	State bank density and Second Bank density across states, 1830	46
4.1	Second Bank portfolio shifts, 1820–1833	77
4.2	Intercity cost of funds and intercity travel time, 1830	78
4.3	Scale economies at Second Bank branches, 1833	80
4.4	Changes in scale and operating efficiency at Second Bank branches, 1818–1833	81
4.5a	Intercity cost of funds (1830) and intercity trade flows (1840)	82
4.5b	Intercity cost of funds and intercity bill volume, 1830	83
4.6	Bank of the United States' remittances and sterling exchange rates, July 1831 to March 1832	87
5.1	Interbank claims held by state banks and the Second Bank as a share of bank money issued, 1820–1832	108
5.2a	Second Bank and state banks' reserve ratios, 1820–1832	113
5.2b	Merchandise import cycle and the Second Bank's reserve ratio, 1822–1832	114
5.3a	Changes in specie holdings of the Second Bank in relation to specie imports, 1821–1832	115
5.3b	Changes in specie holdings of the state banks in relation to specie imports, 1821–1832	116
5.4	Sterling exchange rates and the silver export point in the United States, 1823–1832	116
6.1	Monthly bid-ask spread on Spanish silver coin purchased and sold by the Second Bank	143
6.2	Second Bank silver coin purchases and premia paid (indexed to average for 1825–1829)	144
6.3	Second Bank silver sold and premia received (indexed to average for 1824–1829)	145
6.4a	Gold purchases and premia paid, July 1828 to December 1831	145
6.4b	Silver purchases and premia paid, January 1825 to May 1829	146

Maps

3.1a   The Second Bank's branch network, 1820   35
3.1b   The Second Bank's branch network and major
       US rivers, 1820   36
3.2a   The Second Bank's branch network, 1830   37
3.2b   The Second Bank's branch network and major
       US rivers, 1830   38
3.3   Regions of the United States   39
3.4a   State bank and Second Bank offices in
       New England, 1820   47
3.4b   State bank and Second Bank offices in
       New England, 1830   48
3.5a   State bank and Second Bank offices in the
       Middle Atlantic, 1820   49
3.5b   State bank and Second Bank offices in the
       Middle Atlantic, 1830   50
3.6a   State bank and Second Bank offices in the
       Southeast, 1820   51
3.6b   State bank and Second Bank offices in the
       Southeast, 1830   52
3.7a   State bank and Second Bank offices in the
       Southwest, 1820   54
3.7b   State bank and Second Bank offices in the
       Southwest, 1830   55
3.8a   State bank and Second Bank offices in the
       Northwest, 1820   56
3.8b   State bank and Second Bank offices in the
       Northwest, 1830   57
3.9   The Mechanics' Bank's network of banks, 1833   63
5.1   Number of state banks that treated Second Bank
       notes as specie funds in US cities and
       towns, 1828–1835   102

Tables

2.1	Shifting structure of federal receipts and outlays before and after the War of 1812	16
3.1	Number of state and federal (Second Bank) banking offices by state, 1820 (a) and 1830 (b)	40
3.2	Changes in number of state bank and Second Bank offices by region, 1820–1830	42
3.3	State bank chartering rates by region and decades, 1810–1836	43
3.4	Population shares and banking-office shares, by region, 1820 and 1830	43
3.5	State, federal, and overall bank density by region, 1820 and 1830	44
3.6	Second Bank market share of all banks and all banks in cities, by region, 1820 and 1830	53
3.7	Number of state banking offices in cities with a Second Bank branch, 1820 and 1830	58
3.8	Proximity analysis	59
3.9	Geographic distribution of state banks and Second Bank specie, 1820 and 1830	59
3.10	Banknote discount rates by region, 1818–1833	60
4.1	Second Bank's return on equity, 1820–1833	75
4.2	Second Bank's return on earning assets, 1820–1833	76
4.3	Informational distance and Second Bank spreads on domestic exchange	79
4.4	Profitability of Second Bank branches, by region, January to June 1833	80
5.1	Treatment of Second Bank notes on state-bank balance sheets, 1828–1835	101
5.2	Composition of the stock of money held by the non-bank public, 1820–1831	125
5.3	Change in commercial banking capacity, 1820–1830	128
5.4	Change in paid-in state bank capital (K) per capita, by region, 1820–1830	128

5.5 Changes in monetary aggregates per capita ($), 1820–1830   129
5.6 Changes in leverage and liquidity in the commercial
     banking system, 1820–1830   129
5.7 Second Bank and state banks' consolidated
     balance sheets, 1820 and 1830   130
6.1 Sales and purchases of silver and gold coin and bullion
     by the Second Bank, January 1820 to November 1831   141
6.2 Size of Second Bank specie sales by type of coin ($),
     1820–1831   142
A.1 City database, 1820   161
A.2 City database, 1830   163
B.1 Differences in banking-office headcount between Knodell's
     Master list and Census in Weber (2006)   168
C.1 Bank density by region, 1820   170
C.2 Bank density by region, 1830   172
D.1 Intercity cost of funds at the Second Bank, 1830   175
E.1 Banking aggregates, 1820–1832 ($m)   176
F.1 Sources for banking aggregates   178

Acknowledgments

I would like to acknowledge persons and institutions that have helped me with this project.

First, I thank all of my colleagues in the field of economic history who have shown interest in my work over the years and encouraged me to write this book. I would like to specifically acknowledge John James, David Weiman, Carol Heim, and Richard Sylla. We lost John James too soon and too suddenly, and I regret that this book was not completed in time to talk with John about the book and to try to answer his insightful questions.

I also thank University of Vermont student Jack Kilbride. Jack made the maps in this book and conducted the proximity analysis reported in Table 3.8. Former Arts and Sciences Dean Antonio Cepeda-Benito funded an innovative initiative in spatial analysis at the University of Vermont that helped pay for my research assistant. The University of Vermont provided travel funds that defrayed the expense of travel to archives in Baltimore, Washington, DC, and Philadelphia, for which I am grateful.

I would like to acknowledge Cambridge University Press for allowing publication of the material in Chapter 4 which draws from Knodell, J (2003), "Profit and duty in the Second Bank of the United States' exchange operations," *Financial History Review*, vol. 10, pp. 5–30. The National Historical Geographic Information System provided state boundary information for the maps in this book.

I benefited from expert and friendly assistance from librarians at several libraries and historical societies: the Maryland Historical Society, the Pennsylvania Historical Society, the Library Company of Philadelphia, the Library of Congress, the American Philosophical Society, and the University of Vermont.

Finally, I extend sincere thanks in retrospect to Prof. Emeritus Paul Evans, for helping me understand what high-powered money is, and to Prof. Emeritus Tim Bates, who hired me at the University of Vermont so many years ago and who continues his stewardship of financial history at the University through raising funds for the Mark J. Zwynenburg Green and Gold Professorship of Financial History. Special recognition goes to my husband, Ted Wimpey, who helped keep me going, in so many ways.

Note on primary sources

This note lists all primary sources cited in this book, their location, and the citation methods used for each. The first six collections listed have been little used, or not used at all, in previous work on the Second Bank.

1. John Campbell White Papers, located at the Maryland Historical Society. John Campbell White was the Cashier of the Baltimore branch of the Second Bank between 1821 and 1836. The material is organized by box and contains correspondence and some bank records. Letters are identified by box number, date, and persons sending and receiving the letter.

2. William Jones Papers, located at the Pennsylvania Historical Society. William Jones was the first President of the Bank (1817–1819). The material consists mainly of incoming correspondence. Letters are identified by box number, date, and persons sending and receiving the letter.

3. McAllister Collection, located at the Library Company of Philadelphia. This Collection includes a group of documents which were reorganized in 2005 under the title *Bank of the United States Records* (McA MSS 012). All documents used in this book are from Series II of this collection, Second Bank, Philadelphia: Correspondence, 1816–1842. The records are almost all incoming correspondence. Documents are identified by Box number, folder number, date of document, and, if a letter, persons sending and receiving the letter.

4. Records of the Baltimore branch of the Bank of the United States, located at the Library of Congress. These records consist primarily of legal documents and incoming correspondence. Documents are identified by box number, date of document, and, if a letter, persons sending and receiving the letter.

5. Kelsey Burr Papers, located at the Library of Congress. Documents are identified by box number, date of document, and, if a letter, persons sending and receiving the letter.

6. Girard Papers, located at the American Philosophical Society. Documents and records are identified by reel number.

7. Biddle Papers, located at the Library of Congress. The outgoing correspondence of Nicholas Biddle. Letters are identified by date and recipient.

8. Congressional documents, available in the Serial Set. Documents are identified by session, whether a product of the US House or the US Senate, and document number.

1   Introduction

Central banks are widely credited with effectively managing the global financial crisis of 2007–2008 by developing new lender of last resort programs. The expansion of the social safety net to encompass almost every type of financial intermediary has brought renewed scrutiny to the role of central banks and, in some corners, worry about their solvency. After many decades of quiet consensus, central banking is once again a political issue, as it was 200 years ago, when the federal government chartered the Second Bank of the United States.[1]

The Second Bank was the subject of one of the biggest political fights in US history, one which ended badly for the Bank with President Jackson's veto of the bill to renew its charter. The Bank and the "Bank War" are two of the most heavily researched topics in economic history, much of it centering on the economic consequences of Jackson's veto. The Bank was heavily outnumbered by the 260 state-chartered banks in operation by 1820. But it had powerful competitive advantages conferred by its charter: it was the only federally chartered bank, and the sole fiscal agent for the federal government; it was by far the largest bank in the country in terms of both assets and capitalization; and it was the only bank in the country that was able to establish a nationwide system of branches. The Bank struggled in its early years, but became sound and profitable under its third and final president, Nicholas Biddle, who took office in 1823.

It has been over fifty years since the last significant book about the Bank, but economic historians are still writing about the Bank, trying to figure out whether it was a central bank in the modern sense. In much of this literature, the Second Bank is seen through the lens of the modern Federal Reserve, an institution with which US economic historians are very familiar and which, with its district banks, is seemingly so similar to the Second Bank. A central issue in the economic history literature on the Bank is whether the Bank met the "lender of last resort" benchmark, particularly with regards to its behavior during the monetary crisis of 1825–1826. This book enters the central-banker debate in the literature and also seeks to move beyond it.

Catterall published his comprehensive history of the Bank in 1902, five years before the Panic of 1907, the last in a series of banking crises leading up to the creation of the Federal Reserve in 1913. Catterall gave the Bank high marks for providing a sound national currency and stabilizing the economy during banking crises. During 1825–1826, the Bank was "appropriately conservative" at first, and then "at the moment aid was needed the BUS [Bank of the United States] was able to render it." Catterall charged that

> Jackson and his supporters committed an offense against the nation when they destroyed the bank. . . . It was the overthrow of a machine capable of incalculable service to this country—a service which can be rendered by no bank not similarly organized. Would it not be better for the nation if it could command that service today?[2]

Little was published about the Bank during the decades of the 1920s, Great Depression, or Second World War. In the postwar decades of the 1950s and 1960s, a flurry of books, articles, and theses were written about the Second Bank. By this time, the Federal Reserve had won its independence from the US Treasury and was becoming proficient at stabilizing cyclical fluctuations. Three authors from this period, Redlich (1951), Smith (1953), and Hammond (1957), were more or less convinced that the Second Bank was a central bank. Hammond, the least ambiguous of the three, concluded that the Bank performed a "rounded and complete central banking function" after 1823 (when Biddle was installed as President), acting as a "balance wheel" of the banking system, governing the exchanges, restraining the growth of bank credit, and protecting the money market from disturbances. Hammond thought that the Second Bank's central-banking performance in the 1820s was better than that of the Federal Reserve in the 1930s (which was not very good at all).[3]

Redlich was similarly bullish on the Bank, but more nuanced in his analysis. Redlich called Biddle "perhaps the world's very first conscious central banker," assessed against contemporary thinking about what central banks should do. Redlich saw the Second Bank as a "controlling bank within a system of banks" and, in the end, concluded that Biddle controlled the state-chartered banks more than he assisted them. Yet, Redlich said, Biddle did feel responsible for the health of the national economy and sacrificed Bank profits for national economic stability: "for some critical weeks in 1825 Biddle acted as the lender of last resort, thereby fulfilling a true central banking function."[4] Smith was also somewhat mixed in his assessment of the Bank, concluding that Biddle had the right ideas, but "the activities of the Bank, viewed in their entirety, did not live up to Biddle's version of this conceived policy" in 1825–1826. Smith criticized Biddle for later taking credit for easing the money market by increasing the Bank's discounts, since the Bank was selling securities at the same time, offsetting the expansionary effect of the increase in discounts. Both Redlich and Smith claimed that the Bank lent to state banks in times of crisis, but provided no documented examples.[5]

Three other authors from the golden years of the postwar period were not convinced that the Bank was a central bank. Meerman (1961) concluded that Biddle developed "a theory and practice of central banking well adapted to the US during the first half of the nineteenth century." Ultimately, though, it was the specie standard that regulated money; the Bank just provided time for the banking system to adjust to balance of payments deficits. In 1825–1826, Meerman said, the Bank was relatively skillful in managing credit conditions in New York, but not as a lender of last resort.[6] Timberlake (1961, 1978) agreed with Meerman that the Second Bank was more of a "shock absorber" than a "balance wheel," and that at times it did the opposite of what a central bank would do. Timberlake, like many contemporaries of the Second Bank, had constitutional problems with its chartering. It was not created to be a central bank, just a public bank (that is, the central government's bank) and a commercial bank. But "one would have to be either obtuse or modest in the assumption of power not to recognize and cultivate the central-banking potential of such an institution, even if such power was ultimately subordinate to the discipline of a specie standard."[7] Biddle was not one to be modest in the assumption of power.

Peter Temin (1969) continued the themes of Meerman and Timberlake in his book on the Jacksonian economy. Temin disagreed sharply with the central-bank thesis, arguing that the Second Bank did not assist the state banks in 1825, but that it did what it had to do to keep the Bank in a position of strength and safety. Van Fenstermaker (1965) agreed: the Bank put its own liquidity first in 1825 and was a "controlling" bank, but not a "central" bank. Highfield et al. (1991, pp. 317–18) analyzed the Bank's behavior in short-run monetary fluctuations using time-series econometric analysis, and concluded that the Bank provided "stability to the financial system through its consistently conservative policies," but that it did not exhibit:

> the central bank behavior claimed by its supporters. . . . the animosity directed at the Bank arose not so much because of what the Bank did but because of what its behavior precluded its competitors from doing. By acting as a check on the expansiveness of the financial system, the Second Bank provided perhaps the most important central banking function.

Jumping forward to the twenty-first century, the literature has come full circle. Recent contributions have returned to the view that the Bank was a central bank. According to Bordo (2012, p. 598), under Biddle, the Bank "had developed into a first rate central bank. . . . stabilizing exchange rates, . . . smoothing seasonal and cyclical shocks and acting as a lender of last resort to the banking system." Bordo cited as evidence Redlich's report that Biddle had read Thornton's essay on central banking, so he knew what to do and how to do it.[8] Officer (2002) drew the closest analogy of all between the Second Bank and the Federal Reserve, going so far as to include the notes and deposits issued by the Second Bank in the monetary base in one version of his model of long-run monetary growth.[9]

This book presents a variety of evidence showing that the Bank fell short of the (modern) central-banker test. The Bank was not chartered to fill the need for a lender of last resort, did not behave like a lender of last resort during monetary crises or in selecting branch locations, and its management was philosophically opposed to the idea of a lender of last resort. Neither did the Bank see its function as providing other kinds of services for the state-chartered banking system.

If not a central bank in the modern sense, was the Second Bank, as Dewey (1910a, p. 148) concluded, "nothing more or less than a large commercial bank with practically the same functions as other banks established under state charters, and differed from them little save size and enjoyment of a few special privileges"? The answer offered here is no, the Second Bank was not just another commercial bank, only bigger. The monetary services that its charter required it to provide to the federal government made it qualitatively different from other commercial banks.

This book seeks to understand the Second Bank's role in the national economy and its business model in the context of early nineteenth-century US political economy. Balogh (2009) and other contributors to the "new institutionalist" US history literature provide insight into the challenges facing the federal government when it chartered the Bank in 1816. In the aftermath of the War of 1812, national

> Republican leaders like Jefferson and Madison [were alerted] to the need for organization and infrastructure that could only be provided by a more assertive General Government. . . . they advocated a far-reaching program of military preparedness that included annual funding for coastal and frontier defense, a peacetime army, an expanded navy, and greater control over state militias.[10]

The United States was a young nation with a greatly enlarged territory, but the loyalties of the western populace still in question and its finances and accounts in disarray. The country needed an institution to integrate the west into national commodity markets and to knit together the central government's geographically expanding fiscal affairs. As this book will show, the Second Bank fit the bill. It helped "conquer space," in the words of US Senator, War Secretary, and Second Bank advocate John Calhoun, for two major clients with operations that spanned long distances: the US government and merchants involved in interregional and international trade.

This historically grounded perspective on the Bank calls for spatial analysis. Space mattered in the early nineteenth-century United States: given the state of the country's transportation infrastructure, it was costly, and took time, to move people, commodities, and money around the country, especially between interior regions and the eastern seaboard. In such an environment, the Bank's national branch network gave it a distinct advantage. The Bank's branch network has received relatively little attention in the literature. In this book, the branch network takes center stage: where the Bank located branches, and why; how the head office at Philadelphia managed the branch network; how financial assets circulated between branches; which branches were strategically vital to the Bank's success, and why.

The literature tends to rely, perhaps more than it should, on Nicholas Biddle's public statements for evidence on the Bank's operations. During the Bank War, Biddle was campaigning for the Bank's recharter in his public testimony, seeking to create a positive image for the Bank. This book considers Biddle's correspondence in the Biddle Papers with the cashiers and presidents of the branches as a more reliable guide to the operations of the Bank than Biddle's testimony before

Congressional committees. The book uses the Biddle Papers, as others have done, and also brings new archival evidence to its project, including two collections relating to the Baltimore branch of the Second Bank. Other collections supplement the Biddle Papers with other correspondence between Philadelphia, the head office, and the branches, both outgoing (as with the Biddle Papers) and incoming.

The book's major findings fall into five broad areas: why the Bank was chartered; the factors driving the design of the Bank's branch network; the Bank's role as the central manager of the domestic and foreign exchanges; the Bank's role in monetary stabilization; and the Bank's operations as a dealer in specie markets. In all of these areas, the model of a twentieth-century central bank is shown to be a poor fit for the Second Bank. Rather, the Second Bank was organized, and organized itself, to earn a competitive profit while meeting the public needs of the 1820s: to put the fiscal affairs of the US government on strong monetary footing and to economically integrate the New West into the national economy. Monetary stability, the key mission of modern central banks, was simply a by-product of the Bank's pursuit of duty and profit.

Notes

1 Contemporaries referred to this bank as the Bank of the United States, but it has come to be known as the Second Bank of the United States to differentiate it from its predecessor, also named the Bank of the United States (1791–1811) and now known as the First Bank of the United States. In this book, the terms "the Second Bank" and "the Bank" are used to refer to the Second Bank of the United States.
2 Catterall (1902, pp. 106–7, 476).
3 Hammond (1957, pp. 323, 324, 285).
4 Redlich (1968, pp. 96, 97, 128, 136).
5 Smith (1953, p. 140). Smith believed that Biddle did not tell the whole story in such statements as the following about the Fall of 1825: "I was perfectly satisfied that there was a tremendous squall coming, that there was a scarcity and a dread which unless immediately quieted, would grow into a panic and get beyond our control. . . . the Bank immediately and in the face of the public alarm, increased its discounts, and by this measure averted the greatest disaster."
6 Meerman (1961, p. 30).
7 Timberlake (1978, pp. 30, 32, 38).
8 In fairness, Bordo's objective in this paper was not to explicate what the Bank did, but to speculate on what the Bank would have done if it had continued to operate. This book agrees that the Bank performed all of the stabilization functions listed by Bordo—except lender of last resort.
9 Officer (2002, pp. 116, 119). Just to show how muddy these waters can become, Officer also acknowledged that the Second Bank "did not generally behave as [a lender] of last resort."
10 Balogh (2009, p. 202).

2 Origin and purposes of the Second Bank

In his monograph on the Second Bank, written for the National Monetary Commission in 1910, Dewey (1910a) observed that

> the circumstances which gave rise to the establishment of the Second Bank were altogether different from those which have brought about a discussion of the question of a central bank at the present juncture; . . . . It is difficult, therefore, to find in the experience of this institution, any lessons of importance which may be of special service in the preparation of a plan for a large national central bank at a later period, when business methods have been transformed by the railroad, the telegraph, and by the development of corporate enterprise, to say nothing of the change in banking law through the general substitution of national supervision for state control.

Dewey was right. The challenges that gave rise to the establishment of the Second Bank in 1817 were rooted in the decentralized, disorganized state banking system, postwar public finance problems, and the vast, distant territory under the jurisdiction of the US government. The geographic dispersion of federal authority led US Senator John Calhoun to call on Congress to "bind the Republic together with a perfect system of roads and canals. Let us conquer space."[1] The Second Bank was part and parcel of this federal government project. Concerns about the constitutionality of a federal bank were set aside in order to provide a uniform currency and stronger fiscal controls for the national government's accounts.

State banking and postwar public finance problems

The federal government had a challenging set of fiscal and monetary problems to address in the immediate postwar period. From 1812 to 1815, the government spent roughly $120 m, but collected only $50 m in receipts. Going into the war, customs duties made up over 90 percent of federal revenues. Under the Jefferson administration (1801–1809), the collection of excise and direct taxes was suspended on the grounds that these taxes were burdensome and that their reduction would prevent the development of an oversized central state.[2] As a result, the government was unprepared to collect other kinds of taxes to pay for the war when customs duties fell off by $6 m and military spending increased by $8 m.

The US government financed the gap with a combination of long-term securities, bank loans, and Treasury notes. Annual debt service increased from $2.45 m in the calendar year 1812 to $7.2 m in 1816.[3] The government relied on borrowing from banks and consortia of individuals, primarily in New York and Pennsylvania. New England, where banking was most developed, opposed the war against England and provided little financing for it.[4] By the end of the war, the government increasingly relied on small-denomination Treasury notes, a form of currency finance, as debt issues were only partially subscribed and sold at deeper and deeper discounts. Outside of New England, revenue that was not collected in Treasury notes was collected in state bank currency at varying rates of discount, and the Treasury notes themselves, which functioned as money, were sold at a discount against specie and notes of New England city banks.

During the war, the fiscal operations of the US government promoted formation of a national banking system—using the state chartered banks. Banks in different states that were federal depositories received each other's notes on deposit and in repayment of loans at par. The balance sheet of one Maryland bank that committed a significant share of its portfolio to financing the war demonstrates the breadth of interbank connections fostered by federal wartime spending. By the end of December, 1813, the Commercial and Farmers Bank of Baltimore had committed almost 20 percent of its earning assets to federal debt (Treasury notes, the loan of 1812, and the loan of 1813). The deposits of federal officers in the Commercial and Farmers Bank included those of the Treasurer, the Commissioner of Loans, the Deputy Commissary, and the Army Paymaster, and exceeded individuals' deposits in the bank. Deposits of the federal government brought notes issued by banks in a wide geographic area into the bank, including banks in Philadelphia, Washington, Norfolk, rural Maryland, New York, and various northern and southern cities. Disbursements of the federal government resulted in a broad geographic circulation of the bank's notes as well. This is evidenced by the "due to" accounts the bank had with banks in New York, Philadelphia, Boston, Fredericksburg, Brownsville, and Tennessee.[5]

Mutual acceptance of bank notes within the state banking system broke down after banks outside of New England suspended specie payments in 1814.[6] Notes issued by banks outside of New England circulated at varying rates of discount from par after 1814. In November 1814, Treasury Secretary Alexander James Dallas explained to Congress that:[7]

> The . . . sudden determination of the banks of each State to refuse credit and circulation to the notes issued in other States, deprived the government, without its participation, of the only means that were possessed for transferring its funds from the places in which they lay inactive to the places in which they were wanted for the payment of the dividends on the funded debt and the discharge of treasury notes. It was the inevitable result of these transactions that the bank credits of the government should be soon exhausted in Boston,

New York, Philadelphia, etc where the principal loan-offices for the payment of the public debt were established, and that the government should be unable to satisfy its engagements in those cities, unless the public creditors would receive drafts on banks in other States, or would subscribe the amount of their claims to a public loan, or would accept a payment in treasury notes.

After the suspension of specie payments, banks took great care to differentiate between "current" money, considered a "cash" deposit, payable in cash, and money taken in as a "special deposit," which was not payable in cash. As more and more banks outside of New England "refused to credit as cash any bank notes but those which they had themselves . . . issued," the Treasury opened accounts with more and more state banks, so that it could deposit and withdraw on a cash basis. The number of depositories multiplied further to the point that, by the end of the war, the Treasury was keeping its funds in ninety-four state banks—one of every two state banking offices—each of which segregated Treasury funds into four accounts, one for each form of payment: cash or local currency, treasury notes bearing interest, small treasury notes not bearing interest, and special deposits (deposits and notes of other suspended state banks).[8]

The US government continued to act as if there was a common national currency through the end of the war. It accepted the notes of suspended banks at par in borrowing and in payment of duties and taxes, a practise that increased the specie-equivalent cost of borrowing and resulted in currency losses to the government when the notes were spent in a region with a stronger currency. For example, $1,000 collected at the Philadelphia Customs District covered only $800 of federal obligations payable in Boston. These losses were amplified as merchants diverted imported goods to the port cities where customs duties could be paid with the most depreciated bank notes.[9]

The localization of state bank currency adversely affected the public credit. In 1815, after the cessation of hostilities, Secretary Dallas gave notice that maturing Treasury notes would be paid when due in Philadelphia and Baltimore, but that, because "funds in current money cannot at present be obtained" at Boston or New York, holders of unpaid Treasury notes in the latter two cities could use them to subscribe to a new loan (at the rate of $95 of Treasury notes for $100 of the new loan), could receive drafts on Philadelphia or Boston in repayment; or they could exchange the old Treasury notes for a new issue of Treasury notes. There were adequate funds in the Treasury to repay the notes, but they were stuck in state depository institutions that did not consider it their responsibility to convert local funds into current Boston or New York funds.[10]

In February 1815, Dallas sought, but did not receive, Congressional authorization to pay a "reasonable rate of exchange upon the transfer of its revenue from the places of collection and deposit to the places of demand and employment." Instead, Congress authorized a new issuance of Treasury notes, almost half of which were issued in small denominations, conceived to function as a national circulating medium and vehicle for the collection of new and higher excise taxes on a wide range of commodities.[11] The Treasury notes were not viewed as equivalent to specie, or as the highest and best form of money in the national economy. In mid-1815, large-denomination Treasury notes, along with all non-specie-convertible paper money, were received and sold at a discount from par in Boston. Secretary Dallas was insulted that some non-specie-paying state banks were refusing "to receive, credit, re-issue, and circulate, the Treasury notes . . . in deposites [*sic*], or in payments to or from the bank, in the same manner . . . as cash, or its own bank notes," and he publicly directed the collectors and receivers of federal duties, taxes, and dues, not to receive the notes of such banks.[12]

The monetary problems of the immediate postwar period were rooted in short-term public finance problems, not a banking crisis per se—that would come four years later. In this sense, the Second Bank had more in common with the First Bank and with the Bank of England, both of which were the institutional solutions to public finance crises, than with the US Federal Reserve Bank, organized after a long series of banking crises in the late nineteenth and early twentieth centuries. Although the long-term prognosis for federal revenue growth and successful debt service was positive, the federal government was in partial default by 1815. William Gouge, contemporary financial journalist, summed it up as follows:

> Such was the state of affairs that, although there was a balance of $22 m in the Treasury, the government was compelled to borrow $500,000 . . . to pay the interest due on the public debt at Boston on the first day of January, 1817.[13]

Potential solutions to the currency problem

The chartering of a second national bank was one solution to the national government's monetary problem, but it was not the only solution. The government could have continued to issue and retire Treasury notes as it made outlays and collected taxes, as it had during the War of 1812. Regional sub-Treasuries could have managed the Treasury currency and specie issuance and holdings, and reallocated notes or specie from areas of excess supply (where spending was concentrated) to areas of excess demand (where taxes were collected). This option was ruled out. The consensus in Congress was that the federal government did not have the constitutional authority to issue currency, a problem that they were prepared to overlook in a time of war, but not in a time of peace.

In March 1815, Secretary Dallas approached twenty of the leading state-chartered banks in eastern seaboard cities (Boston, Hartford, New York, Philadelphia, Baltimore, Washington, Richmond, Charleston, Savannah, Raleigh) with a proposal under which they would, on an exclusive basis, hold the public deposits, and their notes would be receivable in all payments to the United States for revenue. The banks agreeing to the plan would "open accounts, each with the rest of them, for the purpose of accommodating the treasury in the manner hereafter stated"; they would accept each other's notes and deposits as cash; but they were not obliged to accept the notes of all banks as cash. The Treasurer would be able to transfer funds by drawing drafts in one place, on deposits in another place. In some sense, Dallas was trying to build on the interbank networks created during the war and create a national banking system, starting with the strongest state banks.[14]

This proposal was not accepted by the state banks, possibly because, as Dallas (1871) put it,

> the charter restrictions of some of the banks, the mutual relation and dependence of the banks of the same State, and even of the banks of the different States, and the duty which the directors of each bank conceive they owe to their immediate constituents upon points of security or emolument, interpose an insuperable obstacle to any voluntary arrangement upon national considerations alone for the establishment of a national medium through the agency of the State banks.

Girard's private bank, which was not closely associated with the government of Pennsylvania, also rejected Dallas's proposal, particularly the requirement that his bank

> open and keep account with the several State Banks which should accede to your plan, and also to receive their notes in payment, [which] would be extremely inconvenient to me as a private Banker whose principal object is not to involve myself.

Girard offered to handle the US government's banking needs through an association with a small group of old, established banks in Philadelphia, New York, Charleston, and Savannah, which Dallas rejected because "the plan of the Treasury must necessarily be a general one."[15]

The challenges were significant enough, and workable alternative solutions were limited enough, for a campaign to charter a second Bank of the United States to finally succeed.[16] This was a campaign waged by congressional leaders, federal government executives, and leaders of commerce. In contrast to the story of the founding of the Federal Reserve, there is no evidence that any of the more than 200 state-chartered banks lobbied Congress to charter a large national bank. On the contrary, five New York City banks presented a memorial to Congress opposing an 1814 proposal for a national bank, and stating their preference for Treasury notes over notes of a federal bank. Nor were the state legislatures clamoring for a national bank, as they were discovering the fiscal benefits of state-chartered banking.[17]

Congressional leaders who had opposed the rechartering of the First Bank, such as President James Madison and Speaker of the House Henry Clay, now saw the utility of such an institution. Leaders of commerce who were significant creditors of the federal government were also key players in the chartering of the Bank. John Jacob Astor, Stephen Girard, and David Parish had stepped forward to subscribe $9 m toward a $16 war loan in 1813; as the price of government stock fell in the following year, these individuals became very involved behind the scenes in an effort to establish a national bank (and to capitalize it at least in part with outstanding government debt, thereby increasing the value of their debt holdings).[18]

The bill to charter the Second Bank of the United States was signed into law in April 1816 after a failed attempt with a different bill in 1815. The capitalization of the Bank brought a rapid improvement in long-term debt yields and prices—an advantage to both debt holders and the government. The Bank raised $35 m in equity (350,000 $100 shares), $7 m from the US government and $28 m from private investors. The US government was to pay for its shares in either specie or new issues of 5 percent debt. Private investors could buy Second Bank shares in three instalments (30 percent of the total purchase in the first instalments, and 35 percent in the second and third). At least $25 of each share was to be paid in specie and up to $75 could be purchased with funded US debt securities. Debt was accepted at premia of 18–25 percent over market prices in payment for Bank shares, creating a strong incentive to pay for as much of stock as possible with debt. The effect on the US debt market was dramatic. Between 1816 and 1817, the total outstanding stock of funded debt remained about the same (it fell from $127 m to $123 m), but the average annual yield fell from 7.25 percent or 5.86 percent, as $21 m in funded debt, or almost 10 percent of the outstanding stock, was taken off the market and absorbed into Second Bank equity.[19]

In subscriptions to Second Bank stock, US debt was accepted at a premium over its market value, but specie was accepted at par value when it was valued at premia of 16–18.5, reducing the incentive to pay with specie . This problem was solved in the second and third instalments, when Second Bank notes and checks, and those of specie-paying state banks, were considered equivalent to specie. This was viewed critically by some, including the authors of a Congressional Committee to inspect the Bank, but was certainly welcomed by the state banks, since much of the specie that would have been paid into the Bank would have come from their vaults.[20]

The Bank was established to do what the state banks had opted not to do. Under the Bank's charter, it was required to

> give the necessary facilities for transferring the public funds from place to place, within the United States, or the Territories thereof, and for distributing the same in payment of the public creditors, without charging commissions or claiming allowance on account of difference in exchange.[21]

The Bank was also to take on loan office duties in all states where it had branches, which included the semi-annual payment of pensions.

Congress did not direct the Bank, through its charter, to provide liquidity assistance to commercial banks; nor did it require the Bank to provide a uniform currency for all households and businesses in the monetized economy—only for itself. A uniform currency for the national government was essential for two reasons. As Albert Gallatin, Treasury Secretary to Presidents Jefferson and Madison, and later New York City banker, noted in the context of the debate over the rechartering of the Second Bank, a variously depreciated paper currency violated the constitutional requirement of uniformity of federal duties and taxes.[22] Secondly, currency losses on interstate transfers weakened the fiscal condition of the US government. The Second Bank was given the authority to establish branches any-where "within the United States, or the Territories thereof," so that revenue earned anywhere in the area under control of the United States could be effectively spent anywhere else in that geographic area—and beyond, to financial capitals across the Atlantic Ocean—with no currency losses.

Postwar reforms in public administration and the Second Bank

In 1816, between the depreciation of the state bank currency in which duties were collected and the unsettled accounts of federal officers, it was difficult, if not impossible, to discern the fiscal health of the nation from the account books of the federal government. The year after it chartered the Second Bank, the federal government adopted administrative reforms to bring better management and oversight of spending to the two large disbursing departments, the War and Navy Departments. Alongside these administrative reforms, and supporting them, the government used the fiscal services of the Bank to improve the quality and time-liness of budget information available to the top of the federal bureaucracy. John Calhoun, Secretary of War (1817–1827), and William Crawford, Secretary of War (1815–1816), and Secretary of the Treasury (1816–1825), and William Jones, Secretary of the Navy (1813–1815), Acting Secretary of the Treasury (1813–1814), and President of the Second Bank (1816–1818), were actively involved in shaping the relationship between the Bank and the federal government bureau-cracy in its early years and beyond.

The sheer volume of government spending managed by the War and Navy Departments, and central government generally, had increased significantly during the War of 1812. Annual spending in the War and Navy Departments averaged $1.6 m in 1801–1811, and increased to a peak of $20 m in the War Department and $9 m in the Navy during the war.[23] The central bureaucracy failed to adapt its staff-ing or procedures to the larger volume of work and continued to use inefficient, duplicative, and time-consuming administrative procedures for settling balances with disbursing and collecting officers, and for collecting unpaid balances. An accountant in the War Department wrote to the Secretary of War in January 1814 in response to the Secretary's request for a statement of unsettled accounts, saying that more time was needed to complete the task, and pointing out that

> where the expenditures of the Department exceed so far in amount those of ordinary years, the business of accounts must necessarily increase in a corre-spondent degree, even if the system according to which the business is trans-acted were as well calculated for the one as the other. This I cannot avoid stating is not the case.[24]

The unsettled accounts were concentrated in the War and Navy Departments, which is where much of the federal spending on goods and services, as distinct from outlays in the form of transfer payments (interest payments and pensions), took place.[25] These departments had their own auditors and comptrollers, in addition to those in the Treasury Department. Disbursing officers submitted their spending reports, with documentation, to the auditor, who examined each expenditure. Then virtually the same work was done by the comptroller, who determined what was owed to or by the disbursing officer. The result of this work was sent to the accountants in the Treasury Department for further review and validation. The collection of accounts from disbursing or collecting officers that remained unpaid, once the accounting was settled, could only be done by bringing lawsuit against the officer, a prolonged process that delayed final settlement even further.[26]

The administrative reforms adopted by Congress in 1817 addressed both contracting authority and oversight over spending. Under the previous, highly decentralized system, the Army contracted with a number of civilian agents at military posts to procure a wide range of supplies. In the estimation of one military historian, the supply system "was in the hands of private contractors . . . . There was no unity of administration and no uniform system of discipline."[27] In the War and Navy Departments, administrative reform brought more centralized management over procurement. In the Navy, the Secretary himself had supervised all of the naval agents in the field, who in turn, from their dispersed locations, contracted with businesses to procure naval supplies (materials for building and equipping ships; armaments; provisions and clothing for the crew). These activities became the responsibility of a newly created Board of Navy Commissioners in 1815.[28]

The reforms of 1818 consolidated oversight over spending in the War and Navy Departments in the Treasury. The accounting officers in the Navy and War Departments were eliminated, and all account settlement was to take place in a reorganized and better-staffed Treasury Department. Administrative procedures such as forfeiture of bonds and the withholding of salary were substituted for legal proceedings against delinquent officers. "Accountable officers" (the disbursing and collecting officers) were required to make more frequent, more punctual, and more standardized returns to Washington.[29]

After 1817, disbursing and collecting officers located in cities with Second Bank branches were required to do their banking business with the Bank, or otherwise at one of the thirty-four specified depository institutions. The Second Bank's reports to the Treasury provided an independent check on the reports of the collecting officers and disbursing officers, and a more consolidated and current picture of current receipts and payments than had been available during the more decentralized fiscal and monetary regime. During the war, reports from the Treasury's ninety-four depository institutions came up to Washington with varying frequencies and in various forms, contributing to the problem of unsettled, confusing accounts. As central fiscal agent, the Bank submitted weekly statements, in a consistent format, to the US Treasury of the sums received from the collecting officers, in three categories, customs, internal revenues (excise taxes and fees), and direct taxes (land taxes, slave taxes, and poll taxes). To spend, the Treasury drew drafts on the cashier of the Bank of the United States (at Philadelphia), payable at a designated branch or depository institution, and provided weekly reports to the Bank of all payment warrants issued. The branch offices returned all drafts drawn by the Treasury to the head office in Philadelphia, which ultimately returned the drafts to the Treasury.[30]

William Jones, first President of the Bank and former member of Cabinet, saw great advantage in the new system:

> Thus would the whole of the transactions of the Treasury with the Bank of the United States, be condensed into one account on the books of the Bank, and the same on those of the Treasury, instead of 40 or 50 accounts, and as many distinct sources of correspondence, which the present system requires of the Treasury Department; and, in this way, by a single instruction, preparation might be made in due time to meet the views of the Treasury at any point, and the bank would be in full possession of all the information necessary to enforce those views, and to regulate the conduct of its agents, so as to ensure a prompt and faithful execution of the duties required.

Jones welcomed the Treasury's proposal to regulate the conduct of the collecting and disbursing officers of the US government; "whatever may be the additional labor which it will impose upon officers of the bank, that service will be performed with great cheerfulness."[31] The Bank worked with the Treasury to draw a bright line between personal and official finances of federal officers. The cashier of the Charleston Office wrote to the Treasury Secretary in early 1819 that there were two federal officers (a Navy agent and the Marshal) who

> have accounts in our books in their individual private names, but not in their official. If a list of all the public officers, who may be instructed by the Department to keep an official account in this branch, could, without inconvenience, be transmitted to me, it would be in my power to keep you informed of any deviations that might occur.

In a similar vein, Bank President Langdon Cheves wrote to Crawford later in 1819:

> Is the bank to understand that, when a Treasury draft in favor of a navy agent, shall be presented, it shall go to his credit only, and as agent, and not be withdrawn but upon a check which has a receipt endorsed thereon?

If this practise were followed, "the agent will always be obliged to deposite [*sic*] his draft, which is now frequently thrown into the market, and cannot withdraw the money deposited to his credit but for government action." By drawing as many "foreign bills" into its own holdings as possible in all locations where it had offices, the Bank would earn the exchange premium, instead of the navy agent, and accumulate a large and geographically diverse holding of short-term bills in its own portfolio.[32]

The Treasury brought back some of the same methods it had used with the First Bank to improve the punctuality of customs collections. Immediately upon assuming office in 1816, Secretary Crawford

> told the collector at Philadelphia to . . . deposit in the BUS, for collection purposes, all the customhouse bonds outstanding on Jan 1 1817, and the following spring he informed all collectors of new procedures resulting from the agreement between the treasury and the BUS by which the latter assumed responsibility for collection of the bonds for import duties.[33]

Having the bonds deposited with the Second Bank improved the punctuality of collections in two ways. First, the Bank became the monitor and enforcer of the payment obligation upon maturation of the bond—not the customs collector, who, while a federal official, operated with a high degree of independence and tended to be closely connected to the local community of merchants, which may have resulted in some laxness at some times and in some places. Second, the Bank had the discretion to lend to import merchants unable to retire their bonds on schedule, with the loan proceeds deposited immediately in the Treasury's account with the Bank. Very soon after the organization of the Second Bank, much of the customs revenue was collected in liabilities of the Bank or of specie-paying city banks.

The Second Bank and its branches, centered around Philadelphia, were the fiscal representatives of the "headquarters" of the federal government, extending the fiscal controls of Washington to the field agents. This role for the Bank was particularly important in regard to the primary spending and collecting departments: the War Department, the Navy, and the customs. The Second Bank became part of the machinery of the federal government. It helped integrate and consolidate federal fiscal operations in a world where some central-government public goods (security, internal improvements) were provided far distant from the center of bureaucratic authority.

The shifting functional and spatial structure of federal outlays and receipts

The geographic territory under the control of the United States expanded after the Louisiana Purchase, the settlement of the War of 1812, and the Spanish cession of Florida. As a result, the geographic scope of the federal government, and its budget, expanded westward on both the spending and revenue side of the ledger. Activity associated with the security, defense, and development of the interior, organized by the War Department, pushed the spending frontier to the west; the Land Office pushed the revenue frontier to the west, with returns that lagged, region by region, behind the spending in the War Department. The Bank's job was to integrate the "western country" into federal fiscal operations.

After the War of 1812, a larger share of federal outlays was expended on the War Department than in the twenty-year period prior to the war (see Table 2.1).

Table 2.1 Shifting structure of federal receipts and outlays before and after the War
of 1812

Annual average, 1791–1811	$m	Share	Annual average, 1791–1811	$m	Share
Outlays			Receipts		
War	1.70	0.21	Customs	9.20	0.91
Navy	1.51	0.19	Internal taxes plus misc.	0.87	0.09
Pensions			Public lands		
Interest	3.1	0.38			
Misc. (including pensions)	1.85	0.23			
Total outlays	8.13		Total receipts	10.07	
Annual average, 1816–1833	$m	Share	Annual average, 1816–1833	$m	Share
War	5.09	0.28	Customs	21.96	0.86
Navy	3.48	0.19	Internal taxes plus misc.	1.61	0.06
Pensions	1.46	0.08	Public lands	1.93	0.08
Interest	3.94	0.22			
Misc.	3.93	0.22			
Total outlays	17.91		Total receipts	25.49	

Source: Dewey, 1903, pp. 110–11,123–4, 168–9.

Note: Dewey's data from 1903 vary slightly from the more recent series constructed by John Wallis (Table Ea588-593 in *Historical Statistics of the US*), largely in the "other" or "miscellaneous" receipts category after 1830, for reasons that are hard to determine, but the discrepancies are not large enough to affect the long-term averages.

To make its territorial control effective, the state needed an on-going military presence on its borders, both the eastern seaboard and the ever-shifting southern and western frontiers.[34] Along with this functional shift came a spatial shift. Prior to the 1810s, virtually all federal outlays were directed to recipients and services located on the eastern seaboard (creditors, pensioners, Navy); in 1816–1833, spending in the War and Indian Departments, virtually all directed to the shifting frontier, made up about one-third of federal outlays.[35]

Army field personnel were located primarily on the shifting northwestern and southwestern frontiers of the public domain, where they constructed and staffed forts; constructed roads; defended the border between US and Indian lands through military engagements with Indians; blocked British traders' access to Indian populations; and (with limited success) moved white squatters out of Indian territory. The purpose of the forts was to show the white settlers, the Indians, the Spanish, and the British that the United States would enforce its treaties.[36] In the year the Bank was chartered, there were thirty forts along the full range of the western frontier, from Fort St. Philip south of New Orleans to Fort Mackinac, near the Canadian border.[37]

Although the geographic territory expanded westward, most of the federal outlays and receipts continued to be recycled within the eastern core, where manufacturing and banking were more developed. Under administrative reforms adopted in 1818, the military supply system was reorganized to create greater central authority and control over contracting. Within the War Department, centers of bureaucratic authority were established for supplying different kinds of goods and services, in place of the previous reliance on local contracting. Five bureaus were established: the commissary general for subsistence (rations), the ordnance department (arms and ammunition), the commissary general of purchases (clothing), and the Corps of Engineers (construction of roads). The Quartermaster General Department had oversight over the procurement of building material for facilities and fuel, and managed the logistics of moving troops and supplies to field locations. Contracts for rations and ordnance were advertised nationally and managed from Washington; contracts for clothing were advertised in and managed from Philadelphia. Only agricultural goods, building material, and some transportation services were purchased from local suppliers in the west.[38]

Customs revenue was large enough to cover expenditures on war, the navy, pensions, interest, and much of the government's "miscellaneous" spending. By the early 1820s, 90 percent of all customs revenues were collected primarily in five districts, New York (far and away the largest), Philadelphia, Boston, Baltimore, and New Orleans.[39] The banks of New York, Philadelphia, Baltimore, Richmond, and Norfolk entered into a joint agreement with the Second Bank to collectively resume specie payments by July 1, 1817.[40] The banks of these cities maintained specie payments successfully after resumption (the banks of Boston having never stopped paying specie), and their notes were receivable at par at home, and near par in the other eastern cities. Because state banks in these cities exchanged their liabilities for Second Bank liabilities at par, federal revenue collected in state bank notes in these cities was applied to federal outlays with no currency losses. By 1823, essentially all of the interest payments on the domestically held debt were made at offices of the Bank of the United States, primarily offices on the eastern seaboard.[41] Similarly, the naval yards were all located in cities with more developed state banking systems.

Two departments of the federal government made disbursements and collections in frontier areas, the Department of Indian Affairs and the General Land Office. As land was transferred from Indian to US sovereignty, superintendents of Indian Affairs were established to implement the terms of treaties, including gifts and annuities. These officials operated on the outer edge of the frontier, where there were no banks. Their monetary disbursements took a variety of forms, including drafts drawn on branches of the Second Bank, drafts drawn on the Treasury or collecting officers of the US government (land office receivers), drafts drawn on themselves, and specie. Indian nations insisted on payment in specie in the treaties they negotiated with the US government, while drafts drawn by the US government were happily received by domestic merchants and transportation companies.[42]

Congress established the General Land Office in 1812 as a separate bureau within the Treasury Department to manage the growing level of activity: surveying the land; mapping out townships and defining ownership units; auctioning and selling the land. There was a boom in the western lands following the War. In 1817, there were twenty-three district land offices (five in Alabama, three in Illinois, two in Indiana, three in Louisiana, one in Michigan, one in Mississippi, seven in Ohio, one in Tennessee).[43] Land sales increased dramatically in 1815–1819, particularly in land districts which had recently been opened for US settlement through Indian, British, and Spanish removal. The state banks located in the interior, many of them recently chartered, had loaned on real estate collateral for land purchases and related investment during the boom. The western banks were unable to resume specie payments in 1817–1818.

Prior to the chartering of the Second Bank, land office receivers and collectors of the internal revenue had deposited the notes issued by western state banks to the credit of the Treasury in the eighty-nine state bank depositories of the US government. In 1817, these balances were transferred to the Second Bank. The question was, were these balances "good money"? Could they be converted into specie or its equivalent, how long would it take, and who would bear any losses associated with this conversion? In 1817 and 1818, these questions were the subject of extensive disagreements and negotiations between the Bank and the Treasury. At the end of the day, the Bank won, but at the expense of its relationship with the Treasury, and with its fiscal duties yet to be fully discharged.

Revenue collection by the Second Bank in the west in the early years: conflict and failure

In May of 1817, the first President of the Bank, William Jones, wrote to Secretary of the Treasury William Crawford that

> [t]he receipt of the paper of the country banks may be a measure of necessity on the part of the Government; but if the interest of the public shall render the measure expedient, the public, and not the bank, it is respectfully conceived, ought to sustain whatever loss or delay may be incurred.

Jones felt that the Board was not able "to enter into a sound discrimination" between the country banks of good credit, with "means of either paying their notes in specie or of procuring paper or credit, which would be deemed equivalent," and those not of good credit. Jones complained that

> [i]t would really appear . . . that the State banks, instead of putting their shoulders to the wheel, indulge the most extravagant expectations of relief from the operations of this bank, and calculate upon replenishing their vaults by transferring to us their debtors; and, by this ingenious kind of transmutation, convert their paper into solid coin, without the expense or inconvenience attending the ordinary process.[44]

Consequently, the Bank treated the deposits of banks of unknown credit the same way that the state banks themselves had after the suspension of specie payments in 1814, as "special deposits," not as cash. These deposits would become a point of contention between the Second Bank and the western state banks, and between the Bank and the Treasury. In January, Jones wrote to Crawford that

> [i]t is true that the 16th section [of the charter] prohibits the bank from suspending or refusing to pay specie on money deposited; but the question recurs whether the deposits are money? The proposition of the bank to hold the deposits specifically subject to the order of the Government was distinctly understood to deny that they were money.[45]

Given the geographic scope of customs, public land sales and the "internal revenue" of the federal government, it was not possible for all revenue to be paid into the Bank or one of its branches. The Treasury wanted its revenue deposited in a bank, not lingering in the hands of receivers and collectors. Treasury Secretary Crawford pointed out that if a Collector,

> residing at a great distance from the bank or its branches, should be required to deposit in them, they would necessarily deposit not more than two or three times in the year; and in the mean time [*sic*], the temptation to apply it to individual uses is greatly increased. . . . If they were required to deposit at short intervals in banks at a great distance from their . . . residences but few would continue in office [in light of the modest emolument and high expense].

The Treasury instructed the Bank to select a group of

> State banks as the places of intermediate deposit for the public money collected in the interior of the large States, and in those States where no branch shall be established. As long as the internal revenue shall be continued, such intermediate places of deposit will be indispensably necessary.[46]

In setting up the system of state bank depositories, the Treasury was trying to protect itself, and also to improve the quality of the stock of bank notes. The Treasury identified the districts where it saw the need for state bank "offices of deposite [*sic*]," and the Bank was to select the banks that would serve as depositories. The Bank asked the Treasury to share information about "the fidelity with which" the banks had "discharged the trust hitherto confided in them," to guide the selections of the Bank's Board of Directors. Secretary Crawford wrote to the cashier of a western bank that "measures will be adopted to guard the Treasury against the receipt of bills which will not be received" at the offices of the Bank of the United States, or at the offices of states banks to be designated as "offices of deposit." He acknowledged that this measure may be inconvenient to some citizens, but "that inconvenience must be attributed to the State Legislatures," which were responsible for the "imprudent multiplication of State Banks, unconnected with each other"—and "not to the Treasury of the United States. The public interest, as well as that of the Treasury, requires that paper of extremely limited currency should give place to that which is really an advantageous substitute for coin."[47]

In April 1817, the Bank identified an initial group of state banks to the Treasury for its approval. The banks were located, for the most part, in relatively "safe" places in the "hard money" area, second-tier cities of New England, the Middle Atlantic, and the South Atlantic without Second Bank branches.[48] The state bank "offices of deposite [sic]" were to make detailed returns to the Bank, not to the Treasury, as had been the practise for the deposit banks in the interregnum between the First and Second Banks. The statements were to delineate the type of revenue received; money deposited by collecting officers was to be placed to the credit of the Second Bank; Treasury drafts were to be drawn on the cashier of the Philadelphia office of the Second Bank and were to be returned to the Treasury through the Bank. The state banks no longer interacted directly with the Treasury, as they had during the war, but with the Bank instead.

The Bank deferred and delayed when it came to identifying state bank offices of deposit in frontier areas in Ohio, western Pennsylvania, and Kentucky, and had to be prodded by the Treasury to do so. In October of 1817, the Bank identified two banks in western Pennsylvania and one bank in the Missouri Territory, but asked the Treasury "to dispense with the employment of State banks northwest of the Ohio" (in Ohio, Illinois, Indiana, and Michigan), since

> the state of the western currency (notwithstanding the ostensible resumption of specie payments) and the magnitude of the collections on account of the public lands seem to require greater circumspection on the part of this bank, and a more effectual control of the Receivers of Public Money than has hitherto existed. A gentleman . . . has assured me that he was witness to the sale of good bank paper by the Receiver at Vincennes at a high premium, in exchange for the worst in the country, which he no doubt deposited to the credit of the Treasurer.[49]

The Treasury, on the other hand, was anxious to establish branches or offices in the western country: "The sums received by the officers attached to the Land Offices are too large to be permitted to remain long in their hands, and ought not to be exposed to the dangers of a distant transportation." As the Bank opened its western branches, it moved to get land office receipts deposited at the branches in Pittsburgh, Chillicothe, and Cincinnati, and to forestall the appointment of more western banks as offices of deposit. In late December, the Treasury instructed its collectors of internal revenue

> to receive the bills of no bank which will not be credited as specie in the Bank of the United States, its offices, and State banks employed as places of deposite [sic], where they are respectively required to make their deposites [sic].[50]

The new system for collecting, depositing, and disbursing federal funds throughout the national domain was barely in place when it broke down. During 1818, the Second Bank set about collecting some of the "special deposits" which had been transferred to it. Officers of the Second Bank's branch in Pittsburgh visited a number of banks in the interior, presenting their notes and demanding payment in notes of the Bank of the United States, its branches, or of state banks in the cities of Philadelphia, New York, Baltimore, Richmond and its branches, Pittsburg (with one exception), and the District of Columbia (again with one exception). The Bank was not satisfied with the results; many banks did not pay, refused to pay, or made only a partial payment.[51] The Bank's demands seemed unfair to many of the western banks. The President of the Fayetteville branch of the State Bank of North Carolina wrote to the President of the Second Bank in March of 1818, inquiring as to whether the Bank would accept in payment and deposit, "checks on banks in Baltimore, Philadelphia, New-York, Boston, or Charleston, on the Bank of the United States or its branches, or the notes of the two latter, and whether you will take drafts or bills of exchange for collection?" He pointed out that the state bank and its branches had been a depository for the "General Government" during the war,

> during which time, the notes of most of the chartered banks in the United States were received in deposite [*sic*], not from a choice, but from the particular situation of the country demanding as general extension of credit to the notes of chartered banks in circulation in the state, as would enable the citizens to pay their taxes.

Now that these credits were being transferred to the Bank of the United States, they were "likely to become, in great degree, a specie debt." The state banks of Cincinnati also wanted the Bank to know that during the war "they were induced by the embarrassments under which the Treasury Department then labored to make larger advances than under other circumstances they would have thought justifiable."[52]

At the same time the Bank was failing to convert special deposits into "good funds," its notes went to a discount in Boston, the hard currency center of the country, and its ability to maintain specie payments came into question. The Bank pulled in its resources, and, among other measures, terminated some state banks as depositories. The Bank notified the Treasury that it would no longer receive the notes of these state banks as "cash," but only as a "special deposit," meaning only funds of like quality could be withdrawn. The Bank did not want to be responsible for guaranteeing the solvency of the state banks whose notes and deposits were presented in payments to the US government.[53]

The Bank also washed its hands of the problem of special deposits. These were the Treasury funds received at the state bank depositories which had held Treasury deposits up to the opening of the Second Bank; bank notes, according to Treasury Secretary Crawford,

> which were refused to be entered to the general credit of the Treasury by the 89 banks in which the public money was then deposited; notwithstanding all

those banks, with the exception of a few in the Eastern States, did not at the time discharge their own notes in specie.

The $3.3 m of special deposit was transferred to a Washington, DC, bank for collection.[54]

The Bank took further steps to protect its own position when it notified the Treasury, at the height of the boom in western land sales in 1818, that it would receive from the public land offices "nothing but its own notes, and the current coin of the Union, except as special deposite [sic]." This put the Treasury squarely between a rock and a hard place. In Secretary Crawford's words, "It was manifest . . . that this determination of the Bank would greatly reduce the receipts into the Treasury from that important branch of the public revenue." He continued:

> To have permitted the distress and ruin in which the purchasers of the public lands would have been involved, . . . without an effort by the Executive department to avert them, would have excited feelings in a large and meritorious body of citizens, which no prudent government, even if despotic, could have seen with indifference.[55]

The Treasury then renewed arrangements with state banks to serve as depository institutions—without the Second Bank as intermediary between the Treasury and the state bank. This was particularly pressing in the public land states of Indiana, Illinois, Missouri, Mississippi, and Alabama, where there were no Second Bank offices. As the Second Bank stopped receiving state bank notes as cash, so did the state banks selected to be "offices of deposite [sic]." The cashier of St. Stephen's Bank in Tombeckbe (in the Alabama Territory), wrote to Secretary Crawford in 1820 that St. Stephen's Bank had been informed by the Savannah branch of the Second Bank that it would no longer receive the notes of either the Bank of the State of Georgia or the Planters' Bank "to the credit" of the US Treasury. Consequently, St. Stephens

> will prefer . . . to receive the public moneys on special deposit, unless the bills of those banks can be received in payment of Treasury drafts. . . . the bills of those banks constitute almost entirely the circulating medium in this State.

In 1822, Secretary Crawford, seeking to justify the losses from receiving payment in notes of banks that subsequently failed, explained to the House of Representatives that

> it was found impracticable for the [land office] receivers to make their deposites [sic] in [the Second Bank], without incurring an expense nearly equal to the amount of their salary and emoluments. . . . The only alternatives left . . . were, to suffer the public money to remain in the hands of the receivers until it could be expended, or direct it to be deposited in some of the local banks.[56]

In 1818, the Treasury chose the latter option, and identified thirteen western banks, located in the cities where receivers of the most active land districts were located. Of the thirteen, eight failed between 1820 and 1825. To add insult to injury, the federal government's own officers in the western districts may have contributed to some of these failures, and to the losses suffered by the federal government as a result. The cashier of the Bank of Steubenville, Ohio, wrote to Treasury Secretary Crawford in March of 1820 that the land office Receiver located in the same town made deposits infrequently, did not deposit all of the returns that he received, and retained much of the specie and "foreign bills" (stronger, eastern currency) that he received for his own use.[57] After 1820, when two of the larger banks in St. Louis and Cincinnati failed, the Treasury became more restrictive in its payment policy, authorizing the land offices to accept only specie, notes of the Second Bank, the notes of the state-chartered banks of Boston, New York, Baltimore, Richmond, South Carolina, and Georgia, plus the specie-paying banks in the state where the land office was located. The notes of specie-paying banks in public land states were, from that time forward, only accepted at land offices in their home states, which restricted their ability to circulate broadly in the region, deepening the recession and slowdown in land sales which was well under way.[58]

Eighteen months after the Second Bank went into operation, the credit risk associated with accepting the notes and deposits of the "country banks" in payment for public lands, excise taxes, and direct taxes had been shifted from the Bank onto the Treasury, leaving the Treasury in the same position it had been in prior to the chartering of the Bank. This was not what the Congress had in mind when it created the Second Bank. In its early years, the Bank had to choose between two conflicting directives: to create a uniform currency for the national government or to ensure the specie convertibility of its own notes and deposits. It chose the latter.

Conclusion

The Second Bank was chartered for the purpose of creating a uniform currency for the national government. Its own currency issue was not large enough to accomplish this goal; federal revenue would continue to be collected in state bank currency. To fulfil its fiscal duty, then, the Second Bank had to create a currency union with the state banks whose geographic scope matched up with the borders of the central government's reach. In this, the Bank failed, after it retrenched and insulated itself from western banking. This was not a permanent solution. While public land sales were depressed in the recession and slow western recovery of the 1820s, they averaged a not-insignificant 8 percent of total receipts on an annual average basis, and the government looked to land sales as a vital fiscal source, and means of populating the west with US citizens (and slaves) into the future.

The Bank's early failure and later success as the national government's fiscal agent in the western country can be illustrated by example. In July of 1819, Lewis Cass, Governor of the Michigan Territory and Superintendent of Indian Affairs at Detroit, Michigan, presented a draft of the US government at the Bank's branch in

Chillicothe, Ohio, for payment in specie, needed to fulfill the terms of an Indian treaty. Payment was refused.[59] A decade later, in May of 1831, the Bank advanced Governor Cass $39,075 for the execution of Indian treaties for which Congress had failed to make the requisite appropriation.[60] The Bank became a superb fiscal agent over the course of the 1820s, able to mobilize funds on short notice at any and all points in the Union—after it established a dominant market position in western banking markets and an extensive operation in domestic and foreign bills of exchange.

Notes

1 Quoted in Balogh (2009, p. 130).
2 The Federalists in Congress had argued that it was "inexpedient to destroy the adminis-trative machinery organized for the collection of [internal] taxes, which had been brought into good working order through ten years of experience"; Dewey (1903, p. 120).
3 Ibid., pp. 111, 131–42. The yield on long-term federal debt reached 9.22 percent in 1814, the highest of the nineteenth century; Homer and Sylla, (1991, p. 299).
4 Adams (1978, pp. 45, 50). Of the $1.87 m in dividends payable on the domestic-funded US debt in January 1815, $.38 m was payable in New England and $1.49 m in Mid-dle Atlantic and Southeast cities. Four-fifths of the "floating debt" of Treasury notes and temporary loans was also held in the Middle and Southern states. Gallatin (1831, p. 44); 13th Cong., 3d Sess., Pub. 453, p. 880.
5 William Jones Papers, Box 1.
6 Perkins (1994, p. 340) argues that banks outside of New England suspended payments because noteholders in those states lost confidence in their banks after the successful British invasion of Washington in August. According to Adams (1978, pp. 77–81), suspension was triggered by the breakdown in the "cooperative spirit which had char-acterized interbank transactions in more peaceful times" as "the New England banks (in particular those of Boston) called for payment in specie." Adams (1978) shows that the drain to New England began early in 1814, after the floating of the $16 m loan the previous year, which led to the accumulation of Middle Atlantic notes in Boston banks without offsetting claims on New England in Middle Atlantic banks.
7 Dallas (1871, p. 271). The quote is from a letter from Dallas to the Chairman of the Committee on Ways and Means.
8 Phillips (1900, p. 20); Adams (1978, p. 50); Dewey (1903, p. 145). See also Mooney (1974, p. 96). On the number of state banks in 1814, see Weber (2006, p. 443).
9 In December 1814, Boston bank notes sold at a 20 percent premium over Philadelphia banknotes; Phillips, R. (2013, p. 18).
10 14th Cong., 1st Sess., Pub. 454, p. 29.
11 Dallas (1871, p. 271), from February 20, 1815, letter from Dallas to the Chairman of the Committee on Ways and Means; Timberlake (1978, pp. 14–18); Kagin (1984).
12 14th Cong., 1st Sess., Pub. 454, p. 29.
13 Gouge quoted in Phillips, J. (1900, p. 22).
14 Dallas (1871, pp. 285–7).
15 Dallas quoted in Dewey (1903, p. 146). On Dallas's plan, see also Adams (1978, pp. 83–5).
16 See Hammond (1957, pp. 233–41) for a summary of the Congressional debate on the Bank bill, prefaced by his observation that "the question of constitutionality, which had so much sincere prominence in 1791, and so much insincere prominence in 1811, had none at all in these debates of 1814, 1815, and 1816."
17 Broz (1999, pp. 55–7); Hammond (1957, p. 241); Sylla et al. (1987).
18 Brown (1942); Walters (1945); Broz (1997). Broz argues that a "small group of rent-seeking investors" were the primary movers in the campaign for a new national

bank, a view substantiated by Brown and Walther's well-documented historical accounts. For Broz, the private benefits to the investors were more than matched by the public benefit of enhanced public credit and sound money.

19 Dewey (1910, pp. 268–9). In Boston, the 6 percent coupon bonds were accepted at par, or $100 for every $100 of face value, and had a market price of $80; the 3 percent bonds were taken at $65 and had a market price of $50; and the 7 percent bonds, at $106.51 when their market price was $90; Martin (1969, p. 14). Federal debt outstanding from Carter et. al. 2006, Table Ea650-651 contributed by John Joseph Wallis; yields from Homer and Sylla (1991, p. 286).

20 On July 1, 1816, American gold and silver sold at a premium of 16–17 percent, and Spanish silver at 18–18.5 percent, in Philadelphia; Phillips, R. (2013, p. 23);15th Cong., 2d Sess., H. Doc. 92, p. 7.

21 From Sec. 15 and 17, respectively, of the Bank's charter, in Catterall (1902, pp. 487, 305).

22 "The uniformity of duties and taxes of every description, whether internal or external, direct or indirect, is an essential and fundamental principle of the Constitution. It is self-evident that that uniformity cannot be carried into effect without a corresponding uniformity of currency. Without laws to this effect, it is absolutely impossible that the taxes and duties should be uniform, as the Constitution prescribes; such laws are therefore necessary and proper, in the most strict sense of the words"; Gallatin (1831, pp. 79, 81–2).

23 Dewey (1903, pp. 111, 141).

24 13th Cong.-2d Sess., Pub. 408, pp. 813–14.

25 The greatest backlog of accounting work was in the accounts of the War Department, where there were unsettled accounts going back to 1798. The accounts in the Indian Department and the Post Office had been unsettled since 1798 and 1810, respectively; White (1951, p. 166).

26 White (1951, ch. 12).

27 Prucha (1969, p. 135).

28 In 1814, a position of naval purveyor was created at the request of then-Secretary William Jones, to allow him to time to take on "the great and efficient objects of the establishment." White (1951, pp. 273, 291). In the early 1820s there were six naval yards, in the cities of Portsmouth, Charlestown, New York, Philadelphia, Washington, and Norfolk, all of which had branches of the Second Bank.

29 White (1951, pp. 171–80, 291).

30 Catterall (1902, pp. 458–64).

31 18th Cong., 1st Sess., H. Doc. 140, p. 614; 18th Cong., 1st Sess., Pub. 705, p. 822.

32 18th Cong., 1st Sess., H. Doc. 140, pp. 790, 812.

33 Mooney (1974, p. 102). Credit was granted to importers upon the issuance of bonds for the payment of duties within a certain period; Dewey (1903, p. 239). Discounts of 4 percent were given for cash payment of duties.

34 According to Balogh (2009, p. 202), in the aftermath of the War of 1812, national "Republican leaders like Jefferson and Madison [were alerted] to the need for organization and infrastructure that could only be provided by a more assertive General Government. . . . they advocated a far-reaching program of military preparedness that included annual funding for coastal and frontier defense, a peacetime army, an expanded navy, and greater control over state militias."

35 This is based on an estimation that one-fifth of what is categorized as "miscellaneous" in Dewey's tables consisted of spending in the Indian department on agents' salaries, gifts, and annuities, as was the case in the late 1810s. In the early 1820s, 11 percent of the value of all Revolutionary War pensions were payable in western states; 18th Cong., 1st Sess., S. Doc. 3, p. 4.

36 According to Prucha (1969, p. 179), "The western forts for the most part did not need to serve as military fortresses awaiting attack from an enemy force. They were primarily stations to house and care for the soldiers, whose very presence served to convince

the Indians that the US government intended to exert its jurisdiction and to enforce its decisions on the western frontier." The military posts were a "means of blocking the channels by which British traders could introduce goods into the Mississippi and Missouri regions from Canada", Prucha (1953, p. 18).

37 Between 1821 and 1835, "40–50% of the army was stationed in the West; another third patrolled the Southeast and Florida"; Wooster (2009, p. 70). The mission of the Army in this period was closely tied to the westward migration of the white and enslaved populations.

38 Miller (1991, pp. 442–4, chs. 5–8).

39 There were eighty-four customs districts in the early 1820s and ninety-six by 1828. Customs receipts in 1823, by district/city or town, from 18th Cong., 1st Sess., S. Doc. 5, December 3, 1823. A small share of customs duties were received at customs districts in southern cities whose banknotes circulated at a discount in the financial and commercial centers of the country.

40 Congress spurred this agreement with its joint resolution of 1817 requiring all payments to the United States to be made in specie, Treasury notes, notes of the US Bank, or notes of specie-paying banks. 18th Cong., 1st Sess., H. Doc. 140, p. 578. The Second Bank agreed not to collect payment for the Treasury deposits transferred to it until it had created the means for the state banks to make payment through its own lending. The Bank's first loans were to "those who may have (customs) bonds to pay . . . on account of the revenue arising from imports in the principal commercial cities."

41 18th Cong., 1st Sess., S. Doc. 5. Of $5.64 m in domestic interest payments in 1823, all but $15,000 was paid out at an office of the Second Bank.

42 In the early 1820s, Superintendents of Indian Affairs at Detroit and St. Louis withdrew specie from land office receivers with drafts on the Secretary of War's and the US Treasury's accounts at the US Bank branches in New York and Louisville; 17th Cong., 2d Sess., H. Doc. 80. This document lists "the names of all Persons to whom Money, Goods, or Effects, have been delivered, . . . for the benefit of the Indians." In 1822, about half of all outlays went to annuities, and the balance to Indian agents and sub-agents, which included presents for Indians and "pay of interpreters and blacksmiths, repairs of buildings, medicine and provisions for emigrating and visiting Indians, transportation of specie and merchandise, expenses of smiths' shops, of expresses, laborers, etc etc."

43 Carstenen (1963, pp. 499–504).

44 18th Cong., 1st Sess., Pub. 705, p. 764.

45 The Board of the Second Bank "did not . . . intend to contract the obligation to pay the drafts of the Government drawn upon those deposits in gold or silver, or in its own bills." 18th Cong., 1st Sess., Pub. 705, p. 497.

46 18th Cong., 1st Sess., Pub. 705, p. 506. Excise taxes were levied on a wide range of consumer goods, including: stamps; carriages; refined sugar; furniture; horses for the saddle and carriage; gold watches, silver watches; boots, saddles and bridles; paper; candles; playing-cards; tobacco and snuff; hats; beer, ale, and porter; and a few producer goods such as leather, iron, nails, and business licenses. The direct tax was apportioned to the states according to population, which were collected by the states.

47 18th Cong., 1st Sess., Pub. 705, p. 544. In a letter to Jones written soon after this one, Treasury Secretary Crawford frankly states that his aim is to "curtail the circulation of all bank paper the credit of which is not supported by arrangements for the redemption of their bills"; ibid., p. 553.

48 18th Cong., 1st Sess., H. Doc. 140, pp. 613–16. The state banks that were selected were in Maine (2), New Hampshire (3), Massachusetts (1), Connecticut (2), Rhode Island (3), New York (2), New Jersey (1), Virginia (3), North Carolina (6), Georgia (2), Tennessee (2), Indiana (1), District of Columbia (1).

49 18th Cong., 1st Sess., Pub. 705, p. 821.

50 18th Cong., 1st Sess., Pub. 705, p. 821; 15th Cong., 1st Sess., Pub. 512, p. 232.

51 18th Cong., 1st Sess., Pub. 705, pp. 856, 859–60. Bankers in Cincinnati objected strongly to the Bank's demand that the balances due to the Cincinnati branch be repaid in five months with notes of the Second Bank, specie, or eastern funds, none of which could be had. Because the notes of the state banks had been used to buy land, this paper "accumulates in the branch and returns upon us in a few months after it is issued; and . . . we find none of the paper of the United States Bank in circulation here to use in retiring the debt [to the United States Bank]."

52 18th Cong., 1st Sess., H. Doc. 140, p. 750. The cashier of the Fayetteville branch of the Second Bank responded that he could not say that "we will take the notes of the mother bank, or its branches, to an unlimited amount, . . . we will take a check on Charleston, for ten thousand dollars, and on New-York or Boston, for twenty-five or thirty thousand dollars. . . . We are willing to accommodate dealers and the public, in exchanges of this kind, to a moderate amount, for individual purposes, but not in large sums for bank or speculative ends in other states."

53 18th Cong., 1st Sess. H. Doc. 140, p. 632.

54 17th Cong., 1st Sess., Pub. 637, pp. 720–1; 15th Cong., 2d Sess., Pub. 547, p. 322.

55 17th Cong., 2d Sess., Pub. 671. Communicated to the House of Representatives February 26, 1823.

56 18th Cong., 1st Sess., Pub. 705, p. 745; 17th Cong., 1st Sess. Pub. 637, p. 719. Crawford referred to the federal law requiring the "principal disbursing officers" to, whenever practicable, "keep the public moneys in their hands, in some incorporated bank." The idea was that the "banks furnished an additional security, not only in the collection but in the disbursement of the public revenue." In the late 1830s, after a wave of bank failures following another land boom and bust, and after the demise of the Second Bank, the US government adopted the Independent Treasury System to avoid using the state banks as depositories for federal revenue.

57 17th Cong., 1st Sess., Pub. 637, pp. 719–20, 741. The thirteen depository banks were located in public land district centers in Ohio (Steubenville, Chillicothe, Columbus, Cincinnati), Indiana (Madison, Vincennes), Illinois (Shawneetown, Edwardsville), Missouri (St. Louis), Kentucky (Louisville), Mississippi (Natchez, St. Stephens), and Alabama (Huntsville). Information on closing dates is from Weber (2011).

58 Prior to this declaration, two land offices in Illinois received the notes of banks in Missouri, Kentucky, Virginia, North Carolina, Tennessee, Alabama, and Indiana, as well as notes of the Bank of the United States, New York City banks, and specie (gold and silver coin). Sixty percent of the receipts collected at these two offices in early 1820 would have been rejected under the new policy. 17th Cong., 1st Sess., Pub. 650, p. 817.

59 Phillips, J (1900, p. 33).

60 22nd Cong., 1st Sess., S. Doc. 98, p. 49.

3   The Second Bank's branch network and the state banking system

The Second Bank was the only bank in the country that was authorized to establish branches in more than one state. The Bank established nineteen branches when it started operations and had twenty-six branches by the end of its tenure. Much can be learned about the character and priorities of the Second Bank from its decisions about where to locate its branches. Toward this end, this chapter examines the respective roles of the US government's preferences, the Bank's commercial interests, and the geography of the state banking system in shaping the Bank's branch network.

Historians of the Bank have been critical of where the Bank chose to locate branches. Catterall believed that the initial "locations were badly selected and in defiance of correct banking principles. Thus, the new, thinly settled, and poor western states had as many offices as the whole of rich and populous New England or the middle states." Dewey (1910a) tended to agree, observing that

> at the outset commercial considerations had less weight in the selection of places, and the needs of the Treasury Department were an influential factor. . . . fiscal necessities were the most urgent in the newly settled sections where local banks were under less control and where sound business practice had not yet been established.

As this chapter will show, the Bank did open new branches disproportionately in the 1820s in less-populated, less-banked areas of the country. But these branches did, most certainly, serve the Bank's commercial interests, as well as its fiscal duty.[1]

The first section analyses the characteristics of cities chosen for branches in 1820 and 1830. This information is supplemented with qualitative data from the Bank's correspondence, particularly letters between the Bank's Presidents and the US Secretary of the Treasury. Both kinds of evidence show that the Bank was more likely to open a branch in a given city if federal revenue collections and deposits there were large, and if the city was relatively underbanked (had less state banking capital in relation to the demand for commercial banking services). In the second section (Shifts in the economic geography of the dual banking system, 1820–1830) the geographic expansion of the Bank's branch network during the Biddle administration is compared with that of the state-chartered banking system. This data shows a dramatic and growing geographic disconnect over the 1820s between the growth of the state-chartered banking system and the growth of Bank's branch network.

The third and fourth sections evaluate the Bank's branch network from the perspective of the lender of last-resort function of modern central banks. Under the heading Branch location and the Bank's effectiveness as a lender of last resort, the Bank's branch network is assessed as a delivery system for emergency lending to state banks, and this third section concludes that the Bank would have opened branches in different cities in the 1820s had emergency lending been its top priority. The fourth section (Branch location and the quality of state bank currency) presents information on the effect of the Bank's branch network on the quality of currency issued by state banks in different regions. Greater access to a Second Bank branch did not bolster the value of western banks' currency in eastern money markets.

Branch location decision-making

The Bank's charter left the choice of where to establish branches up to the Directors of the "parent" Board of the Bank at Philadelphia, with some exceptions. Congress could require the Bank to locate a branch in the District of Columbia, or in any state where at least two thousand shares of the Bank were held and whose legislature petitioned Congress for a branch.[2] No branch was established by Congressional action. Not every state received a branch: in 1817, five states did not get a branch (Vermont, New Jersey, Delaware, Tennessee, Indiana), while four states had two branches (Pennsylvania, Virginia, Kentucky, and Ohio). The Bank received a number of petitions from citizens for branches, and was sensitive to political considerations, but in the final analysis created a branch network that served both duty and profit.[3]

There are no records of the Board's deliberations on where to locate branches, but the driving factors can be inferred from their decisions and from correspondence of the two Bank Presidents who were in office when branch location decisions were made, William Jones (1817–1819) and Nicholas Biddle (1823–1836). Treasury Secretaries William Crawford (1816–1825) and Richard Rush (1825–1829) lobbied Jones and Biddle, respectively, on the matter of branch locations. Their advice was followed in some, but not all instances.

Secretary Crawford wrote a number of letters to Bank President William Jones in 1816 and 1817 on the subject of the Bank's branches. In his way of thinking, branches were most needed where there was a state or regional imbalance between federal revenues and expenditures.

Crawford urged the early placement of branches in Kentucky, Ohio, and Louisiana. In the Southwest,

> the concentration of the military force of the South Division to the neighborhood of New Orleans, and of Mobile, on account of the doubtful relations

between this country and Spain, will require an expenditure in that Section much beyond, the revenue collected there.

Crawford also asked for a branch in Augusta, Georgia, telling Jones:

> During the continuation of hostilities with the Creek Indians, considerable funds will be required in the State of Georgia to meet the military expenditure in that quarter. I . . . request that the Treasury moneys at Savannah may be reserved for that purpose, and that one hundred thousand dollars may also be placed at Augusta, without delay. You will be pleased to inform me when the Office of Discount and Deposit at Augusta is in operation.[4]

Conversely, in Kentucky, Ohio, and the Territories north of the Ohio River, the sale of public lands and the internal taxes "will greatly exceed the disbursements there," and the "currency in which it has been collected render it useless in a great measure, any where [*sic*] else."[5]

The Bank and the Treasury both hoped that the Bank would displace some of the existing state banks, and deter the formation of new ones in some sections of the country. In July 1817 Treasury Secretary Crawford wrote to Jones, urging the prompt opening of the Louisville, Kentucky, branch in light of "the favorable disposition which is manifested in that Section of the union to the national bank," and also to prevent the "multiplication of the state banks." He hoped that, once the Bank was established, some of the state banks would not seek renewal of their charters when they expired. In March 1818, during the land boom in the "New West," Bank President Jones wrote to Secretary Crawford that

> [c]ontrary to every rational expectation, the liberal diffusion of the capital of the Bank of the United States, which it was alleged would not only superside [*sic*] the necessity and desire for new banks, but induce many of the old ones to withdraw,

has instead "has been followed by arbitrary and unconstitutional amercements" and the formation of many new banks.[6]

The Second Bank was concerned about all of the new banks for two reasons: they would reduce the Bank's market share, and they would potentially expose the Bank to credit risk from holding the paper of these new banks (the latter, a fear that turned out to be justified). The Bank delayed the opening of the branch in Augusta in light of the tax imposed by the State of Georgia and because the "creation of vast numbers of banks in various sections of the Union" created new demands on the Bank's specie resources. Similarly, Nashville, Tennessee, was also selected for a branch, but the establishment of the branch was postponed in 1818 after the Tennessee Legislature imposed a financial penalty of $50,000 on any office of the Bank of the United States doing business in Tennessee and chartered ten new banks, which "greatly impaired . . . the inducements to establish a branch within the State of Tennessee."[7] The branch at Nashville was established almost ten years later, when there were only two chartered banks in the entire state. As will be shown, the Panic of 1819 helped achieve the desired goal of state bank suppression in the west.

The Bank avoided opening new branches in well-banked markets.[8] Consider the case of Albany, New York. In July 1827, a number of leading citizens and businesses of Albany presented a petition requesting a branch of the Bank of the United States, on the grounds that they expected a large increase in business activity after certain canals were completed. In their view, state banking capital in Albany was insufficient

> to afford the facilities to commercial enterprise, which the business of the place would warrant . . . instances are not wanting, of active, intelligent, and enterprising merchants, removing from this place to the city of New York, to participate in the benefits of the increased banking capital there, although their business, principally, has been continued with the interior of the state.

The Bank, however, concluded that the "field of banking operations seems to be preoccupied," on top of which the US government did not receive "revenue of any importance there," while "those of the State being naturally deposited in the State institutions." The Bank did open a branch in Utica, New York, a city further west on the Erie Canal, on "business principles entirely."[9]

A similar logic was at play in the Bank's choice of Fayetteville over Raleigh for a branch in North Carolina. In a July 1817 letter to President Jones, Treasury Secretary Crawford made the case for Raleigh, on the grounds that Raleigh was more central, it was "surrounded by a rich country," more internal revenue was collected there than anywhere else in the state, it was the state capital, "a better direction could be obtained there than any where [*sic*] else," and its location on the "great post route from North to South . . . of course furnishes the same facilities for the transmission of the public money as Fayetteville." Crawford added that most of the members of Congress from North Carolina would prefer Raleigh. In the end, Fayetteville was selected, not Raleigh. Fayetteville had fewer banks in relation to population than Raleigh in 1820, it had more growth potential than Raleigh, and the Bank's leadership knew that the State of North Carolina would conduct its business with one of the state-chartered banks, not the Bank of the United States branch.[10]

The Bank would have opened more of its new branches in New England after 1820 had its objective had been to maximize its ability to provide services to state banks, as New England was the most densely banked region of the country. The Boston branch of the BUS faced significant competition from other "monied institutions." US Senator James Lloyd (Massachusetts) wrote to Biddle to explain why the discounts of the Boston branch were in decline:

> several new Banks and Insurance Companies have been recently incorporated by the Legislature, which seems to have thrown open its doors to all applicants of this character; these possessing Capitals each of from 3 to 500.000 dollars have brought much new money, seeking investment, under active and zealous directions into the market, . . . for the employment of which, the generally unproductive state of foreign commerce offers little inducement, together with the payment of the 7% stock, and the receipt of about 1.300.000 dollars, from the awards under the Spanish Convention, have altogether, rendered the supply for the money market so abundant, and the aggregate of funds to be employed so large, as to have reduced the rate of interest . . . this is the secret of the reduction of the debt of the Branch . . .; several of its debtors having without doubt paid off their debts . . . by funds procured elsewhere at a lower rate of interest.[11]

The merchants of St. Louis, Missouri, petitioned for a new branch in 1826, appealing to the needs of trade and the central government. The merchants pointed out that the state had been altogether without any banking facilities for five years; as a result, "[a]lmost the only circulating medium in this part of the Country is Specie. Such currency always circumscribes and impedes that march of commercial enterprise by depriving it of that ease and dispatch which are essential to its very existence," especially in "a new Country . . .where the roads are indifferent and the means of conveyance neither safe nor numerous." The petition pointed out that the use of specie caused problems for the US government as well: "The sums of money transmitted to St. Louis for the purpose of being disbursed to the Troops stationed in the Missouri and Mississippi Rivers, and to the Surveying and Indian Departments, have generally exceeded 200,000 $ per annum." The cost of transporting these funds averaged 5–7 percent of the value of the specie shipped. St. Louis got its branch.[12]

The US Treasurer sought "safety," "certainty," and "unity of the moneyed operations of this department": that is, a better alternative to specie, state banks, and federal officers. Federal officers on the frontier were sometimes used as de facto banks, even though, as Treasury Secretary Richard Rush acknowledged, "this mode is not so convenient or agreeable to those to whome [sic] the moneys are to be paid."[13] The records of the Franklin, Missouri, Land Office Receiver's "accounts current" with the US government show how banking with federal officers worked. The Receiver recorded receipts and disbursements, made periodic deposits in the New Orleans branch of the Bank of the United States, and paid bills of exchange drawn by US officials such as the army quartermaster, army paymaster, and the Treasurer of the US (in the latter case, in favor of the Superintendent of Indian Affairs at Detroit, Michigan). The long time lags in communication created predictable problems: in one instance, the receiver received instructions to pay coin for a large bill of exchange (to be used for soldiers' wages) just after he had sent the specie to one of the Bank's western branches. In another example from 1828, the St. Louis Receiver made a deposit in the Louisville branch of the Bank of the United States and then immediately withdrew it and moved it back to St. Louis.[14]

Secretary Rush liked banking with the Bank because it " lessens the number of officers, and makes the accounts more clear, and easier to be understood." In his letters and presentations to Congress, Rush often referred to the problem of "bad agents," and clearly believed the Bank was a much safer, and more accountable agent, than many others that the Treasury had used over the years, whether in collecting or disbursing public funds.[15] In May 1826, Rush wrote to Biddle requesting new branches in Mobile, Detroit, St. Louis, and Maine, which would "remove the necessity of employing any other than the Bank of the US and its offices as depositories of the public moneys throughout the United States." Rush's goal was " not to extend its connexion [*sic*] with the local or State banks in any case, if it can be avoided." Rush's request for new branches was granted, with the exception of Detroit.

Table A.1, in Appendix A, presents the characteristics of the US cities that had offices of the Second Bank branch in 1820 and 1830 with those that did not. The "cities" of the United States (defined by the US Census as urban places with population greater than 2,500) are listed, along with information on population (a proxy for the size of the market for commercial banking services), whether the city was the administrative center of a customs district, the relative volume of customs duties collected, the size of each city's state-chartered banking sector, and whether the city had a Second Bank branch. All of these city properties were interrelated, making it difficult to isolate their individual effects.

City size mattered, but more so in 1820 than in 1830. In both 1820 and 1830, the Bank placed branches in the major cities that were centers of high-volume customs districts, which also had large banking sectors. In 1820, the Bank put fourteen of its nineteen offices (the "parent" office in Philadelphia plus eighteen branches) in cities within the top quartile of population size, and ten in cities within the top quartile of banking sector size (measured by the number of state banking offices). In 1830, fourteen of twenty-six branches were in the top 25 percent of cities by population, and ten of twenty-six In the top 25 percent of cities by banking sector size. In 1830, almost all of the smaller cities that had Second Bank branches were located in places strategic for settlement of the upper Mississippi Valley, or for settlement of areas served by the Erie Canal, the most active settlement frontiers at the time.

The set of cities chosen for branches matched up well with the Bank's fiscal duty to collect and transfer the federal revenue, again, more so in 1820 than in 1830. Of the nineteen Second Bank offices in 1820, thirteen were customs office district cities. There were eleven cities that were also centers of customs districts, but did not get branches. These cities were primarily located in well-banked New England. In 1830, fourteen of the twenty-six cities with Bank offices were centers of a customs district. All six cities with a naval yard in 1820 and 1830 had a Second Bank branch.[16] The cities selected for a Second Bank branch that were not centers of a customs district were, for the most part, again, located in areas recently "opened" to US settlement west of the Appalachian Mountains (with the exception of Fayetteville).[17]

The Second Bank selected western cities for branches that were actual or potential centers of commodity distribution. Only two of these cities also had land district offices (Cincinnati and Louisville), where public land sales were managed. By the early 1830s, there were forty-nine western towns with land district offices, and only ten had a banking office (federal or state). The land receivers (the officials that received payment for the lands) were expected to forward receipts to the closest Second Bank branch, in specie, Second Bank money, or notes issued by "specie-paying" state banks in the Second Bank's estimation.[18]

Locating branches in western cities served two primary goals for the national government, revenue collection (public land sales) and nation-building. In an 1818 Resolution of the Second Bank's Philadelphia Board explaining why the Board had decided to postpone the opening of its branch in Nashville, Tennessee, the Board somewhat piously stated that the Directors' decisions about offices in the interior were

> influenced more by considerations of public duty than immediate pecuniary advantage, and by an earnest desire to renovate the currency of the country, facilitate the financial operations of Government, and afford to commercial intercourse those facilities in exchange without which the agricultural and commercial interests of the western country in particular must ever be subjected to great loss and inconvenience.

The Board may have learned from the experience of the First Bank of the United States. Petitions for branches of the First Bank of the US from Natchez and Louisville had not been successful, which "was probably a fundamental political mistake on the part of the [First] Bank in view of the rising importance of the New West."[19] Although the population and commerce of some of the western cities was modest in 1817, they would see impressive growth in the 1820s. The Bank began operations two years after the first successful steamboat run up the Mississippi River from New Orleans to Louisville, which had a transformative effect on the western economy—and on the Bank. Maps 3.1 and 3.2 show the contours of the Bank's branch network in 1820 and 1830. As shown in Maps 3.1b and 3.2b, the Bank's branch network was water transportation based; each branch was either on a coast or river. The Bank's asset growth in the 1820s was driven by its role in financing the movement of western commodities to market over rivers and oceans, most notably cotton.

 This analysis of the Bank's correspondence and characteristics of the cities chosen for Second Bank branches has pointed to the importance of fiscal duty and commercial profit in the Bank's decisions. Colocating with state-chartered banks was less and less important to the Bank over time, as shown in the next section.

Map 3.1a The Second Bank's branch network, 1820

Shifts in the economic geography of the dual banking system, 1820–1830

Over the 1820s, the Second Bank expanded its branch network in those places where the state-chartered banking system contracted. As a result, there was a growing divergence between regions that were state bank dominated and those that were Second Bank dominated. This section documents these shifts in the economic geography of the dual (state and federal) banking system between 1820 and 1830,

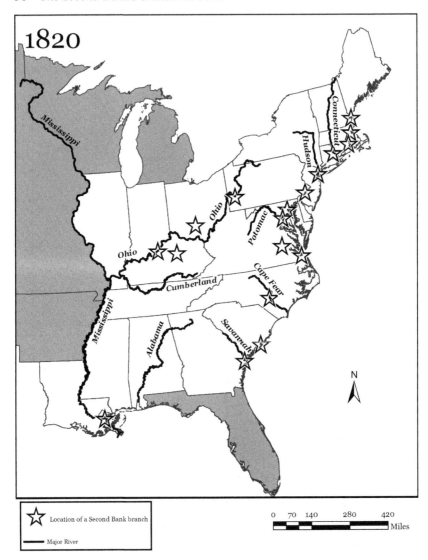

Map 3.1b The Second Bank's branch network and major US rivers, 1820

using a data set of the number and location of federal and state banking offices (including branches of state banks within their home states) by city and state.[20]

The US economy of the 1820s consisted of five regions: three older regions including the original states, New England, the Middle Atlantic, the South Atlantic or Southeast; and two new regions, the Southwest and Northwest (see Map 3.3), states that were organized after 1791.[21] The states and regions were the same in 1820, with the exception of one state, Missouri, in the Northwest, which became a state in 1821. Table 3.1 shows the number of federal (Second Bank) and state

Map 3.2a The Second Bank's branch network, 1830

banking offices (including branches) by region as defined by groups of states in 1820 and 1830.

When chartering the Second Bank, the federal government agreed not to charter any more banks, so any new banks that formed would do so under a state charter.[22] State bank regulations varied from state to state, and in this pre-free-banking period, all banks operated under charters granted by the legislature, as opposed to general banking law. State governments had incentive to charter banks, as they received fiscal benefits from chartering banks through ownership, taxation,

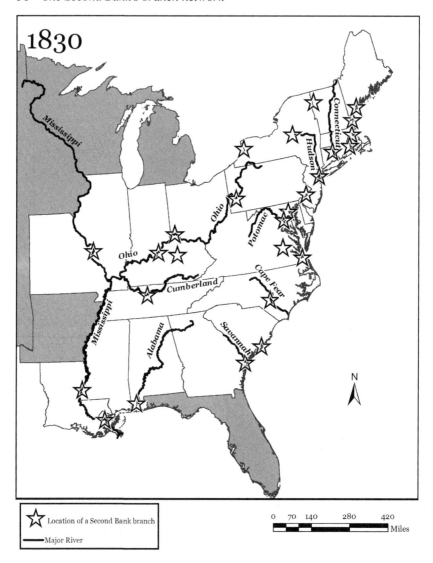

Map 3.2b The Second Bank's branch network and major US rivers, 1830

and/or access to credit (Sylla et al. 1987). For this reason, three states (Tennessee, Kentucky, and Ohio) passed prohibitively protective taxes or penalties on branches of the Second Bank located within their borders; Maryland imposed a more modest tax on branches of the Bank for revenue purposes. In February 1819, *McCulloch v. Maryland* found that state governments lacked the authority under the US Constitution to tax branches of the Bank, removing this kind of constraint on the Bank's ability to expand and operate.[23] If these efforts had been successful, the dual banking system would have developed much differently than it did.

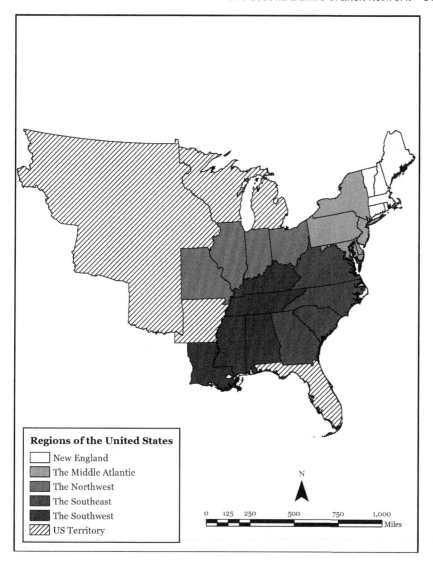

Map 3.3 Regions of the United States

Between 1820 and 1830, the number of banking offices in the nation increased from 360 to 429, or about 2 percent on an annual average basis. Table 3.2 shows the net change (number of entrants minus number of exits) in the number of state and federal banking offices between 1820 and 1830. Nationally, the rate at which states chartered new banks was lower in the 1820s than either the 1810s, when chartering was stimulated by the exit of the First Bank of the United States, the War of 1812, and the suspension of specie payments in 1814–1817 and 1819–1820, or the 1830s, when chartering was stimulated by the closure of the Second

Table 3.1 Number of state and federal (Second Bank) banking offices by state, 1820 (a) and 1830 (b)

(a)

	1820		Total no. of bank offices
	Second Bank branches (n)	State bank offices (n)	
New England			
Connecticut	1	11	12
Maine		13	13
Massachusetts	1	26	27
New Hampshire	1	10	11
Vermont		2	2
Rhode Island	1	30	31
Total	4	92	96
Share of national total	0.21	0.27	0.27
Middle Atlantic			
Delaware		9	9
DC	1	12	13
Maryland	1	23	24
New Jersey		14	14
New York	1	34	35
Pennsylvania	2	37	39
Total	5	129	134
Share of national total	0.26	0.38	0.37
Southeast			
Georgia	1	10	11
North Carolina	1	17	18
South Carolina	1	6	7
Virginia	2	18	20
Florida			0
Total	5	51	56
Share of national total	0.26	0.15	0.16
Southwest			
Louisiana	1	3	4
Alabama		6	6
Mississippi		3	3
Tennessee		8	8
Kentucky	2	16	18
Arkansas			0
Total	3	36	39
Share of national total	0.16	0.11	0.11
Northwest			
Illinois		3	3
Indiana		7	7
Ohio	2	21	23
Missouri		2	2
Michigan			0
Total	2	33	35
Share of national total	0.11	0.10	0.10
National	19	341	360

(b)

	Second Bank branches (n)	State bank offices (n)	Total bank offices (n)
New England			
Connecticut	1	17	18
Maine	1	20	21
Massachusetts	1	63	64
New Hampshire	1	20	21
Vermont	1	10	11
Rhode Island	1	43	44
Total	6	173	179
Share of national total	0.23	0.43	0.42
Middle Atlantic			
Delaware		10	10
DC	1	9	10
Maryland	1	17	18
New Jersey		18	18
New York	3	49	52
Pennsylvania	2	36	38
Total	7	139	146
Share of national total	0.27	0.34	0.34
Southeast			
Georgia	1	17	18
North Carolina	1	16	17
South Carolina	1	8	9
Virginia	2	18	20
Florida		2	2
Total	5	61	66
Share of national total	0.19	0.15	0.15
Southwest			
Louisiana	1	4	5
Alabama	1	4	5
Mississippi	1	3	4
Tennessee	1	2	3
Kentucky	2	1	3
Arkansas			0
Total	6	14	20
Share of national total	0.23	0.03	0.05
Northwest			
Illinois		0	0
Indiana		0	0
Ohio	1	13	14
Missouri	1	0	1
Michigan		3	3
Total	2	16	18
Share of national total	0.08	0.04	0.04
National	26	403	429

Source: Catterall (1902, pp. 376–7); Master list of state banking offices. See Appendix B.

Table 3.2 Changes in number of state bank and Second Bank offices by region, 1820–1830

1820

	Second Bank branches (n)	State bank offices (n)	Total offices (n)
New England	4	92	96
Middle Atlantic	5	129	134
Southeast	5	51	56
Southwest	3	36	39
Northwest	2	33	35
National	19	341	360

1830

	Second Bank branches (n)	State bank offices (n)	Total offices (n)
New England	6	173	179
Middle Atlantic	7	139	146
Southeast	5	61	66
Southwest	6	14	20
Northwest	2	16	18
National	26	403	429

1820–1830 change

	Second Bank branches (n)	State bank offices (n)	Total offices (n)
New England	2	81	83
Middle Atlantic	2	10	12
Southeast	0	10	10
Southwest	3	−22	−19
Northwest	0	−17	−17
National	7	62	69

Sources: See note to Table 3.1.

Bank (see Table 3.3). Chartering rates were lower in 1820–1829 compared with 1810–1819 in all regions except New England. It was less attractive to open a bank in the 1820s; the Bank's operations limited the duration and size of monetary expansions, resulting in a slower annual average pace of money growth and lower expected profits from banking.

After the Panic of 1819, when bank failures imposed losses on noteholders and shareholders, state legislatures were less interested in chartering new banks as well. Regionally, the slowdown in bank chartering was largest in the Southwest and Northwest, where bank failures were concentrated, where there was a lull in public land sales, and where the Second Bank became a powerful competitor with the ability to meet much of the demand for credit and money. The high rate of bank failures, combined with few new banks chartered, resulted in a reduction of the number of state banking offices in frontier regions from sixty-nine in 1820 to only thirty in 1830.[24]

Table 3.3 State bank chartering rates by region and decades, 1810–1836

	Number of banks chartered per 10,000 growth in population			Mean annual change 1810s to 1820s (%)	Mean annual change 1820s to 1830s (%)
	1810–1819	*1820–1829*	*1830–1836*		
New England	37	38.0	83	0.27	19.74
Middle Atlantic	16	4.0	20	–7.50	66.67
Southeast	3	2.0	15	–3.33	108.33
Southwest	11	0.6	5	–9.45	122.22
Northwest	6	0.7	4	–8.83	78.57
National	12	5.0	14	–5.83	30.00

Sources: Van Fenstermaker (1965, Appendix A); Bureau of the Census (1960), Series A195; Knodell (2006, Table 7).

Table 3.4 Population shares and banking-office shares, by region, 1820 and 1830

	Share of population	Share of Second Bank branches	Share of state banking offices	Share of state banking capital
1820				
New England	0.17	0.21	0.27	0.36
Middle Atlantic	0.34	0.26	0.38	0.30
Southeast	0.25	0.26	0.15	0.16
Southwest	0.14	0.16	0.11	0.16
Northwest	0.09	0.11	0.10	0.02
1830				
New England	0.15	0.23	0.43	0.39
Middle Atlantic	0.33	0.27	0.34	0.34
Southeast	0.23	0.19	0.15	0.19
Southwest	0.16	0.23	0.03	0.08
Northwest	0.13	0.08	0.04	0.005

Source: Bureau of the Census (1960); Master list of state banking offices; see note to Table 5.7 for state banking capital data and method.

Table 3.4 shows each region's share of population, state banking offices, state banking capital, and Second Bank branches in 1820 and 1830. In 1820, the more developed regions were somewhat underserved by the Second Bank, and the less developed regions, somewhat overserved. New England and the Middle Atlantic were home to 65 percent of all state-chartered banks, and 47 percent of all Second Bank branches. Per capita incomes, and per capita demand for money, were higher in these states, where agricultural productivity was higher and the more monetized manufacturing sector was larger. The frontier regions, the Southwest and the Northwest, had 21 percent of all state banking offices and 27 percent of all Second Bank offices.

By 1830, the relationship between share of state banks and share of Bank branches is notably looser: the Southwest had only 3 percent of all state banks, but 23 percent of all Second Bank branches, while New England had 43 percent of all state banks, but the same 23 percent of all Second Bank branches. The Northwest's share of all Second Bank branches fell, but was still almost twice its share of all state bank offices. The Second Bank added seven net new branches between 1820 and 1830, and placed four of them in New England and the Middle Atlantic, which gained ninety-one state bank offices (eighty-one of these in New England alone), and three in the Southwest and Northwest, which lost thirty-six state bank offices.[25] All of the new branches were added after 1826; six of these served the western market either from the Mississippi River route (Natchez, Mississippi; Mobile, Alabama; Nashville, Tennessee; and St. Louis, Missouri) or the Erie Canal route (Utica and Buffalo, New York).

Bank density gives information about the size of the banking sector in relation to population. Density is defined here as the number of banking offices per 10,000 people; a higher number denotes greater density and access. Table 3.5 shows the density of the federal segment of the dual banking system (number of

Table 3.5 State, federal, and overall bank density by region, 1820 and 1830

	Second Bank offices per 10,000 pop. (n)		State bank offices per 10,000 pop. (n)		Total no. of banking offices per 10,000 pop.	
	1820	1830	1820	1830	1820	1830
New England						
n	0.24	0.31	5.55	8.85	5.79	9.16
Index (regional density/national density)	1.21	1.50	1.55	2.79	1.53	2.71
Middle Atlantic						
n	0.16	0.17	4.02	3.36	4.17	3.52
Index	0.78	0.82	1.12	1.06	1.10	1.04
Southeast						
n	0.21	0.17	2.11	2.09	2.31	2.26
Index	1.03	0.84	0.59	0.66	0.61	0.67
Southwest						
n	0.22	0.29	2.65	0.68	2.87	0.97
Index	1.11	1.42	0.74	0.21	0.76	0.29
Northwest						
n	0.23	0.12	3.85	0.99	4.08	1.12
Index	1.17	0.61	1.07	0.31	1.08	0.33
National						
n	0.20	0.20	3.59	3.18	3.79	3.38

Sources: Appendix C, Tables C.1 and C.2.

Second Bank branches per 10,000 people), of the state segment (number of state banking offices per 10,000 people), and of dual system as a whole (number of banking offices per 10,000 people), by region and nationally, for 1820 and 1830. (The underlying state-level data is presented in Tables C.1 and C.2, Appendix C.)

In 1820, the most developed banking systems, as measured by the overall density index, were those of New England, the Middle Atlantic (both older regions), and the younger Old Northwest. Between 1820 and 1830, the density of the banking system (state plus national banking offices) fell 10 percent, as the number of banking offices did not keep pace with population growth. All of the contraction in density took place in the state-chartered sector. Bank density rose in New England, fell somewhat in the Middle Atlantic and Southeast, and fell significantly in both the Southwest and Northwest. In both of these newer regions, the fall in bank density is driven by the contraction of the state banking sector.[26] The "density gap," the ratio of highest to lowest regional bank density, rose from 3.5 banking offices per 10,000 people in 1820 to 8.2 in 1830.

In 1820, the Second Bank was somewhat more likely to open a branch in cities with more state banks per capita. This is shown in Figure 3.1, a scatter plot with state bank density on the vertical axis and Second Bank density on the horizontal axis. The relationship was generally positive if the two outlier states are eliminated (Delaware, with a Second Bank density index of 0, and Louisiana, with a very high Second Bank density index of 3.27). That is, the Second Bank's branch network was relatively more dense in the same states that had relatively more dense state banking sectors. By 1830 (see Figure 3.2), the relationship between the two indices is roughly inverse, showing that there were more Second Bank branches per capita in states with fewer state banks per capita. In other words, in 1820, the Bank tended to colocate with the state banks; by

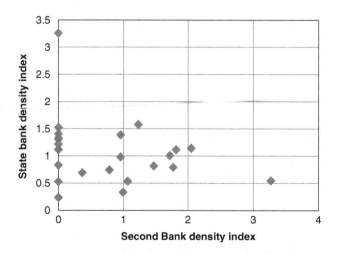

Figure 3.1 State bank density and Second Bank density across states, 1820.

Sources: Appendix C, Tables 3.1 and 3.2.

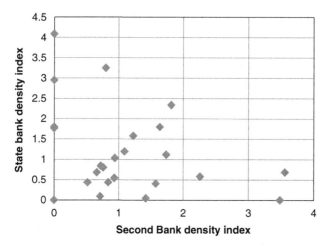

Figure 3.2 State bank density and Second Bank density across states, 1830.

Sources: Appendix C, Tables 3.1 and 3.2.

1830, the Bank had built up its network in those regions where there were fewer state banks. Finally, a comparison of the scatter plots for 1820 and 1830 shows divergence in the mix of state and federal banking offices across states over the decade. In 1820, there is closer clustering around the point where the density of a region's banking system was exactly at the national average density (of one) for both sectors.

The geographic disconnect between Second Bank and state bank offices is also seen in the regional maps of the dual banking system. Maps 3.4–8 show the location of Second Bank branches in relation to state banking offices in each region in 1820 and 1830. In the older regions in 1820, there is a reasonably close spatial clustering of the state banks and the Second Bank branches. By 1830, the state banking system had expanded into interior regions in the Northeast, reflecting the greater market orientation of agriculture in those areas, and, by implication, greater levels of internal trade between the major cities and their agricultural hinterlands. But the Second Bank branch network did not follow this interior expansion of the state-chartered banking system; instead, it expanded along the major rivers into the interior, particularly the southwestern interior.

Greater regional divergence in the mix of state and federal banking offices also shows up in market share data. Table 3.6 shows the Second Bank's market share, by region and for all cities within each region, in 1820 and 1830. Nationally, the Bank's market share rose slightly, both for cities and for all areas. Between 1820 and 1830, the older regions became more state-bank dominated, and the newer regions, more Second Bank dominated. In the older regions, the Bank's overall (urban and rural) market share fell slightly in New England and the Southeast, and rose slightly in the Middle Atlantic. In the newer regions (Southwest and Northwest), the Bank's market share rose dramatically. In the Southwest, Second Bank

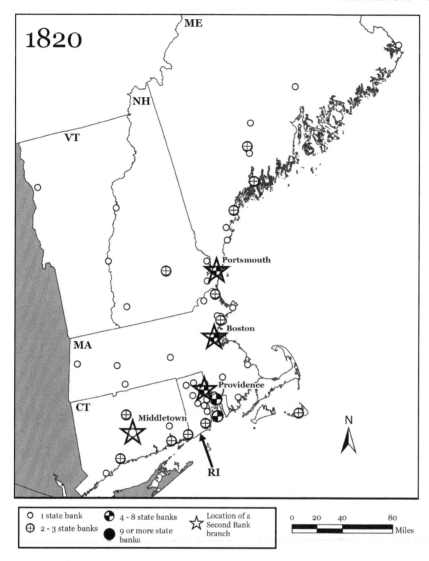

Map 3.4a State bank and Second Bank offices in New England, 1820

branches made up 7.7 percent of all banking offices in 1820, and 30 percent in 1830. In the Northwest, the Second Bank's overall market share rose from 8.6 percent in 1820 to 18 percent in 1830. The dramatic contraction of the state banking sector in the Southwest and Northwest after the Panic of 1819, and the dominance of the Second Bank in western money markets by 1830, is dramatically displayed in Maps 3.7 and 3.8.

The Bank's market share in the cities of the west was particularly large. It doubled between 1820 and 1830, and was much higher than its share of eastern

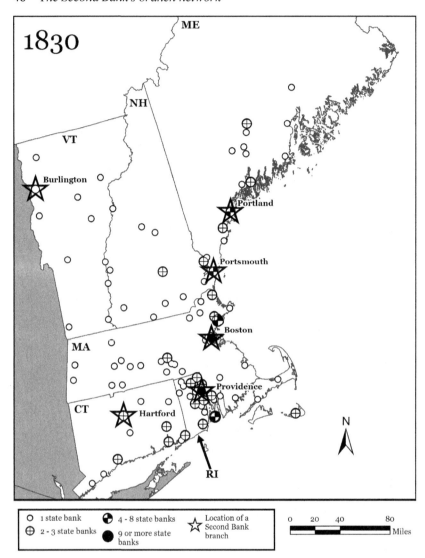

Map 3.4b State bank and Second Bank offices in New England, 1830

city banking markets. In 1830, the Bank operated almost one-half of all banking offices in Southwest cities, and 75 percent in Northwest cities (see Table 3.6).[27] Table 3.7 shows the number of state banks in all US cities with an office of the Second Bank. By 1830, the Second Bank was operating in eleven cities with one or no state-chartered banks, all except Utica (in western New York state, on the Erie Canal) in the Southwest or Northwest. The Bank's large urban market share in the Southwest and Northwest positioned the Bank to become the dominant dealer in domestic and foreign bills of exchange.

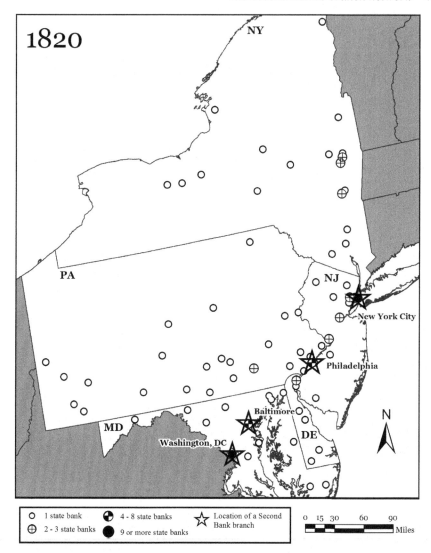

Map 3.5a State bank and Second Bank offices in the Middle Atlantic, 1820

Branch location and the Bank's effectiveness as a lender of last resort

In the twenty-first century, central banks can transfer liquidity instantaneously to any bank within their regulatory zones. In the 1820s, the time and expense required to move liquidity (especially in its "hard" form) from one place to another limited the Bank's ability to provide emergency liquidity assistance to state banks in a timely way. Whether the Bank lent specie from its vaults or its own notes or drafts, these instruments had to be physically delivered—quickly—from the

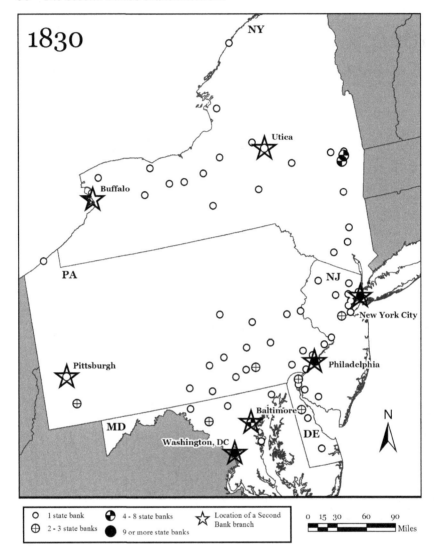

Map 3.5b State bank and Second Bank offices in the Middle Atlantic, 1830

Second Bank branch to the state bank in need of assistance. The Second Bank could respond quickly to a state bank with a liquidity crisis that was located in the same city as a Second Bank branch. But to reach banks located outside of these centers, specie or paper (a banknote or draft) had to be carried by road, river, or sea. Cities along the eastern seaboard from Washington to Boston had (at least) daily mail service by the 1830s. The roads connecting the major cities of New York, Philadelphia, Boston, and Baltimore were the best roads in the country; it was possible to travel seven miles an hour in 1820, and eight miles in 1830.[28]

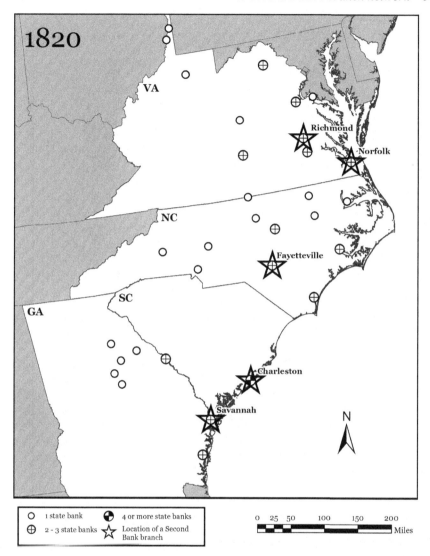

Map 3.6a State bank and Second Bank offices in the Southeast, 1820

Travel times were much longer on roads connecting these cities with smaller towns in their trading areas, and outside the Northeast.

Table 3.8 shows the number and percentage of state banks in and within a twenty-five-mile radius of the cities in New England and the Middle Atlantic regions that had Second Bank branches, in 1820 and 1830.[29] A bank experiencing a run located in Philadelphia, for example, had same-day access to the Bank's liquid assets. A bank located outside Philadelphia, but within twenty five miles, had one-day access: it could send a courier to the city, secure specie or drafts, and return

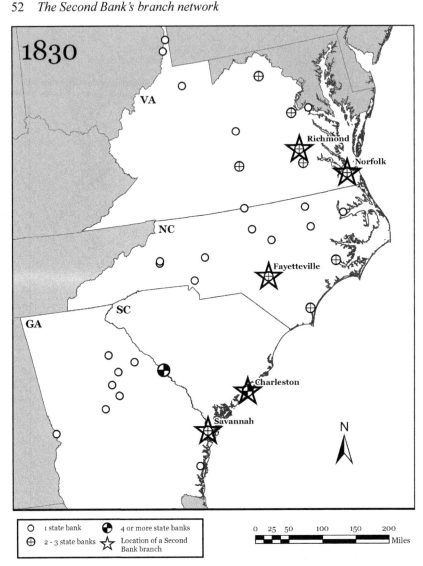

Map 3.6b State bank and Second Bank offices in the Southeast, 1830

within twelve hours. Table 3.8 also displays the number of state banks located in other cities with Second Bank branches. (Transportation linkages between these cities and their hinterlands were not good, so it is assumed that no banks outside these cities had one-day access.) In both 1820 and 1830, about one-fourth of all state banks had same-day access to a Second Bank office. In 1830, about half of all state banks could have potentially accessed Second Bank specie or drafts within one day.

If the Bank's top priority had been to provide timely liquidity support for the most state banks possible, in the manner of a modern central bank, it would have

Table 3.6 Second Bank market share of all banks and all banks in cities, by region, 1820 and 1830

	1820	*1830*
New England		
State banks in cities (*n*)	44	66
Second Bank branches in cities (*n*)	4	6
Second Bank share of all city banks	0.083	0.083
Second Bank share of all banks in region	0.042	0.034
Middle Atlantic		
State banks in cities (*n*)	56	64
Second Bank branches in cities (*n*)	4	6
Second Bank share of all city banks	0.067	0.086
Second Bank share of all banks in region	0.037	0.048
Southeast		
State banks in cities (*n*)	21	21
Second Bank branches in cities (*n*)	5	5
Second Bank share of all city banks	0.192	0.192
Second Bank share of all banks in region	0.089	0.076
Southwest		
State banks in cities (*n*)	11	7
Second Bank branches in cities (*n*)	3	6
Second Bank share of all city banks	0.214	0.462
Second Bank share of all banks in region	0.077	0.30
Northwest		
State banks in cities (*n*)	5	1
Second Bank branches in cities (*n*)	3	3
Second Bank share of all city banks	0.375	0.750
Second Bank share of all banks in region	0.086	0.18
National		
State banks in cities (*n*)	137	159
Second Bank branches in cities (*n*)	19	26
Second Bank share of all city banks	0.122	0.141
Second Bank share of all banking offices	0.053	0.061

Source: Appendix C, author's calculations of number of state banks in US cities. Pittsburgh, PA, included in Northwest region in this table. "Banks" refers to banking offices (branches included).

located its branches so as to maximize proximity to the most state banks. This it did not do. Between 1820 and 1830, second-tier banking centers arose in New England, the Middle Atlantic, and the Southeast. In 1820, the Directors passed over cities such as Lancaster, Pennsylvania, Albany, New York, Raleigh, North Carolina, and Portland, Maine, which had between two and four banks, in favor of Norfolk, Virginia, Louisville, Kentucky, and Lexington, Kentucky, which had one or no banks. In 1830, the Directors passed over Salem, Maryland, with six banks; Albany, New York, Troy, New York, and Newport, Rhode Island, each with four banks, and

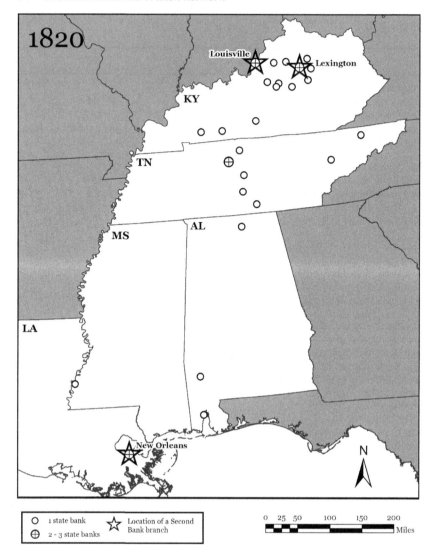

Map 3.7a State bank and Second Bank offices in the Southwest, 1820

Augusta, Georgia, with five banks, in favor of ten interior and frontier cities with one or no state banks.[30] If these six cities had received branches instead of six cities that had no banks or one bank, one-half of the state banks in the country would have had same-day access to the Bank's specie by 1830, instead of one-fourth.

For the Bank to have actually provided liquidity to the state banks across the nation in this fashion, it would have had to locate its specie where the state banks were, whether it lent the physical specie or notes that needed to have a reserve behind them. The location of the Bank's specie did not match up well

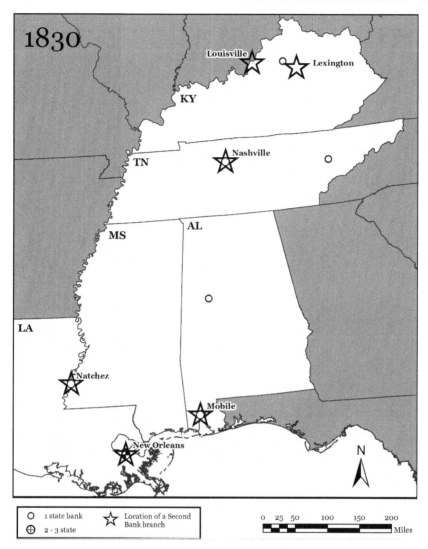

Map 3.7b State bank and Second Bank offices in the Southwest, 1830

with the geographic distribution of the state banks. Table 3.9 compares the allocation of the Bank's specie across its branches, by region, with the geographic distribution of state-chartered banks located in cities, in 1820 and 1830. In both years, a disproportionately small share of the Bank's specie was located in one of its New England branches, and a disproportionately large share in one of its Southwest branches. Between 1820 and 1830, the Bank's specie was relocated from the Southeast and New England to the Middle Atlantic, home to the Bank's main office and the country's financial center (Philadelphia and New York).

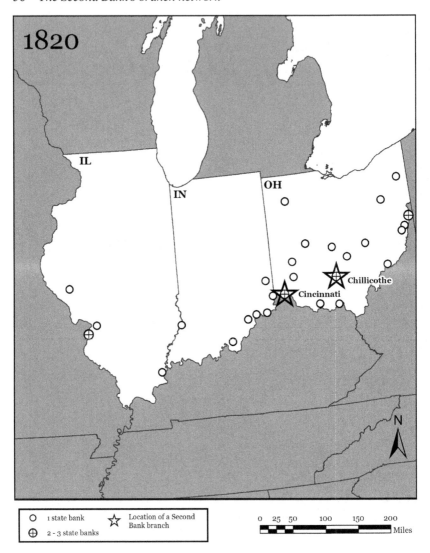

Map 3.8a State bank and Second Bank offices in the Northwest, 1820

As Chapters Five and Six will show, the Bank placed half of its specie in two of its branches, New York and Philadelphia, because the Bank's foreign exchange and specie market operations were centered in those two cities.[31]

Branch location and the quality of state bank currency

The Second Bank is frequently credited with improving the quality of the currency (banknotes) issued by the state-chartered banks. The Bank did not have supervisory authority over the state banks; this resided with the state banking

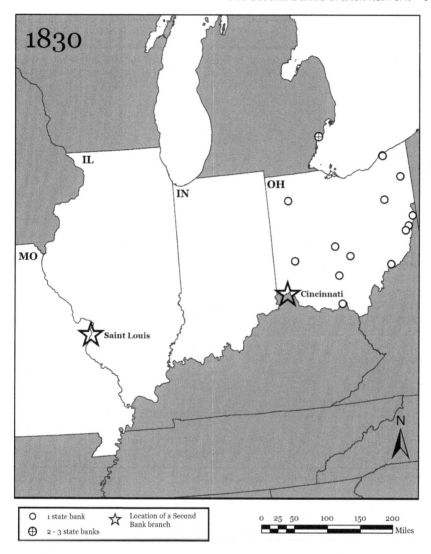

Map 3.8b State bank and Second Bank offices in the Northwest, 1830

authorities. However, the Bank did enforce regular clearing and settlement of interbank debt at all of its branches, and it had the power of determining which banks were "specie-paying" and which were not, for the purpose of meeting tax and customs duties payments to the US government. This section uses banknote discount rate data to understand whether the Bank had a salutary effect on the quality of state-bank notes in regions where it played a large role in the commercial banking system.

Markets for banknotes had developed in the major cities by the time the Bank was chartered. Small financial firms, variously called private bankers, lottery and

Table 3.7 Number of state banking offices in cities with a Second Bank branch, 1820 and 1830

Cities with Second Bank branch in 1820	State banking offices in 1820 (n)	Cities with Second Bank branch in 1830	State banking offices in 1830 (n)
New York City	9	New York City	18
Philadelphia	8	Philadelphia	11
Baltimore	8	Baltimore	7
Boston	6	Boston	16
New Orleans	3	New Orleans	4
Charleston	4	Charleston	5
Washington DC	12	Washington DC	8
Richmond VA	2	Richmond VA	2
Providence RI	7	Providence RI	10
Cincinnati	3	Cincinnati	0
Norfolk VA	2	Norfolk VA	2
Savannah	2	Savannah	3
Portsmouth NH	4	Portsmouth NH	6
Pittsburg	2	Pittsburg	1
Lexington KY	2	Lexington KY	0
Louisville KY	2	Louisville KY	0
Fayetteville NC	2	Fayetteville NC	2
Middletown CT	1	Hartford CT (removed from Middletown)	3
Chillicothe OH	3	Utica NY	1
		Natchez	1
		Mobile	1
		Buffalo	0
		Burlington	0
		Nashville	1
		St. Louis	1
		Portland ME	4

Sources: Master list of state banking offices (see Appendix B).

exchange offices, and exchange dealers, bought and sold notes issued by "foreign" (non-local) banks, both "current" notes, that were accepted by local banks, and "uncurrent" notes, which were not. The dealers could deposit the current notes in the bank, and either resell the uncurrent notes or return them for redemption into specie or some preferable form of paper. These dealers operated alongside the state-chartered banks, and supplied a service complementary to theirs. Banknote discount rates were published in the local newspaper or in periodicals specializing in market information about banks.

Table 3.10 compares banknote discount rates quoted in Philadelphia in 1818, 1823, 1828, and 1833 (early January dates).[32] A $10 Ohio bank note with a 1 percent discount rate sold for $9.90 in Philadelphia funds; one with a 10 percent discount rate sold for $9.00. Low discount rates signaled the market's perception that the issuer was easy to access, liquid, and solvent. The banknotes are divided into three broad groups, those issued by banks in states and cities within

Table 3.8 Proximity analysis

Major cities with a Second Bank branch	1820		1830	
	State bank offices in city (n)	State bank offices in and within 25 mile radius of city (n)	State bank offices in city (n)	State bank offices in and within 25 mile radius of city (n)
New York City	9	14	18	25
Philadelphia	8	17	11	19
Boston	6	12	16	32
Providence	7	28	10	43
Portsmouth	4	9	6	13
Baltimore	8	9	7	9
Middletown	1	5		–
Washington	12	13		9
Portland		–	4	8
Hartford		–	3	5
Total	55	107	75	163
State banks in other cities with a Second Bank branch *(n)*	23	23	27	27
Total no. of state banks proximate to Second Bank branch	78	130	102	190
Total no. of state banking offices	341	341	403	403
Share of state banks in proximity to the Second Bank	0.23	0.38	0.25	0.47

Source: Master list of state banking offices and maps of state banks; see Appendix B.

Table 3.9 Geographic distribution of state banks and Second Bank specie, 1820 and 1830

	1820			1830		
	State banks in cities (n)	Share of state banks in cities	Share of Second Bank specie	State banks in cities (n)	Share of state banks in cities	share of Second Bank specie
New England	44	0.33	0.10	75	0.48	0.07
Middle Atlantic	56	0.42	0.42	71	0.46	0.58
Southeast	21	0.16	0.23	28	0.18	0.11
Northwest	5	0.04	0.03	4	0.03	0.05
Southwest	7	0.05	0.21	7	0.04	0.19
Total	133			185		

Sources: State bank data from author's calculations from Master list of state banking offices (see Appendix B); Second Bank branch specie data from 22nd Cong., 1st Sess., H. Doc. 147.

Table 3.10 Banknote discount rates by region, 1818–1833

	January 1818			January 1823			January 1828			January 1833		
	Average	Upper	Lower	Average	Upper	Lower	Average	Upper	Lower	Average	Upper	Lower
Boston	1.75	1.5	2	1.5	1	2	1			1		
Massachusetts												
New York, city banks	0			0			0			0.25	0	0.5
New York, country banks	3			3.25	1.5	5	2	1.5	2.5	1	0.75	1.25
New Jersey	0			0.75	0	1.5	0.5			0.5	0	1
Philadelphia	0			0			0			0		
Other Pennsylvania	2.75	2	3.5	2.5	0	5	0.5			1	0	2
Delaware	1.5			0								
Baltimore				0.5			0			0.25		
Other Maryland	8	6	10	1	0.5	1.5	0.75	0.5	1	0.5		
District of Columbia	0			1.25			0.5			0.25		
Average in eastern core (New England and Middle Atlantic)	1.89			1.08			0.58			0.53		
Richmond	0											
VA				2			0.75	0.5	1	0.75	0.5	1
Northwestern VA				5			4			2.5	2	3
NC	2.5	1.5	3.5	6.5			6			2.75	2.5	3
SC	0.75	0.5	1	4.5			1			2.5	2	3
GA	1			6.5			2			8	6	10
Average of Southeast states	1.06			4.90			2.75			3.3		

Tennessee	4.75	4.5	5	35	10			4.5	4	5
Kentucky	4.75	4.5	5	70	30	25	35	22.5	20	25
Ohio	4.75	4.5	5	6	4			2.25	1.5	3
New Orleans				5.5	4			4		
Alabama					22.5	20	25	7	6	8
Mississippi					6			5.5	5	6
Michigan (Detroit)					3			1.75	1.5	2
Other Louisiana								4.5	4	5
Average of Southwest and Northwest states	4.75			29.13	11.36			6.5		

Source: Phillips (2013, vol. 4, pp. 26, 42, 54, 64).

the eastern core (New England and the Middle Atlantic), those issued by banks in the Southeast, and those issued by banks on the western frontier (north and south). The Bank's share of all banks, and of all city banks, was smallest in the eastern core and largest on the western frontier.

Over the period as a whole, the state bank currency did improve during the Second Bank era—in the eastern core, where the Second Bank had the smallest share of the banking market. In New England and the Middle Atlantic, banknote discount rates fell continuously over the period, reflecting the effect of state banks' settlement systems and redemption networks on banknote prices.[33] These networks were most advanced in the New England and Middle Atlantic regions, where transportation networks, banking systems, and internal markets in food-stuffs and manufactured goods were also most advanced.[34] By the mid-1820s the Suffolk Bank System had evolved into a multilateral net-settlement system in which the notes of any participating bank could be used to settle interbank debt, with the Suffolk Bank acting as a banknote clearing house.[35]

The state-chartered banks in New York, Baltimore, and Philadelphia organized redemption networks in which country banks held redemption accounts with a city bank, the central node of the network.[36] The city banks at the center of the network determined the terms on which the notes of the country banks would continue to be received in the center. As long as the country bank's balance did not fall below a stipulated level, the city bank would accept its notes at par. Virginia banknotes were at a discount in Baltimore and other Northeast cities until 1823, when the Bank of the Valley, and presumably the other Virginia banks as well, set up redemption accounts with banks in Baltimore, Philadelphia, and New York. The Bank of the Valley reported to Congress that it "made arrangements with the Baltimore banks, by which its notes were received by those banks at par in all *business transactions* [italics in the original]." The bank's notes "were not only good at home, but could be used, without loss in all business transactions in Balti-more, Philadelphia, or New York."[37] The Mechanics' Bank of New York was one of the city banks that organized a redemption network with a broad geographic scope. Map 3.9 displays the locations of banks in the Mechanics' Bank's network in 1833, right before the federal government started moving its deposits out of the Second Bank and into state institutions.[38]

Outside the core, average discount rates for the western region were higher in 1833 than they were in 1818 (but did fall between 1823 and 1833). In 1833, the average discount rate on western banknotes was 6.5 percent; on notes issued by banks in the Northwest (Ohio and Michigan), the rate was only 2 percent, com-pared with 8 percent on notes issued by banks in the Southwest (Kentucky, Tennes-see, Alabama, Mississippi, Louisiana). Maps 3.7b and 3.8b (banking offices in the Southwest and Northwest, respectively, in 1830) show that many of the banks in the Southwest were located in cities with a Second Bank branch, while none of the banks in the Northwest were. On the frontier, proximity to a Second Bank branch did not translate into lower banknote discount rates in eastern money markets.

The Bank's behavior reinforced the gap between the quality of "core" and "periphery" banknotes. The Bank kept 60 percent of its specie in its Middle

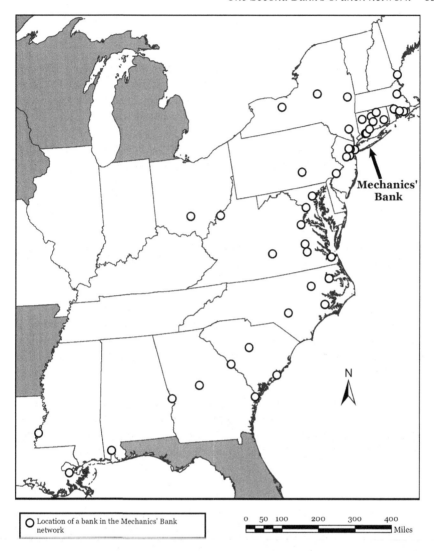

Location of a bank in the Mechanics' Bank network

0   50 100   200   300   400
Miles

Map 3.9 The Mechanics' Bank's network of banks, 1833

Atlantic branches, and it insisted on weekly settlement of balances due from the state banks in specie in the major eastern cities. In contrast, in the Southeast, Southwest, and Northwest, the Bank expected weekly settlement, but, acknowledging the lower liquidity of state banks in the agricultural regions, was willing to accept less liquid assets in settlement.

Evidence from one western branch, Louisville, suggests that the western branches of the Second Bank did not accept the notes of "foreign" state banks, including those in nearby states. Receiving and exchanging notes of other banks was the way the Second Bank "regulated" the state banks. In November 1832, the Cashier of the Philadelphia office asked the Cashier of the Louisville office to

> give me the names of the State banks with which you correspond, and particularly of those whose notes you receive on deposite [*sic*], with a statement of the nature and value of their accounts. The policy of receiving any distant State bank paper on deposite [*sic*], is a point to be discussed.

In his reply, the Louisville cashier listed a number of banks in Ohio, Virginia, Pennsylvania, Maryland, Connecticut, and New York, and explained that

> With these banks we have no other business than to collect for them . . . . *We do not receive the notes of any of those banks, nor indeed of any bank except the Bank of the United States and its branches* [emphasis added]. This regulation excludes all other notes from circulation, and it meets the entire approbation of our citizens.[39]

The Bank was more interested in displacing state-bank notes with its own notes than in improving the state bank currency, particularly in the west and south. The higher discount rates on western state bank money in eastern markets benefited the Bank by making its own $5 notes all the more attractive to merchants and farmers. In an 1830 letter to Gallatin about proposals in Congress to change the Bank's charter, Biddle wrote:

> I should not think it advisable to diminish the $5 notes of the Bank of the US which keep out the notes of equal amount which would otherwise be issued by the State Banks. It is a good illustration of the manner in which extremes touch that after all the financial troubles of Kentucky, that State professes a better currency than any other of the Union, consisting as it does entirely of Specie and notes of the Bank of the United States.[40]

During the Madison administration (1824–1828), the Treasury shared the goal of suppressing state-bank notes. It issued a circular to receivers of public money in February 1826, stipulating that "No bank note of a less amount than five dollars is to be received." Five dollars was the smallest note the Second Bank was authorized to issue.[41]

Conclusion

Smith (1953, p. 40) thought that the Second Bank's "branches were established with an eye to the convenience of the Treasury as well as the needs of business and there was ordinarily little or no conflict of interest between these two objectives." The evidence presented here provides support for Smith's view. In locating branches, the Bank took both duty and profit into consideration. Some of the cities received branches to maximize the Bank's effectiveness as the depository for customs duties, and other cities received branches because they had fewer state banks and high growth potential. Colocating with state banks so that it could best support them as a modern-style central bank would was not the driving force behind the selection of cities for branches, especially after Biddle took charge. The new branches established in the less-populated, less-banked frontier areas after 1826, which Catterall said were "in defiance of correct banking principles," were well placed from the point of view of the Bank's expanding business in domestic and foreign exchange, the subject of the next chapter.

Notes

1 Catterall (1902, p. 379); Dewey (1910a, p. 196). The Bank also established agencies at Chillicothe, OH, Cincinnati, OH, and Macon, GA. The agencies are not discussed here.
2 Section 14 of the Act to incorporate the subscribers to the Bank of the United States, reproduced in large part in Catterall (1902), Appendix I.
3 In light of President Andrew Jackson's later war on the Bank, it is worth noting that in August of 1821, in his role as Military Governor of the Florida Territory, Andrew Jackson lobbied the President of the Bank for a branch at Pensacola. The Board felt that more time was needed for the area's trade to develop and for business people to become well established and well known to the Philadelphia bank managers, "at least by reputation." 23rd Cong., 2d Sess., S. Doc. 17, pp. 249–51.
4 Crawford was able to manage without the branch at Augusta by using the services of the Milledgeville branch of the Bank of the State of Georgia, as "considerable sums of money must necessarily be expended in the settled parts of the State nearest to the theatre of war . . . It will, no doubt, be more convenient for the offices who have to disburse the public money for transporting the baggage, etc., of the troops, to obtain it at Milledgeville than at Augusta or Savannah." Crawford, who spent his youth and young adulthood in and around Augusta, knew that the rate of exchange between Milledgeville and Savannah was in favor of Savannah "at this season of the year," so he presumed that it would be "advantageous for the bank at Milledgeville to take the drafts of the Government payable in Savannah by the Branch Bank of the United States established there." 18th Cong., 1st Sess., Pub. 705, pp. 575, 833; Mooney (1974, pp. 4–5).
5 William Jones Papers, November 17, 1816, letter from William Crawford to William Jones.
6 William Jones Papers, July 19, 1817, letter from Crawford to Jones; 18th Cong., 1st Sess., Pub. 705, p. 833.
7 18th Cong., 1st Sess., Pub. 705, p. 836.
8 Note that the Federal Reserve's business model created the incentive to locate branches where there were more banks, since the capital of the district reserve banks came from the commercial banks that joined the Federal Reserve (by 1913, there were commercial banks operating under national charters, and they were required to join the Federal Reserve, or lose their national charter).
9 On the Albany branch decision, see 23rd Cong., 2d Sess., S. Doc. 17, pp. 251–2; Biddle Papers, October 27, 1826, letter from Biddle to Martin Van Buren. Wilburn (1967) suggests that the Bank's refusal to open a branch in Albany came back to haunt the Bank during the Bank War, when the state government was a strong opponent of the Bank even though, according to Wilburn, many of the New York banks in the western district and New York City supported the Second Bank (albeit quietly). On the Utica branch, see Biddle Papers, September 15, 1830, letter from Biddle to James Bennett. Biddle added that the Utica branch "cannot fail to be useful, and in case any trouble should grow out of the present system of banking in your State, may be highly necessary to the Community." Biddle was referring to the new bank legislation adopted by New York

in the 1829 Safety Fund Act. Utica's bank density was higher than Albany's (3.4 banks per 10,000 population compared with Albany's 2.4), which was offset by high expected growth in trade volume and loan demand as the Erie Canal lowered transportation cost on the west–east route.

10 William Jones Papers, Box 2, July 19, 1817, letter to Jones from Crawford. The Bank may simply have wanted to demonstrate the Bank's independence from political pressure. Fayetteville had 5.7 banks per 10,000 inhabitants in 1820, and Raleigh had 11.2. Fayetteville's population grew between 1820 and 1830, while Raleigh's population fell. See Appendix A.

11 McAllister Papers, Box 2, Folder 97. Letter of August 11, 1824, to Biddle from James Lloyd.

12 Biddle Papers; January 21, 1830, letter from Biddle to Hemphill, which reproduced the February 1826 memorial from the citizens of St. Louis requesting the establishment of a Branch. Biddle dispatched Thomas Cadwalader, of Philadelphia, to Nashville and St. Louis to assess the need for Second Bank branches in those cities. His report on St. Louis was sent in March 1827 and concluded that an office there would "afford certain conveniences to the Government" and "facilitate, in frequent instances, the mercantile operations of the place," but that there was no "source from which business of a regular banking character would flow in sufficient amount" as to serve the interests of the stockholders. He went on to say that, since the board might take a different view, or as circumstances might change dramatically "in the rapid movements of a new country," he advanced a list of prominent gentlemen who could potentially serve as directors of a branch in St. Louis. 23rd Cong., 2d Sess., S. Doc. 17, pp. 5–9.

13 23rd Cong., 2d Sess., S. Doc. 17, p. 254. The St. Louis petitioners observed that to meet expenditures other than wages, "Drafts have to be given on the different Receivers of Public Money residing in this and the adjoining State, and on the Branches of the US Bank at Louisville and New Orleans, the whole of which is attended with considerable delay and risk."

14 20th Cong., 1st Sess., S. Doc. 193.

15 23rd Cong., 2d Sess., S. Doc. 17, pp. 254–5. By 1827, land office receivers made deposits only in branches of the Bank of the United States with the exception of those in Alabama; 20th Cong., 1st Sess., S. Doc. 193, pp. 58. By 1834, naval pensions were paid only at Bank of the United States branches with the exception of a state bank in Delaware and one in New Jersey; 24th Cong., 1st Sess., H. Rep. 585, p. 756. On the matter of "bad agents," see 20th Cong., 1st Sess., S. Doc. 195, p. 4, where Rush told Congress that using the Bank as the government's fiscal agent allows "bad agencies" to be "completely avoided."

16 These cities were New York, Charlestown, MA (a suburb of Boston), Philadelphia, Portsmouth, Washington, and Norfolk; White (1951, p. 287).

17 In 1820, these were Pittsburg, Cincinnati, Louisville, Lexington, Fayetteville, and Chillicothe; to these were added, by 1830, Natchez, MS, Mobile, AL, St. Louis, MO, Nashville, TN, Utica, NY, and Buffalo, NY. Burlington, VT, a northern frontier town and center of a customs district, also received a branch by 1830 but had a population under 2,500.

18 From Master list of state banks, Appendix B, and Rohrbough (1990).

19 The Board's statement is from 18th Cong., 1st Sess., Pub. 705, p. 836. Of course, pecuniary returns did matter, since the reason for the postponement was the penalty tax the state of Tennessee had imposed on out of state banks. See Wettereau (1942, pp. 78–81, 83–4, 85, 88). On 1815 as the date of first successful steamboat run up the Mississippi, see Hunter (1949, pp. 17–18).

20 See Appendix B for a detailed discussion of the sources and methods used to construct the Master list of state banking offices used in this study.

21 The Missouri, Arkansas, Michigan, and Florida territories are not considered in this analysis, since these governments could not charter banks.

22 Section 21 of the charter did allow Congress to create more banks in the District of Columbia.

23 Catterall (1902, pp. 64–5); Ellis (2007, p. 65). In the opinion, Justice Marshall wrote, "The exigencies of the nation may require that the treasure raised in the north should be transported to the south, that raised in the east conveyed to the west, or that this order should be reversed. . . . The great duties of the bank are prescribed; those duties require branches; and the bank itself may we think, be safety trusted with the selection of places where those branches shall be fixed." Georgia levied a tax on out-of-state bank stock owned by individuals. Indiana and Illinois included provisions in their state constitutions in 1816 and 1818, respectively, prohibiting establishment of any banks not chartered by the state. These provisions were not challenged.

24 Van Fenstermaker (1965, p. 90) reports a much larger contraction of western banking after 1820, because he includes in his 1820 count 47 banks chartered by Kentucky in 1818 whose charters were repealed in 1820. These are not included in Weber's count, presumably because there is no evidence these banks ever were capitalized. Bodenhorn (2003, p. 240) refers to 63 western banks closing after the Panic of 1819; this is apparently taken from Van Fenstermaker's table showing the number of western banks falling from 80 in 1820 to 17 in 1825.

25 The Bank opened nine new branches and closed two. These data allocate banking offices to regions as defined by groups of states. Regions are perhaps more meaningfully defined in terms of transportation and distribution networks, but population data is collected on a state level. One of the Bank's branches, that at Pittsburg, was in the Middle Atlantic region as a city of Pennsylvania, but it was in the Northwest insofar as it was on the Ohio River and part of the larger Mississippi River Valley economy.

26 In the Northwest, the density of both the Second Bank and state bank sectors fell between 1820 and 1830, but the fall in state bank density was proportionally larger.

27 In this table, Pittsburg is considered part of the Northwest, not the Middle Atlantic.

28 Pred (1973, pp. 85–93).

29 Table 3.8 assumes that roads connecting cities with their hinterlands were about half as good as the roads connecting the major cities; see Pred (1973, p. 86).

30 See Table A.1.

31 The Bank's management may have felt that its specie was not needed in New England and the Southeast due to the liquidity concentration and mobilization provided by the Suffolk Bank System in Boston and the branch networks in Virginia, North Carolina, and Georgia.

32 Over this time, the population of banks in this data source changed as banks entered and exited. Nile's Register, a Baltimore newspaper, published banknote prices in the Baltimore market in August 1818 at Mr. Cohen's Lottery and Exchange Office. The notes of New York, Boston, and Philadelphia banks were quoted at par; others at various discounts from par (banks in New Jersey, Pennsylvania, Delaware, Maryland, Virginia, North Carolina, South Carolina, Georgia, Kentucky, and Ohio).

33 Van Fenstermaker (1965, p. 43), argued that "interbank deposits thus helped to create a more uniform currency for the nation," generally. The evidence presented here suggests that this was more true for certain regions than for others.

34 See Meyer (2003).

35 Bodenhorn (2003, p. 99).

36 Other commercial cities, such as Providence, RI, also organized redemption networks, but those in New York, Baltimore, and Philadelphia were the largest and most important.

37 25th Cong. 2d Sess., H. Doc. 79, p. 414. The bank was proud to report that "Between the funds kept in redemption accounts in other banks and the notes of other banks on hand, the Bank of the Valley was enabled . . . to meet every return of its notes by other banks since the year 1823." That is, it met all its debts to other banks without the need to ship any specie from its vault. Van Fenstermaker (1965, p. 43) cites an 1823 issue of

Niles' Register that the "bank notes of Virginia, District of Columbia, and Pennsylvania were received for deposit without discount at Baltimore banks" in that year.

38 On the Mechanics' Bank, see Redlich (1968, Part I, pp. 51–2).
39 22nd Cong., 2d Sess., H. Rep. 121, pp. 145–6.
40 Biddle Papers, September 9, 1830, letter from Biddle to Gallatin.
41 Kelsey Burr Papers, Box 2, cited in a June 21, 1830, letter from Biddle to the Cashier of the Boston branch of the Second Bank.

4 The Second Bank and the "exchanges"

Conquering space

Over the 1820s, more and more of the Bank's resources were shifted into the western and southwestern regions, where, as Biddle explained to Congress, "the production of the great staples seemed to require most assistance in order to get them into the market."[1] Although Biddle framed the Bank's western focus as a public service, it also served the profit-seeking side of the Bank's mission. In interior cities such as Nashville, Mobile, Natchez, and St. Louis, the Bank enjoyed a large wedge between the cost of making payments with specie, and its own cost to supply paper exchange. These were underbanked markets with a high growth in demand for financial services due to the introduction of steamboats and the expansion of slave production of the "great staples."

In the pre-canal and -railroad era, distance translated to long and costly time lags in transmission of information and in the movement of liquidity (specie). Through its "exchange" business, the Bank lowered the cost of making interregional payments, eliminated seasonality from long-distance payments, and provided a highly elastic supply of trade finance. The Bank stimulated the growth of interregional trade, particularly the "triangle trade" through New Orleans which drew in areas of recent US settlement on the western frontier. The New Orleans branch and its tributary branches in the upper Mississippi Valley (Natchez, Nashville, Louisville, Lexington, Cincinnati, St. Louis) became even more important to profit generation after the Bank entered foreign exchange dealing on a large scale. These were the cities where the Bank opened new branches after 1825 and enjoyed little competition from the state-chartered banks.

The Bank's exchange business was organized around the needs of its two primary clients: wholesale merchants in long-distance trade, and the US government.[2] This chapter discusses the monetary barriers to trade on the frontier before the entry of the Bank; the organization and management of the exchange business; the central role of New Orleans within the Bank's business model; and synergies between the exchanges and the Bank's fiscal duties to the national government.

Monetary barriers to trade on the frontier

By the 1810s, there were relatively well developed markets for intercity bills of exchange linking Boston, Philadelphia, New York, and Baltimore; the rate of thirty-day exchange at Boston on Baltimore, Philadelphia, and New York was

0.5 percent in 1812–1814. Bank checks circulated among the better- and mutually known banks of these four cities in payment of intracity and intercity mercantile debts.[3] The state banks' Suffolk System, redemption networks, and branch systems created the means of making payments within the New England, Middle Atlantic, and South Atlantic regions. But the monetary infrastructure in and linking the interior and the frontier to the eastern seaboard was far behind that within the commercial core of the country.

There were limited vehicles for the low-cost, low-risk transfer of value from interior and southeastern seaboard locations to the northeastern seaboard centers of commerce. The prohibition on interstate branching by state-chartered banks prevented the formation of national branch banks, within and between which interregional payments would have otherwise cleared. Further, neither the notes of, nor checks drawn on, the young, modestly capitalized banks located in newly settling cities were accepted in the eastern cities without large discounts; instead, payments had to be made with specie, eastern banknotes, or bills of exchange drawn on merchants in eastern cities. Each of these instruments had limitations as a means of remittance.

The cost of moving specie was prohibitively high, particularly between the coast and interior points. The cost of transporting specie to make payments from cities on the Ohio River to New York has been estimated at around 4 percent (of the value of the specie transported) in 1830; the cost was even higher in 1820, before the decade of improvement in inland river steamboat service. Due to the risk of theft and accidents on the rivers or oceans, insurance comprised a large portion of the cost of shipping specie.[4] Few marketable commodities had margins that could cover the cost of moving specie over long distances to pay for imports into the region, and the seasonality in the production and marketing of agricultural commodities meant alternating months of feast or famine in terms of cash earnings. Eastern banknotes were cheaper to transport, but they were in very short supply in interior cities, making bills of exchange the main alternative to specie as a means of long-distance remittance.

A bill of exchange was an order issued by one person, a drawer, to another person, the acceptor, or maker, requiring the acceptor to pay, at some certain time, a certain sum to the order of a specified individual or the bearer. Typically the drawer and the acceptor were business associates involved in wholesale trade. The acceptor confirmed the promise to pay by signing or "accepting" the bill, making it "two-name" paper. The drawer could present the bill in payment to a third party, who could hold the bill to maturity, or endorse it and present it in payment to a fourth party, and so on. In this way, negotiable bills of exchange passed "like currency from debtor to creditor, almost indefinitely."[5] As a means of remittance, bills of exchange were uncertain and inconvenient. Whoever held the bill at maturity was exposed to the risk that the acceptor may not pay when the bill was presented; for bills drawn on commodities, a fall in price between the time the bill was drawn and the date it was payable could cause the acceptor to default. Endorsers were also exposed to legal liability in the event of nonpayment by the maker.[6] Bills were not necessarily drawn in the same denomination needed by the merchant with remittances to make, nor were they necessarily payable where remittances had to be made. Both of these "inconveniences" resulted in additional transactions costs.

The price of bills of exchange in the interior was high and highly variable; at times, paper exchange was altogether unavailable. In June 1819, before the exchanges were placed on a sound footing under Biddle, Bank of the United States President Cheves wrote to Treasury Secretary Crawford:

> We find the most insuperable difficulties in obtaining the means of remitting revenue from Charleston and Savannah. The price of exchange is not only very high, but safe bills are not to be had at all except in very small amounts, and only occasionally. Possibly public stocks might be obtained in these places at the current rates; however onerous it might be, it might, nevertheless, be the interest of the bank to bear the loss of the difference between the market prices and the prices at which the Commissioners of the Sinking Fund are authorized to purchase. . . . Would you, therefore, authorize the Bank to purchase, for the use of the Sinking Fund, to the amount of revenue to be remitted from Charleston or Savannah, or for any part thereof?

Similarly, a Charleston merchant reported, in 1830, that prior to the formation of the Second Bank the rate of exchange between Charleston and New York swung between 8–10 percent in favor to 8–10 percent against Charleston, reflecting the extreme seasonality of trade flows between the two cities and the absence of private arbitrage capital. Merchants in Louisville and Nashville paid 10–15 percent for bills on New York or Philadelphia at the time the Bank was chartered.[7]

The Board Committee in 1817 had seen that the Bank would provide a valuable service to merchants if it conducted its exchange operations with "facility, promptitude, and regularity" (features which were notably absent from the domestic exchanges at the time).[8] The Bank seized the market opportunity by purchasing bills of exchange as earning assets, thereby taking them out of the role of a circulating medium, and financing these purchases by issuing its own drafts, which came to replace bills of exchange as a means of long-distance remittance. The spread that the Bank earned on this activity reflected the value that merchants placed on the lower risk and greater convenience of Second Bank drafts. The Directors of the Bank affirmatively identified the profit potential in the exchange business soon after the chartering of the Bank in 1816. A committee of the Bank's Board of Directors was appointed to "devise and report a plan for the transaction of exchange business," and it reported the results of its work in an 1817 report which reveals how the Bank's leadership perceived its market position and how it thought it could best be exploited. The committee reported that merchants lacked a means of remittance that was "cheap, certain, and convenient," and recommended that the Bank provide such an instrument, to the mutual benefit of the Bank and the merchants. The committee had to be thinking particularly of eastern merchants developing western markets.[9]

The purpose of the Bank's exchange operations was to facilitate the clearing of debts among merchants, not debts among banks. In a letter to the president of the New York branch of the Second Bank written in 1817, Bank President William Jones directed the New York Board to "decline receiving for collection the drafts or checks of the banks in your city, upon the banks in other cities." Jones explained that "it has never been the contemplation of this board to furnish to the state banks all the facilities of exchange, . . . while the bank and its offices should undertake the invidious task" of collecting the debts. (The Bank would, however, buy bills from, and sell its own drafts to, state banks.) Jones went on in his letter to the New York Board to explain that

> the real object of the Bank of the U.S. is to supply the *individual* demands for exchange; to afford the merchant the means of remitting without loss; and, by facilities and advantages he cannot obtain elsewhere, to make it his interest to transact his business with the bank and its offices." Such accommodation of the state banks (clearing debts among state banks), Jones said, would "remove the inducement which good customers would otherwise have, to give the bank and its offices the preference.

The Bank, with its branch network, was an interregional intermediary for clearing debts between merchants—not debts between state banks.[10]

During the debate over the rechartering of the Bank, Biddle touted the benefits of its exchange business, writing in 1830 that

> They who complain . . . are not the merchants but the large Capitalists and Bankers to whom the incessant fluctuations of exchange between all the towns of the US were the sources of extraordinary profit, which is now taken from them by the very low rate at which the Domestic exchanges are managed by the Bank.

Biddle mentioned specifically the benefits to the "Southern planter" who

> when he sold his crop to the Merchant was obliged to wait the returns from abroad incurring meanwhile the risk of the solvency of his merchant. Now the Merchant draws his Bill, receives the amount from the Bank and the planter gets his money without delay or risk.[11]

Organization, management, and evolution of the Second Bank's domestic exchange operations

During the Biddle presidency, the Bank organized and mobilized its nineteen-office branch network to become the dominant supplier of long-distance payments services within the national economy.[12] This section discusses the role of the branches and the head office in the domestic exchange business; the growth of this line of business within the Bank and on the western frontier; and pricing, costs, and profits in the domestic exchange business.

Organization and management of the domestic exchanges

The Bank's exchange business operated on both the asset and liability side of its balance sheet. On the asset side, branches discounted intercity domestic bills of exchange; on the liability side, branches sold drafts on other Second Bank branches, or on the Bank's international bankers. For example, the Cincinnati branch discounted bills drawn by merchants on shipments of pork to New Orleans, and sold drafts drawn on the New York, Philadelphia, and Baltimore branches, which Cincinnati merchants used to pay for goods purchased in those cities.[13]

The Bank faced the problem of "competing with itself," as western merchants had a choice between Bank of the United States notes and Bank of the United States interbranch drafts to make payments in eastern cities. Drafts sold at a premium, and notes were exchanged at par. Bank officials touted the advantages of Bank of the United States drafts over Bank of the United States notes as a means of long-distance payment. In one of his many long letters to Sen. Hemphill in the run-up to the Bank War, Biddle pointed out that an individual who chose to transfer funds from St. Louis to Philadelphia with notes issued by the St. Louis Bank of the United States branch would incur risk of theft if the notes were carried on his person, or mailed, and, in addition, he could not be sure that the Philadelphia office of the Bank of the United States would receive the St. Louis Bank of the United States notes at full face value. By drawing a draft payable to his order, in duplicate, he is "not liable to any hazard," the draft would be honored at full face value, without doubt, all for a premium of only 0.5 percent (at St. Louis on Philadelphia).[14]

The domestic exchanges were managed jointly by the central office in Philadelphia and the boards of the branches. Prices, terms to maturity, and bill volume were set centrally, with some room for local board discretion. The rates of domestic exchange were set administratively and did not vary in response to shifting supply and demand over the course of the year. This practise eliminated the seasonal spikes and troughs in domestic exchange rates.

Exchange markets in the west and south were highly one-sided, alternating from a market of all buyers and no sellers, to one with all sellers and no buyers, due to the highly seasonal nature of agricultural commodity trade flows in the pre-railroad era. Merchants in southern and western cities had debts to clear in eastern cities at different times of year than those at which they accumulated credits in eastern cities from selling cotton and produce. Biddle touted the public benefits provided by the Bank as it "[adapted itself] to the wants and interests of each section of the Union, by [being] alternately a large purchaser among the sellers of bills, and a large seller among the purchasers." Biddle explicitly noted the benefits to the south, where "the presence of a large and constant purchaser thus gives greater steadiness and uniformity to the demand for bills, on which the profit of the southern merchant and planter depends." These counterseasonal market-making operations would routinely involve short-term interbranch borrowing which took the form, essentially, of (interest-free) interbranch overdrafts, since drafts were sold in advance of remittances.[15]

At each office, there was a posted set of prices at which Bank of the United States drafts on other offices were sold, and bills of exchange payable in other branch cities were sold. The Bank did not charge commissions in addition to exchange.[16] In instructions for the Nashville branch, Biddle directed the management not to

> charge less than the rates established by resolution of the Board . . . ; it could charge more at its discretion. No bills longer than 6 months when drawn on N.O. [New Orleans], and not longer than 4 months if drawn on other places.

The Bank was a heavy user of the US Postal Service, as it mailed bills of exchange and letters recording the credits and debits to the running accounts between branches.[17]

Local boards were in charge of reviewing credit quality based on directors' knowledge of prospective borrowers.[18] This policy was expressed in a letter from Biddle to the cashier of the Nashville branch. Biddle had received a letter from a customer of the Nashville branch who was unhappy that his bill had been refused. Biddle said:

> I explained to Mr Dwyer's friend who brought me the letter that it was impossible for us at so great a distance to judge of the degree of credit which a person in Nashville ought to have in the Office, so well as the gentlemen who were on the spot—that we never interfered to give directions as to loans to individuals.

In direct correspondence with the Nashville Cashier, Biddle wrote, "The Board rely upon the prudence of your Direction, not to expand too suddenly, but to follow gradually and cautiously, the progress of the real business, and the real Commercial wants of the community around you."[19]

An important operating principle in the domestic exchange business was that the drafts drawn by one branch on another branch had to be "covered" with remittances of an equal amount, typically from bills of exchange payable at that branch. In his instructions to the Nashville branch, which can be taken to reflect Bank policy for the western branches generally, Biddle directed that the bills of exchange be

> mainly confined to such as can be collected and paid, at or through, the Bank and the Offices. Although, you can extend them to other places, if the Convenience of the Office or its customers should render it expedient. You can draw checks on the Bank and the Offices whenever you have balances there, or have the means of covering your checks by early remittances, so as not to incommode the Bank or the Office on which you draw.[20]

The Bank's branch network and its large capital base allowed it to manage the information costs and credit risk associated with holding a portfolio of domestic bills of exchange. These costs were significant in the light of rapidly expanding internal trade, the entry of new mercantile firms to mediate this trade, and the difficulty of getting reliable information about the firms upon which domestic bills were drawn. The Bank's network of branch boards played the important role of collecting and sharing information about the makers and endorsers of bills of exchange presented for purchase by the Bank.

Growth of the domestic exchange business

The Bank held three kinds of earning assets: bills of exchange, "discounts" (commercial paper payable locally), and funded debt securities of the US government. In addition to its earning assets, the Bank held cash reserves (specie and balances in London and Paris). Between 1821–1824 and 1829–1831, the bank's earning assets grew from $44 m to $82 m, an average annual rate of growth of 8.6 percent, and its overall leverage (assets per dollar of capital) increased from 1.68 to 2.76. The Bank's profitability, as measured by return on equity, rose from 5.16 percent to 8.95 percent, entirely explained by the Bank's rising leverage (see Table 4.1).

The exchange business (domestic and foreign) drove the Bank's asset growth at the end of the decade. In the early 1820s, exchange averaged 16 percent of earning assets; by the end of decade, 45 percent (see Table 4.2). After 1825, US debt occupied a smaller and smaller place in the Bank's portfolio. US debt was an

Table 4.1 Second Bank's return on equity, 1820–1833

	Return on assets (%)	Earning assets/assets	Assets/ Capital	Return on equity (%)	Dividend rate (%)
1820	3.99	0.83	1.53	5.06	
1821	3.64	0.85	1.53	4.73	3.5
1822	3.44	0.87	1.53	4.58	4.75
1823	3.73	0.83	1.76	5.45	5
1824	3.67	0.85	1.89	5.90	5
1825	3.87	0.88	1.96	6.67	5.5
1826	4.03	0.83	2.03	6.79	6
1827	4.02	0.9	1.99	7.20	6
1828	3.98	0.85	2.32	7.85	7
1829	4.02	0.83	2.5	8.34	7
1830	3.98	0.82	2.63	8.58	7
1831	3.5	0.9	3.15	9.92	7
1832	3.54	0.87	3.66	11.27	7
1833	3.33	0.87	3.51	10.17	7
1821–24	3.62	0.85	1.68	5.16	4.56
1825–28	3.98	0.87	2.08	7.13	6.13
1829–31	3.83	0.85	2.76	8.95	7

Note: Earning assets includes discounts, bills of exchange, and government securities; total assets adds to these real capital and cash. Three-year averages of return on equity may not equal the product of the three-year averages of return on assets, earning assets/assets, and assets/capital due to rounding error.

Sources: Author's calculations based on Catterall (1902, Appendix V), amended by substituting Catterall's estimates for annual bills of exchange in Appendix VI for the smaller, bi-annual amounts reported in Appendix V.

attractive asset, with a favorable risk-return profile, its large denominations, and its low transactions costs. But the Bank had no choice but to replace it as the federal government retired its debt. Bills of exchange replaced the US debt, and then some: between 1825 and 1833, the Bank's holdings of US debt fell $18 m, while its holdings of bills of exchange increased $56 m (see Figure 4.1). If the Bank's leverage had remained at its average level of 1825–1828, its return on equity would have fallen to 6.77 percent in 1829–1831, instead of rising to 8.95 percent.

The Bank's strong profitability performance in its later years was the direct result of the rapid growth in bills of exchange drawn in western regions. Between 1825–1828 and 1829–1831, the share of domestic exchange that originated in western regions rose from 32 percent to 52 percent. The growth of bills drawn at the Bank's western and southwestern branches was the direct result of new transportation technologies (the steamboat and the packet lines connecting New Orleans and Mobile to New York) that fostered, and was fostered by, the rapid growth in slave production of cotton, sugar, and tobacco for export in Mississippi Valley.[21] The specialized producers of these commodities consumed the flour, pork, corn, and whiskey that was shipped down the Mississippi River and also financed with bills of exchange. The reduction of inland exchange rates due to the Bank's exchange operations lowered the cost of getting product to market and increased the volume of marketable output.

Table 4.2 Second Bank's return on earning assets, 1820–1833

	Profit rate on discounts (%)	Portfolio share	Profit rate on exchange (%)	Portfolio share	Yield on Treasury debt (%)	Portfolio share	Weighted return on earning assets (%)
1820	4.4	0.67	2	0.13	3.74	0.21	3.99
1821	4.1	0.58	1.4	0.13	3.74	0.29	3.64
1822	3.9	0.6	1.4	0.17	3.74	0.23	3.44
1823	4.3	0.61	1.8	0.18	3.74	0.21	3.73
1824	4.1	0.52	1.9	0.16	3.74	0.33	3.67
1825	4.5	0.51	2.2	0.19	3.74	0.31	3.87
1826	5	0.49	2.2	0.21	3.74	0.3	4.03
1827	5	0.46	2.6	0.26	3.74	0.28	4.02
1828	5.1	0.46	2.5	0.31	3.74	0.23	3.98
1829	5.5	0.44	2.5	0.4	3.74	0.16	4.02
1830	5.3	0.45	2.6	0.44	3.74	0.12	3.98
1831	4.7	0.5	2.3	0.5		0	3.50
1832	5.8	0.39	2.1	0.61		0	3.54
1833	5.7	0.36	2	0.64		0	3.33
1821–24	4.1	0.58	1.6	0.16	3.74	0.26	3.62
1825–28	4.9	0.48	2.4	0.24	3.74	0.28	3.98
1829–31	5.2	0.46	2.5	0.45	3.74	0.09	3.83

Note: Three-year averages of weighted return on earning assets may not equal the product of the three-year averages of weighted return on discounts, exchange, and Treasury debt due to rounding error.

Sources: Sen. Doc., 17, 23rd Cong., 2d Sess., p. 194; yield on Treasury debt from Adams (1978, p. 118); sources cited in note to Table 4.1

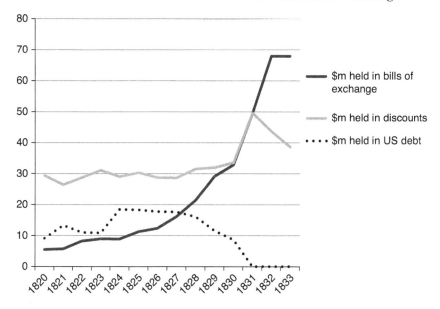

Figure 4.1 Second Bank portfolio shifts, 1820–1833.
Source: Table 4.1.

Costs, prices, and profits in the domestic exchanges

Moving funds over longer distances, which took more time to complete (New Orleans to New York vs Philadelphia to New York, for example), raised the Bank's exposure to credit risk and reduced its liquidity. The maturity of bills was longer on runs between the interior and the eastern seaboard, which created more credit risk. The Bank earned interest on the bills it discounted during the period the bill was transmitted to the point where it was payable (the bill drawn in New Orleans bill, made payable in New York, for example), but with longer time to market, there was more time for commodity prices (e.g., cotton) to change and for debtors' financial condition to change before the bill was paid. The higher cost of domestic exchange to and from the interior can be indirectly measured by the time required to move information and people between cities. The Bank was compensated for this additional credit risk and loss of liquidity with higher revenue per bill, measured either by the level of intercity exchange rates or the bid-ask spread. Figure 4.2 plots the level of intercity exchange rates in the early 1830s against the cost of transferring funds between cities, measured here by a proxy, the intercity travel time. (See Appendix D for a discussion of how intercity exchange rates were constructed.) The Second Bank charged higher rates for slower, longer-distance, more costly transfers.

The Bank's gross earnings from exchange depended on bid-ask spreads, the difference between the discount, or bid price, for exchange on the assets the Bank purchased (bills of exchange) and the premium, or ask price, for the liabilities the Bank sold (interbranch drafts).[22] Table 4.3 compares average intercity bid-ask

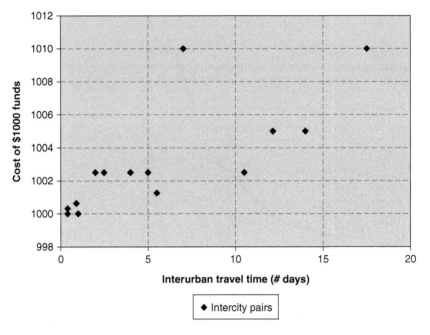

Figure 4.2 Intercity cost of funds and intercity travel time, 1830.

Sources: For intercity travel times, Pred 1973, his Figures 5.1–3, pp. 175–85. For intercity cost of funds, author's calculations from H. Rep. 358, 21st Cong., 1st Sess., pp. 34–7; and Appendix D.

Note: The 14 city pairs plotted include Philadelphia–Baltimore and New York with Philadelphia, Boston, Baltimore, Richmond, Norfolk, Charleston, Savannah, Mobile, New Orleans, St. Louis, Louisville, Cincinnati, Detroit, Buffalo, and Pittsburgh. The correlation coefficient is 0.75.

spreads within the eastern seaboard, and between New York and cities in the Lake Erie, South Atlantic, Ohio Valley, and Gulf Coast regions with measures of informational distance, taken as a proxy for the cost of interregional intermediation, for the same city groups. Not only did spreads rise with informational distance, but they rose more than proportionately when southwestern and western cities are compared with other cities outside the eastern seaboard core.

The costs of intermediation to New York were two to three times as high from the Gulf Coast cities as from the southern Atlantic Coast cities, but the spreads from the Gulf Coast cities were five times larger. Similarly, Ohio Valley cities were roughly twice as far, by these measures, from New York as Buffalo, but their spreads were almost five times higher. The Bank's market power in these western cities explains at least some of these gaps between the spread on domestic exchange and the cost of interregional funds transfer. The Bank had four state bank competitors in the New Orleans market in 1830, but it had only one in Mobile, Natchez, Pittsburgh, and St. Louis, and no competitors at all in Cincinnati, Lexington, and Louisville.

The Bank was aware of its market power and was prepared to use its greater efficiency in providing exchange to drive out the competition. The cashier of the

Table 4.3 Informational distance and Second Bank spreads on domestic exchange

	Average interurban travel time, 1831(n days)	*Average interurban event-publication time lag, 1841 (n days)*	*Average intercity bid-ask spread on domestic exchange, 1830 (percentage face value)*
Within eastern seaboard	0.76	1	0.04
Between New York and Lake Erie	4	4.3	0.25
Between New York and South Atlantic	4	5.9	0.28
Between New York and Ohio River	10	7	1.2
Between New York and Gulf Coast	13	11	1.5

Note: Eastern seaboard cities: New York, Philadelphia, Baltimore, Boston. Lake Erie city: Buffalo. South Atlantic cities: Richmond, Norfolk, Charleston, Savannah. Ohio River cities: St. Louis, Louisville, Cincinnati, Pittsburgh. Gulf Coast cities: New Orleans, Mobile.

Sources: Measures of informational distance from Pred (1973), Figs. 5.1–3, Maps 2.9 and 5.2, Table 2.4, pp. 48–57, 82–93, 175–85. Bid-ask spreads from author's calculations from H. Rep. 358, 21st Cong., 1st Sess., pp. 34–7; see Appendix D.

Louisville branch wrote to the "parent" office in Philadelphia in November 1832 that "Louisville has become the great mart for the western states. . . . This you will see forms a large field for exchange operations, particularly as we have no competition." The same year, the Philadelphia cashier wrote to the Cincinnati cashier that a new state bank in Cincinnati, the Commercial Bank, had

> bought a large amount of bills on New Orleans. If your office can get this business, the Commercial Bank would have to employ its funds in discounting city paper. This is more peculiarly its business as a local bank, while the exchange business properly belongs to your office as a part of the national bank. . . . A reduction in your rates of purchase would probably render the exchange business no longer profitable to that bank; and we know well that our offices can afford to purchase at lower rates than State banks.[23]

The Second Bank offices located in the Gulf Coast and Ohio Valley regions were the most profitable. Table 4.4 shows the average operating efficiency, gross return on earning assets, and operating profit rate of Second Bank branches in five regions in 1833. This table is based on branch-level expense data (itemized as salaries, stationery, transportation of specie, and sundries) and gross revenue data (discounts, exchange, and interest). The Gulf Coast branches had among the highest revenue, and lowest expenses, per dollar of earning assets; the Ohio Valley branches had average revenue, but the highest level of operating efficiency.

Scale economies at the branch level help explain interbranch variations in operating efficiency. Figure 4.3, which plots operating efficiency in 1833 against

Table 4.4 Profitability of Second Bank branches, by region, January to June 1833

Second Bank branches by region	Operating efficiency[1]	Gross return on earning assets[2]	Operating profitability[3]
New England	1.03	6.81	81.6
Middle Atlantic	0.56	2.65	77.6
South Atlantic	0.58	3.34	82.3
Gulf Coast	0.43	5.75	92.2
Ohio Valley	0.38	3.18	88.8

[1]Operating expenses as a percentage of earning assets.

[2]Revenues from discounts, exchange, and interest as a percentage of earning assets.

[3] Revenues minus operating expenses as a percentage of operating revenue.

New England branches include the Portsmouth, Boston, Burlington, Portland, Providence, and Hartford offices. Middle Atlantic branches: New York, Baltimore, Philadelphia, Washington. South Atlantic: Richmond, Norfolk, Fayetteville, Charleston, Savannah. Gulf Coast: New Orleans, Mobile, Natchez. Ohio Valley: Lexington, Louisville, Cincinnati, Pittsburgh, St. Louis, Nashville.

Sources: Author's calculations. Income and expense data from Second Bank Profit and Loss Statements for June 1833, Sen. Doc. 17, 23rd Cong., 2d Sess. Earning asset data for June 1831 from H. Exec. Doc. 147, 22nd Cong., 1st Sess.

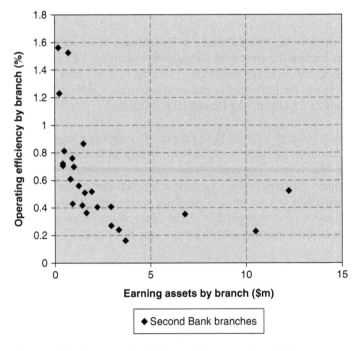

♦ Second Bank branches

Figure 4.3 Scale economies at Second Bank branches, 1833.

Sources: See source note for Table 4.4.

Note: Operating efficiency is measured as current operating expenses as a percentage of earning assets.

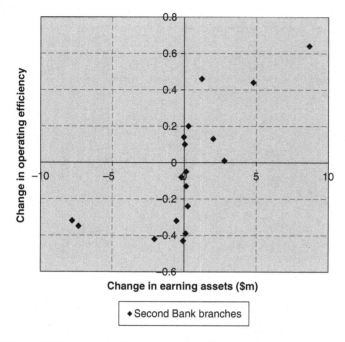

Figure 4.4 Changes in scale and operating efficiency at Second Bank branches, 1818–1833.

Sources: For 1818 expense and earning assets data, Profit and Loss Statement in H. Rep. 92, 15th Cong., 2d Sess., and H. Exec. Doc. 147, 22nd Cong., 1st Sess., respectively. For 1833, see source note to Table 4.4.

Note: Change in operating efficiency is measured as the inverse of the change in operating expenses as a percentage of earning assets.

the volume of earning assets by branch in June 1831, shows that branches with larger portfolios had lower expenses per dollar of earning assets.[24] The largest office, Philadelphia, at $12.23 m of assets, had lower operating efficiency than many smaller offices, probably explained by the fact that the costs of managing the interbranch accounts and the foreign exchange accounts were incurred and expensed at the central office. Figure 4.4 plots the change in the size of a branch's portfolio between 1818 and 1833 against the change in its efficiency, and similarly shows that branches that shrunk in size became less efficient, and branches that grew became more efficient. Branches in the Gulf Coast and Ohio Valley regions experienced the fastest growth in earning assets.

Intercity exchange rates did not vary significantly, or in the expected direction, with the density or thickness of intercity exchange markets. Figures 4.5a and 4.5b plot the intercity exchange rate against two measures of intercity exchange market depth. Bills of exchange were more liquid assets when drawn between cities with higher bill volumes and more frequent trade interactions; consequently, we would expect the cost of funds to fall as market thickness increases. Here the correlation is positive, but in any case weak, capturing the effect of the Second Bank's role

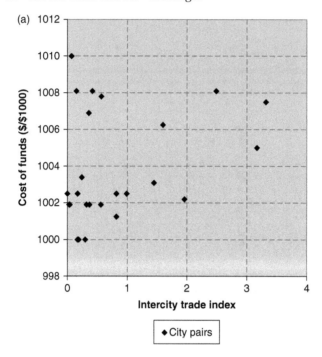

Figure 4.5a Intercity cost of funds (1830) and intercity trade flows (1840).

Sources: For intercity trade index, Pred 1973, his Tables 4.7 and 4.11. For intercity cost of funds, author's calculations from H. Rep. 358, 21st Cong., 1st Sess., pp. 34–7. See Appendix D.

Note: The intercity trade index is Pred's measure of the relative level of shipping interaction between two ports. Correlation coefficient for the 24 city pairs plotted is 0.30. Includes 12 pairs of southern cities: New York paired with 6 southern cities, and Philadelphia paired with 6 southern cities.

as "market-maker" in the domestic exchanges. The Bank's market-making operations in domestic exchange made the frontier money markets function as if they had the depth of those in the eastern seaboard.

In sum, the return on exchange rose slightly with the shift into the west. The higher cost of making payments to and from interior points was more than covered with higher prices, leaving room for a larger profit margin. Some of the higher cost of transferring funds to and from the frontier was offset by economies of scale at the branch level as the volume of exchange business rose at interior branches.

The Bank's foreign exchange operations

The Bank's Board recognized the market opportunity in the foreign exchanges in 1817, when the committee charged with studying the exchange business recommended that "the bank . . . engage extensively and systematically in the purchase and sale of foreign exchange", as a "certain resource for the profitable employment

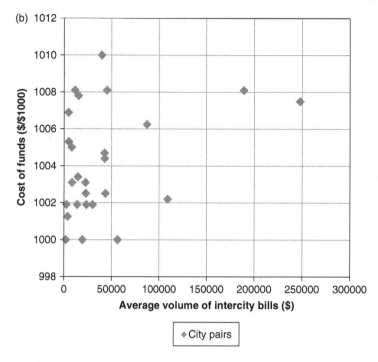

Figure 4.5b Intercity cost of funds and intercity bill volume, 1830.

Sources: Intercity bill volume, from H. Rep. 358, 21st Cong. 1st Sess., Appendix D. For intercity cost of funds, author's calculations from H. Rep. 358, 21st Cong., 1st Sess., pp. 34–7. See Appendix D.

of all the surplus capital of the bank." The committee described the market opportunity for intermediaries growing out of the fact that

> during the busy season, in the south, nearly all the merchants are drawers, and ... [are] compelled to send their bills to the northern cities to be disposed of, and to have their proceeds returned, subject to all the inconveniences of delay and expense consequent on the then existing course of trade.

The Second Bank Board committee proposed that the Second Bank "avail itself of the same advantages" which have allowed "monied men" (private bankers) to carry on "extensive and profitable operations."[25] A leading house among these monied men was the House of Brown, which was active in the foreign exchange market in the 1810s. It was based in Baltimore and, by 1825, had branches or agents in Liverpool, Philadelphia, New Orleans, and New York.[26]

Notwithstanding the presence of capable competitors, the Board committee saw the potential for the Bank to supply prime sterling drafts. The Board committee predicted that the bills of the Bank "would command a preference over the bills of individuals," especially among "foreign agents acting under orders from abroad, and all the cautious and timid acting upon their own account." Since these two groups would form a large proportion of the purchasers of sterling drafts, "the generality of drawers would find it to their interest to sell to the Bank," resulting in a volume of business and a premium over competitors' drafts that would be large enough to amount to "a pretty good profit." The Board directed management to

> facilitate the operations of our merchants by placing within their reach, and at the moment required, the purchase or sale of bills upon Europe, and thus put an end to those forced fluctuations of exchange which have no foundation in the course of trade.[27]

In his economic history of the House of Brown, Perkins confirms that the sterling bills of the Second Bank were the most highly valued and in greatest demand, and therefore sold at the highest rates—but still at rates well within the cost of shipping specie to European ports, allowing the Bank to claim that both the Bank and the public (merchants) were better off. The House of Brown's drafts were in a "second tier" between the Second Bank and "ordinary endorsers" of bills of exchange.[28] The Bank's advantages lay in its more extensive branch network, which allowed for larger operations with greater geographic scope, and its large drawing account with the House of Barings.

Although the market opportunity was recognized in 1817, the Bank did not engage in large-scale foreign exchange dealing until after the monetary crisis of 1825–1826, which made large-scale entry into the market particularly compelling for the Bank.[29] During the crisis, a number of cotton trading houses in both the US and the UK failed, causing their bills of exchange to be rejected by the market. At such a time, "the Second Bank's name on a bill was probably a welcome guarantee."[30] In addition, the auction system of selling imports in the American market broke down and the American import merchant, trading on his own account, resumed his central role in Anglo-American trade. This created a new source of demand for sterling bills to make remittances in London and Liverpool. The import merchants were among the prime borrowers which the Second Bank wanted for its discount portfolio; to attract them, they had to offer the foreign exchange services the import houses could get elsewhere. Finally, the crisis spurred the reorganization of the British discount market in ways that expanded the credit capacity of the Anglo-American trading system and increased the Bank of England's central-banking responsibilities, both of which facilitated the adoption of large-scale operations by the Second Bank.

The Second Bank's foreign exchange operations grew naturally out of its domestic exchange operations, and were modeled after them. The Bank discounted (purchased at a discount) bills of exchange drawn on cotton, tobacco, and other commodity exports to Europe and denominated in foreign currencies (primarily sterling, but also francs and guilders) and sold its own drafts drawn on and payable at its European banking partners. As means of payment, the Second Bank sterling, franc, and guilder drafts drawn "in sums to suit" had less credit risk and were more convenient than the bills of exchange drawn on commodities shipped to commission houses. As an intermediary, the Bank earned interest income on the bills of exchange and a spread reflecting the credit risk differential between the mercantile bills it purchased and the drafts it sold. For example, in November 1831, the Bank purchased sterling bills of exchange at premia of 8.5–9 percent; at the same time it could sell its own sterling drafts for 10 percent.[31] In the foreign exchanges, the Bank moderated but did not eliminate seasonality with its counter-seasonal exchange operations. In the winter and spring, when cotton moved to market and sterling fell to a discount, southern branches purchased mercantile bills on London; in the summer and fall import-buying seasons, when sterling rose to a premium, northern branches sold Bank bills on London. Prior to the entry of the Second Bank, the House of Brown had reportedly added "several percentage points" to its normal profit margin of 1–1.5 percent with the same counterseasonal exchange operations.[32] As more of the Bank's capital was directed to foreign exchange, the seasonal swing in exchange rates, and potential arbitrage returns, fell. Access to external short-term credit was essential to the Bank's counterseasonal exchange operations. The Bank's London correspondent, the merchant banking firm House of Barings, provided an uncovered or "running credit" to the Second Bank. Under this arrangement bills drawn on Baring by the Second Bank could exceed current remittances to the Second Bank's account at Baring.[33]

Biddle's correspondence with branch cashiers and business associates shows how the Bank sought to benefit from seasonal swings in exchange rates at times when the exchange rate was well within the specie export points. For example, on February 6, 1826, Biddle told the Cashier of the Boston Office to "suspend your sales of the Sterling Bills of the Bank in your possession, on the receipt of this, until further advised." In August 1823, Biddle wrote to an associate in New York that

> The Cashier (in Philadelphia) has this day written to Mr Robinson (the Cashier of the New York branch) authorizing him to purchase for the Bank 30 or 40 thousand pounds sterling of Exchange on London and has referred him to you for information and advice . . . Our desire is to avoid unnecessary expense and brokerage, and also to manage it so as not to let the Bank appear as a purchaser, as this might raise the market. The present moment is rather one of Stagnation in Exchange and therefore we hope that you may operate to advantage at a low rate, but we are willing to go as high as 7 1/2.

In September 1827, Biddle wrote to Robert Lenox, a New York businessman:

> "My impression is that exchange ought to rise. For that reason we have been in no hurry to part with our stock of sterling bills but have reserved them for the better price which we expect. Our French Exchange which we have begun during the past year proved a very good business. Since the first of January last we have sold nearly seven millions of francs, on Paris.[34]

Although Biddle welcomed the opportunity to earn profits from seasonal swings in exchange rates, he disapproved of arbitrage operations in foreign exchange that resulted in specie exports. When exchange rates moved outside the corridor created by the cost of shipping specie between two cities, private bankers could earn a risk-free or low-risk return through silver-sterling arbitrage operations. Two periods, 1827–1828 and 1831–1832, demonstrate the interaction between the Bank and the House of Brown when the sterling exchange rate touched the silver export point. In both cases, seasonal pressures combined with high demand for imports to send the price of sterling bills towards the specie export point.

In December 1827, the House of Brown started exporting specie when sterling bills reached 111 percent of nominal parity.[35] The Bank responded in two ways. First, it increased the supply of Bank of the United States sterling drafts by drawing on its line of credit with Baring Brothers in London, which was almost exhausted by March 1828. As the sterling bill rate fell, potential arbitrage profits shrank. Second, the Bank rationed credit away from sterling arbitrageurs. In March of 1828, Biddle wrote to William Patterson, a prominent Baltimore merchant, about coin shipments, observing that, after taking into account the freight and insurance costs,

> the present rate of (sterling) bills leave a small margin of profit and as long as there are shippers of coin at small profits we must expect that they will avail themselves of it. This is a business however that presses with some severity upon the community, and it is therefore proper that those institutions which have the interests of that community especially in their charge, should not voluntarily furnish facilities for such operations.[36]

A similar set of circumstances arose in the Fall of 1831. In October, the House of Brown sold sterling bills at the very high rate of 111 and at same time shipped specie to cover the bills at a lower cost. Silver prices were rising at the time in the London market, which essentially lowered the silver export point as it meant that silver bought more gold, and more sterling, in England. Alexander Brown expected that the Bank of the United States "would lower its rate soon so as to prevent dollars going." Brown understood the Bank of the United States well. Biddle told an unidentified correspondent that

> From Sept 1 1831 to April 1 1832 the Bank undertook to check the exportation of specie by supplying bills at such a rate as left no inducement for individuals to ship it. To do which they exhausted all the funds they could procure from every source. Over $5 million were remitted and still left them with a debt of more than $1.7 million.[37]

In addition to lowering its price, the Bank of the United States increased its supply of sterling bills and sold some of its stock of silver coin in an effort to meet the demand for foreign exchange and moderate the upward pressure on the rate on sterling bills.[38] An 1832 Congressional report provides some detail on how the Bank increased the supply of sterling bills. The report shows the date and location of sterling-denominated bills drawn, the amount, the exchange rate (expressed as a premium over nominal par of $4.44), the drawer, the drawee, the endorser, the time remaining on the bill, and the date the Bank bought the bill, between July 1831 and

April 1832. These were bills the Bank purchased, then sent to London to cover maturing sterling obligations (Bank of the United States sterling drafts).[39]

If the Bank's first priority had been to maximize counterseasonal profits, its bill purchases and remittances would have reached their highest level during the summer months, when the rate on sterling bills was at its lowest point. In 1831 and 1832, however, the Bank's first priority, as signaled by its behavior, was to keep the exchange rate from moving outside the specie export points. The Bank's purchases and remittances of sterling bills of exchange were larger when the sterling exchange rates was higher (Figure 4.6).[40] The bills purchased in October 1831, when the exchange rate and the volume of bill purchases and remittances were at their highest levels, were almost all drawn in Philadelphia (the location of the Bank's head office), by a financial firm, on a London financial firm. Sixty percent of these bills were drawn by one Philadelphia bank, Thomas Biddle & Co., on Gowan & Marx, of London, and endorsed by W McIlvaine, the Cashier of the Philadelphia office of the Second Bank. Also in October, the Bank of the United States purchased a very large bill drawn by the US Treasurer on Baring Brothers (also banker to the US government), payable at sight.

The bills of exchange drawn in October to December, when sterling rates were hovering around or higher than the specie export point, were different in several

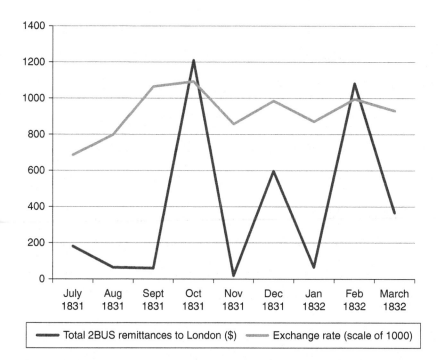

Figure 4.6 Bank of the United States' remittances and sterling exchange rates, July 1831 to March 1832.

Source: Author's calculations from 22nd Cong., 1st Sess., H. Rep. 460, pp. 158–75.

respects from the bills drawn and purchased in the summer months. Almost all of the bills purchased in July, when the rate was the lowest, were true "trade bills" drawn in June and July, in one of the southern cotton ports (New Orleans, Savannah, Charleston, Mobile, Natchez). These can be considered true trade bills in the sense that the parties to the bill were mercantile firms and individuals, as opposed to "finance bills," in which the parties to the bill were financial firms. The finance bills drawn and purchased in October were significantly larger (on average, twenty times larger) than the "true" trade bills, and had longer time to run than the usual sixty days. Some bills ran as long as 125 days, reflecting, possibly, the drawer's intent to cover the account when exchange could be purchased at a lower rate than that at which it was purchased.[41]

The large bills offered by Thomas Biddle & Co. (a private banking house) and the US government made it possible for the Bank to execute a large, quick increase in the supply of sterling in New York, Baltimore, and Philadelphia at a time of year when no new trade bills would be coming on the market to serve as cover. The actions of the Bank of the United States—reducing the price of its sterling bills, increasing the supply of its sterling bills, and cutting off Bank of the United States credit to arbitrageurs—contained the exchange rate and reduced the arbitrage profits that would otherwise have been realized by the House of Brown and others.

The New Orleans branch: linchpin of the Bank's exchange operations

After 1825, the New Orleans branch became the linchpin of the Bank's exchange operations and business model. As the cotton frontier moved west, New Orleans became the gathering point for much of the domestic and foreign (primarily sterling) exchange owned by the Bank. New Orleans was also the port of entry for much of the Spanish silver coin that entered the country in payment for goods sold in Mexico and other southern markets. Finally, it was the branch through which many of the Bank's notes were put into, and remained in, circulation. Biddle came to see the New Orleans branch as "the most important of the whole establishment."[42]

New Orleans had active trading relations in multiple directions, domestic and international. All of this trade had countervailing monetary transactions that were managed by the Bank, the state institutions, and the private bankers. Upriver Bank branches (Louisville, Cincinnati, St. Louis, Nashville) discounted bills of exchange on flour, pork, corn, and whiskey shipments to New Orleans, giving Bank notes in exchange. The bill proceeds accumulated as balances in New Orleans to the credit of western merchants, who used them to remit funds to New York, Philadelphia, and Baltimore, in payment for manufactured goods purchased there. New Orleans exported some of the western foodstuffs to Cuba and Mexico, and received credits in New York (in the case of Cuba, which sold sugar in northern markets) and specie (in the case of Mexico, which had fewer exportable crops) in exchange. The primary way New Orleans generated northern funds was by remitting sterling bills of exchange drawn on cotton, which moved down the Mississippi River in growing volumes in the 1820s, then to the Northeast on the packet lines that were also organized in the 1820s.[43]

Very soon after assuming his office, Biddle saw that the New Orleans exchange business was being run on unsound business practices.[44] Biddle issued a set of new instructions for the branch's bill operations to the cashier at New Orleans (Charles West), whose object, Biddle wrote, was to "give you an influence and control over the monied operations of N. Orleans and an ascendancy over all the State Institutions."[45] Biddle hoped that the New Orleans Office would "increase in usefulness and profit"; toward this end, he wanted the New Orleans office to "possess the best correspondence in New Orleans." Biddle himself and the Philadelphia cashier would write regularly, and, Biddle wrote to West:

> Mr Jaudon (the 2nd assistant cashier in Philadelphia) will address you twice a week on the State of exchange, and the general monied concerns of Phil and New York with such other information as may be deemed useful. These he will send by duplicates to New York—where Mr Robinson (the New York cashier) will be directed to add his information by every packet.[46]

Philadelphia's management of the movements of monetary instruments in and out of New Orleans is captured nicely in a May 5, 1826, letter to the New Orleans cashier, quickly written "before the sailing of the Hercules." Biddle wrote, "We will send to you all the notes we can possibly procure and you will send to us all the Sterling you can purchase and all the specie you can spare." The "greatest difficulty" with this plan was actually procuring enough small notes:

> We sent on the 15th of Feb $125,015, 18th of March 334,370 making 459,385 chiefly of small notes and I hope the Hercules by which this letter goes will take upwards of $64,000 more. We shall continue to forward them to you as fast as we can collect your old issues or sign new ones.[47]

He continued:

> These will I hope enable you to enlarge your purchase of foreign bills which are particularly desireable [*sic*]. At the limits of your last purchase 3 (or even 4 or 5) there need be no bounds except your means to more dealings when the late offers have such prospect of ultimate profit. The supply of notes now furnished will enable you I hope to enlarge your purchases greatly—and if you should find yourself strong enough to forward an additional sum of specie beyond the $400,000 in progress it would be very gratifying as these supplies are always you know very acceptable, and the disbursements of the Treasury on the 1st of July next, accounting for the principal of the 6s of 1813 to $5,030,000 will make it desirable to be as strong as possible here about that period. Your statement of March 6 represents you as having $957,000.

I should think between 3 and 4 hundred thousand with a good supply of paper would be ample. You can confer with Mr Fort and if you concur in opinion that you can, when the notes arrive, safely spare more specie you will please to do so.[48]

As the western offices expanded their purchases of bills, the Bank could not produce enough notes to keep up with the demand, due to the requirement that each Bank note be signed by the President of the Bank and the cashier of the head office. In 1827, the Bank introduced branch drafts, a near substitute for Bank notes. These were orders to pay drawn on Philadelphia, printed in Philadelphia as blank checks, and shipped to the offices. Local officials filled in the names of payees (cashiers or presidents of the local branch) and endorsed the draft "payable to bearer," converting them from checks into circulating notes. The branch drafts were issued by branches outside the commercial core; none by Philadelphia, Boston, New York, Baltimore, Washington, or Richmond. New Orleans, Natchez, Nashville, Lexington, Savannah, Fayetteville, and Mobile were the largest issuers of branch drafts; together they accounted for two-thirds of all branch drafts issued and in circulation in September 1834. The Bank's opponents charged that the branch drafts were illegal; Biddle's view was:

> The Branch drafts moreover are so far injurious to the Bank that they are in fact bills of exchange without any premium. For a large draft the Bank often charges something. For an equal amount of these small drafts no charge is of course made. The Bank would willingly give up the issue of such drafts, if they had the means of substituting notes signed by officers of the Parent Bank.[49]

Synergies with the Bank's fiscal duties

The Bank's branch network was an asset in the exchange business, but it was also a large fixed operating cost. A large volume of exchange business was needed in order to maximize the scope of multilateral book-entry settlement and to reduce the unit fixed cost of the branch network. The Board Committee of 1817 recognized this fact, notifying the full Board that the benefits for the Bank "will require the adoption of a liberal and extensive system of operations." Operating on a large scale would also meet another objective, that of minimizing the costs associated with the fiscal functions the Bank was obliged by its charter to perform for the US Treasury: collecting the federal revenue, in payment of which Second Bank notes were legal tender; disbursing federal funds; servicing outstanding debt and underwriting new debt issues; and holding federal deposits.

The collection and disbursement of funds required intercity, interstate, and interregional transfers of funds, which the Bank was to perform, as noted earlier, "without charging commission or claiming allowance on account of difference of exchange."[50] Although the Bank earned interest on the earning assets funded with the federal deposits, the margin of interest income over fiduciary expenses was not ample, particularly in the early years of the Bank's operation. In 1820, before the

Bank became a large-scale exchange dealer, a Committee of the Board observed that, when the exchanges were adverse, funds had to be transferred with specie, which the Bank was "anxious to avoid . . . as far as possible."[51]

In order to create scale economies, the Bank had to find multiple ways to generate revenues from its expensive collections and payments infrastructure (the branch network). The collection of bills of exchange entailed the same clerical operations involved in the cross-country revenue collection-and-remittance function the Bank performed for the Treasury. By 1832 the Bank had four different kinds of income-earning exchange transactions. In its primary exchange business, the Bank purchased domestic bills of exchange payable at its various branches and sold drafts drawn on its various branches. The Bank supplemented this business by collecting domestic bills of exchange payable outside of its branch network, at state-chartered and private banks, and by selling drafts drawn by its offices on state-chartered and private banks located in areas where there was no Second Bank branch. Drawing drafts on state-chartered banks was an operation the Bank had to perform to meet its obligation to transfer and disburse federal funds at all points. The Bank's subsidiary exchange business, unlike the primary business, was not wholly contained within its branch network. It allowed the Bank to provide geographically comprehensive payments services to its clientele, and made up 35 percent of all income-earning exchange transactions.[52] Scale economies reduced the total cost of the $16.1 m of transfers which the Second Bank performed for the Treasury in 1832, out of a total exchange business of $242 m, well below what they would have cost by themselves.[53]

The administrative reforms adopted by the US government soon after the chartering of the Bank also reduced the cost burden of the fiscal transfers. In the major spending departments (the War Department and the Navy), the centralization of contract issuance and management in Washington increased the average size of transfers on the federal account, reducing the Bank's transaction costs per dollar of fiscal transfer. The concentration of transfers at two branches, Philadelphia and Washington, created cost efficiencies, as clerks in those offices became proficient and specialized. Of the $16.1 m of transfers performed for the US Treasury, $11.9 m took place at the Philadelphia and Washington offices, reflecting the centralization of US budget management in Washington after the administrative reforms of 1818.[54] Another $1.2 m of transfers were located at Norfolk, a major Navy shipyard. These scale economies were offset in part by the Bank's obligation to pay individual pensions, which involved the issuance of many small drafts.

By the late 1820s, under Treasury secretaries Rush and Ingham, the Bank achieved its full potential as the US government's fiscal agent. The domestic exchange business facilitated the Bank's intercity transfer of funds on behalf of the US government. In the early 1820s, the Treasury and the Bank agreed on protocols regarding transfers and the time that would be allowed to accomplish transfers. There was frequent communication about the size, timing, and location of expected revenue collections and warrants.[55] Although the federal government was expected to have funds available when drafts arrived for payment at an office, the Bank was able to extend short-term credit because of liquidity inflows from its bill business. For example, in June 1825, Biddle wrote to the cashier of the Bank of the United States branch at New Orleans regarding certain Treasury drafts which were written

> without the previous notice required by the agreement between the Bank and the Treasury. In a few days however we expect to see Mr Rush when the future drafts will I hope be placed on a more regular footing. In the mean time it is proper to give to the government, every facility for the distribution of its funds, and to do it promptly and cheerfully.[56]

The Bank's foreign exchange operations also supported its fiscal duties to the US government. The Board committee argued that becoming a large-scale foreign exchange dealer

> would afford the means of providing advantageously, for those payments in Europe which the bank has necessarily obligated itself to furnish, and would enable the bank to place the remittances of government on that sure basis, which will relieve them from all the uncertainties and hazards inseparable from the engagements of individuals [meaning individual merchant bankers].[57]

Instead of paying commissions and exchange premiums to private bankers for sterling drafts, the Bank could generate its own supply. Because it held a large share of the stock of sterling bills, the Bank could manage the cost of servicing and retiring foreign-held federal debt by keeping the exchange rate below the specie point, as described earlier.

Under Treasury Secretary Rush, the Treasury's object was to establish a "general system" that would allow the Treasury to dispense, "as far as possible, with the instrumentality of the State banks." To achieve this end, he identified ideal locations for new Bank branches, as seen earlier, and enforced the policy of using the Second Bank as the government's bank. In 1830, the Customs Collector at Boston moved the Treasury deposits from the Bank of the United States branch to one of the Boston banks; Treasury Secretary Ingham immediately directly that they be returned to the Bank of the United States.[58] An 1829 Circular from the Post Office Department directed that

> Postmasters who are not instructed to deposite [*sic*] their proceeds of postage, will make their payments on drafts signed by the same Assistant PG, and countersigned by John Suter, Principal Pay Clerk, or by the Chief Clerk—and in no other manner.

Under Rush, the Treasury preferred to bank with public land receivers than with state banks. The Treasury authorized various federal officers on the western frontier to draw drafts on the Treasury when warrants for spending were issued for them; the receivers were to buy these bills and to use them to make remittances back to Washington "of . . . the public moneys in your hands as Receiver."[59]

In his advocacy for the rechartering of the Bank, and under favorable or acceptable terms, Biddle vigorously defended the Bank's domestic exchange business. In one of his many long letters to Albert Gallatin, Biddle discussed an amendment to the charter to restrict the Bank's buying of bills of exchange. He wrote:

> it would be extremely difficult to devise any sound and safe limitation. If the Bank cannot buy bills, it must transmit the public revenue by taking all the Specie from the State Banks in one place and conveying it to another, thus tearing up by the roots the Local Institutions—it cannot sustain its circulation as it does now—and the exchanges instead of being brought down to the lowest rates, would be in the hands of a few rich capitalists who would regulate them of course for their own personal benefit at the expense of the interior trade.[60]

Conclusion

By the end of the 1820s, intercity exchange rates, particularly those between the eastern seaboard and interior cities and towns, had been reduced to low levels, well below the cost of transporting specie. In making the case for the rechartering of the Bank, Biddle told Congress that "no facilities of traveling and transportation can so completely abridge the wide spaces which separate the parts of this extensive country, as the removal of those great barriers which the want of easy commercial exchanges interpose to their prosperity."[61] As the Bank's business shifted westward, filling the vacuum left by the state banking system, New Orleans became the linchpin of the Bank's business model: it was the place where much of the Bank's specie and sterling bills came into the Bank, and where a large number of the Bank's notes were introduced and maintained in circulation.

As the Bank's branches in the Mississippi River Valley financed a large share of this area's exports to Mexico and Latin America, many of the Spanish silver dollars entering the economy from these markets were "collected" by the Second Bank. The Bank became the single largest holder of specie in the nation, a position which it leveraged in the service of both profit and duty.

Notes

1 Dewey (1910a, p. 200).
2 This chapter draws heavily on Knodell (2003).
3 With a rate of exchange of 0.5 percent, $100 in New York funds was worth $99.50 in Philadelphia, Boston, and Baltimore. Bodenhorn (2000, p. 173); D. Adams (1978, ch. 5); Krooss (1967, p. 116). The large city banks in Boston, New York, Philadelphia, and Boston drew drafts on each other and collected bills through each other, much as the Bank's offices did with each other.
4 Insurance costs were much higher for steamboat travel on the rivers of the interior than on the transatlantic or domestic ocean routes, and made up 70–80 percent of the cost of shipping specie from Ohio cities in 1830; Knodell (1998, pp. 714–30), and Hunter (1949, pp. 271–304). Hunter identified four main causes of steamboat accidents: snags and other obstructions, explosions, fire, and collisions, from the most to least prevalent.

In 1830, there was a large cost differential between paying with specie and paying with Bank exchange even within the eastern seaboard. Biddle provided an example of a $10,000 payment to be made by a company in Philadelphia to a company in Providence, RI, which would cost $25 with a Bank draft and $78.17 with specie, $51 of which was insurance. Biddle Papers, January 21, 1830, letter to Rep. Hemphill.

5 Freyer (1976, pp. 437, 441–3).

6 In *Bank of the United States v. Smith*, 11 Wheaton 75 (1817), the Bank, as the final endorsee on a promissory note, successfully sued a prior endorser on the note because the maker of the note did not make funds available to pay the amount due at maturity. In *Bank of the United States v. Weisiger*, 2 Peters 129 (1829), it was similarly established that if the final holder of the note, in this case the Bank, was unable to recover from the maker of the note, the holder could sue the payee (the person to whom the note was payable) or a subsequent endorser.

7 18th Cong., 1st Sess., Pub 705, p. 885; 21st Cong., 1st Sess., H. Rep. 358, p. 31; authors unknown (1832, p. 259).

8 15th Cong., 2d Sess., H. Rep. 92, p. 53.

9 These interbranch drafts, which sold at a premium, are to be distinguished from the branch drafts, Second Bank notes under a different name, issued after 1827. According to Gallatin (1831, p. 29), who was at the time of writing President of a New York City Bank, so very familiar with actual practice, the interbranch drafts were a kind of currency; they "pass through several hands, and circulate several months, in distant parts of the country, before they are presented for payment." The Board Committee report is in 15th Cong., 2d Sess., H. Rep. 92, pp. 53–7. In 1817, the Board received a memorial from merchants in Philadelphia "interested in the Western Trade" saying that "they labour under considerable embarrassments in consequence of the almost total impracticality of obtaining remittances from thence to their City without incurring enormous loss in the Exchange." The Memorial is reproduced in a January 21, 1830, letter from Biddle to Joseph Hemphill, Biddle Papers.

10 15th Cong., 2d Sess., H. Rep. 92, pp. 46–9.

11 Biddle Papers, July 29, 1830, letter to Gallatin.

12 Knodell (1998, 2003).

13 "Discounting" bills means purchasing the bill at a discount from face value. When (if) the bill was fully paid at maturity, the difference comprised the interest income to the lender.

14 Biddle Papers, January 21, 1830, letter to Rep. Hemphill, who represented Philadelphia. It would have made sense for the Bank to restrict issuance of large notes at its western branches, to force the western merchants to buy drafts instead.

15 This counterseasonal position-taking in the bill market was the necessary companion to administered (versus supply-and-demand driven) exchange rates. See Redlich (1968, p. 129). In contrast, in the post-Second Bank regime, "collecting banks" in southern cities would "agree to furnish drafts only as eastern and northern funds could be procured." Consequently, interior banks holding bills payable in southern cities saw their funds "lie idle" until eastern and northern funds were available, and charged higher discount rates on the southern bills to compensate for the loss in interest income; Dewey (1910b, pp. 175–7). Biddle Papers, August 2, 1830, letter to Gallatin; 22nd Cong., 1st Sess., H. Rep. 460, p. 322.

16 To the contrary, the Bank's "Rules and regulations for conducting exchange business" stipulate that the proceeds of bills of exchange "shall be paid to the depositor free of any . . . charge" other than the discount rate. 15th Cong., 2d Sess., H. Rep. 92, p. 55. Bodenhorn (2000, p. 176) claimed that the "Bank probably disguised its higher than posted exchange discounts with its commission charges . . . (g)iven the spread between the . . . posted exchange rates and its actual returns." See Knodell (2003, pp. 26–8) for a rebuttal to this claim. See also Biddle Papers, March 12, 1830, Biddle letter to Hemphill in which he explained that a commission charged by the Cincinnati Cashier was not on drafts, but was applied to for certain additional services supplied

to "persons at a distance who . . . instead of committing them to the merchants of that place found it was cheaper to write to the Cashier."

17 The posted exchange rates were distributed, and reported to Congress, from Philadelphia. 21st Cong., 1st Sess., H. Report 358, Appendix 2. In some cases no intercity price was posted, reflecting the absence of intercity trading relations. Biddle Papers, September 18, 1834, letter from Biddle to the Cashier of the Nashville branch. According to Pred (1973, p. 79), in 1840 "the use of the mails for transmitting private information over long distances was probably still confined to a relatively small minority of the total population, most of whom were involved in commerce."

18 The Bank operated before the first credit-rating agencies were established.

19 Kelsey Burr Papers, Box 2, December 2, 1829, letter from Biddle to John Sommerville, Esq., Cashier, Nashville, and September 18, 1834, letter from Biddle to the Cashier of the Nashville branch.

20 Kelsey Burr Papers, Box 2, September 18, 1834, letter from Biddle to the Cashier of the Nashville branch. Philadelphia showed some flexibility on pricing by 1834, when state bank entry was increasing in response to the Bank's loss of its federal charter. In a December 2, 1834, letter, Biddle told the President of the Providence branch, "if your Board think it expedient to reduce to par the rates of purchase and collection on Boston New York & Phil they are authorized by my letter of the 24th of Sept last to do so. Whatever they may decide upon the subject will be agreeable to us."

21 See Rothman (2005, ch. 5) and Gudmestad (2011) on the role of the steamboat.

22 This is a somewhat unconventional use of the term "bid-ask spreads," which usually applies to a dealer buying and selling a single financial instrument. Here, there are two different instruments involved (a bill of exchange issued by a merchant and a draft issued by the Second Bank) with different credit risk characteristics.

23 22nd Cong., 2d Sess., H. Rep. 121, pp. 144, 148.

24 Since the Bank's earning assets were larger in 1833 than in 1831, the resulting measures of efficiency are too low in an absolute sense, but this problem should not significantly distort them as measures of the relative efficiencies of different offices.

25 15th Cong., 2d Sess., H. Rep. 92, pp. 57–9.

26 Perkins, (1975, pp. 19–33).

27 15th Cong., 2d Sess., H. Rep. 92, p. 58.

28 According to Perkins (1975, pp. 29–30), the House of Brown welcomed the Bank's commitment to maintaining a continuous market, because it relieved them of the responsibility of accommodating their customers, and "reduced significantly the risk of unforeseen difficulties in the execution of seasonal operations." In a pinch, they could count on being able to buy bills from the Second Bank to cover drafts drawn on their Liverpool account. But to enjoy this benefit, the House of Brown had to share the foreign exchange profits with the Second Bank.

29 22nd Cong., 1st Sess., H. Exec. Doc. 147, Statement B, pp. 56–8, shows the rates at which the Philadelphia, Charleston, Savannah, New Orleans, and Mobile offices purchased foreign exchange, by month, between 1817 and 1831. Purchases were sporadic at all branches until 1826.

30 Parsons (1977, pp. 73, 131, 212–26). These failures followed a large drop in the price of cotton, which rendered cotton houses unable to pay the bills of exchange drawn upon them from the proceeds of cotton sales. This reduced the effective supply of sterling exchange in the US, leading to an export of specie, with associated pressures on US banks.

31 See Officer (1996, pp. 203–7), on the role of the Second Bank's foreign exchange operations in stabilizing and internally integrating the American foreign exchange market. Brown Brothers sold its sterling bills for ten percent; the Bank sold at the same or higher rates; Perkins (1975, p. 30).

32 Ibid., pp. 27–8.

33 Redlich (1968, pp. 131–3); Hidy (1944).

34 Kelsey Burr Papers, Box 1; Biddle Papers, August 7, 1823, letter to Thomas Knox, and September 6, 1827, letter to Robert Lenox.

35 Nominal parity between the US dollar and sterling was 4s. 6d., or $4.44 4/9; but "true" parity was much higher, taking into account the cost of converting silver, the effective US standard, into gold at the higher commercial ratio (the ratio of silver to gold in the world market). In "true parity" terms, the silver export point was 3 percent over par. See Officer (1996) for a careful estimation of true parity, the basis for his gold point estimates. The $4.44 4/9 rate of exchange between the US dollar and sterling originates from the true mint parity (based on assays) between the Spanish dollar (dollar coins minted in Seville and Mexico) and British coin in the early eighteenth century. This nominal par was applied to the US dollar in 1792, when it was pegged to the Spanish dollar.

36 Officer (1996), Table 6.8, White series, Table 5.2, data for true mint parity. Biddle Papers, letter to William Patterson, March 11, 1828. Patterson shipped goods in and out of the West Indies, and would have likely received payment in specie, in part. Biddle may have been trying to convince Patterson not to assist the House of Brown in its arbitrage operations by selling or lending specie to them. According to Govan, "The Browns could not understand why Biddle opposed their export of silver, since it did not interfere with the profits of the Bank"; Govan (1959, pp. 97–8).

37 Perkins (1975, p. 193). In the quote, "dollars" referred to Spanish pesos, not paper US dollars. The Biddle quote is an undated document in Kelsey Burr Papers, Box 2; "debt" referred to the Bank's line of credit with Baring Brothers.

38 On the Bank's supply of foreign exchange, see Parsons (1977, p. 277).

39 See 22nd Cong., 1st Sess. H. Rep. 460, a "Statement of all the remittances made to Europe, since the 1st of July 1831, whether in bills, in specie, or otherwise; and all sums placed at the credit of the bank, by their bankers, stating from whence they came." Remittances to Paris were one-tenth those to London ($.34 m compared with $3.8 m), and remittances to Amsterdam were even smaller.

40 The Bank still earned a small spread on these operations. For example, in November 1831, the Bank purchased sterling bills of exchange at premia of 8.5–9 percent; at the same time it could sell sterling for 10 percent or a bit higher, which was the rate at which Brown Brothers sold its sterling bills; Perkins (1975, p. 30).

41 If this was the case, the Bank would have been financing the private banker's counter-seasonal arbitrage operations. Even though the Bank did not earn the seasonal spread in its 1831 operations, it did profit from the larger US dollar interest income due to the seasonally high exchange rate and longer term to maturity (meaning a larger discount at the time of purchase). In October 1831, the Bank bought 120 pounds sterling of bills drawn by Biddle and Co. at a dollar/sterling exchange rate of $4.93 (11 percent premium over $4.44 nominal par), which yielded an additional $22,000 of US dollar bill value compared with a dollar/sterling rate of $4.75 (7 percent premium over $4.44 nominal par). At this time, the Bank was seeking alternative earning assets to replace the US government debt which was being retired.

42 Kelsey Burr Papers, Box 2, September 11, 1827, letter from Biddle to Charles West and January 4, 1826, letter to R. Gilmore, at the Baltimore branch about mismanagement at New Orleans. In latter letter, Biddle wrote, "We regard the office at N. Orleans . . . from its intrinsic importance, and from its being the key of the Western Offices, as the first of the whole establishment, decidedly superior to any other office."

43 Albion (1965, pp. 49–76).

44 On February 19, 1823, Biddle wrote to John White, cashier of the Baltimore office, "We have made also a vigorous effort to correct the exchange operations of the New Orleans office which during the last year were conducted on principles equally unsound and unprofitable. . . . For instance the Office at N. York collects on N. Orleans at 3 per cent [sic], but as the exchange is now conducted the Office at N Orleans repays it in 60 or 90 day bills at par without interest. Allowing then the 30 days for transmission, the

60 day bills are in fact at 1½, the 90 day bills at 2. So that really the profit is scarcely a compensation for the risk and trouble, even when you receive your funds back immediately. But when it is considered that they sometimes remain for a considerable time at N Orleans, it is perhaps better to keep them at home where they can be employed more profitably, unless bills are obtained at a considerable discount"; Biddle Papers.

45 Kelsey Burr Papers, Box 1, February 11, 1823, letter from Biddle to Charles S West, Cashier of the New Orleans branch. The instructions included the minimum discount on domestic bills, when to enter the market, the level of operations, and how to proceed with sterling bills. Biddle explained, "In the course now directed you will probably be aided by the State Institutions. They have hitherto complained that the Exchange operations of the Office have injured them by spoiling the Bill market, and they will be prepared to cooperate with you. But if they do not, if they are even willing to repeat our operations of the last year, they can never safely undertake it unless you assist or participate in it."

46 McAllister Collection, Box 6, Folder 231, April 8, 1826, letter from Biddle to Thomas Wilson Esq., Cashier, Office of Discount & Deposit at New Orleans; May 5, 1826, letter from Biddle to Wilson.

47 Ibid.

48 Ibid.

49 Biddle complained to Daniel Webster that "to make two millions of five dollar notes, it would be necessary to sign my name 400,000 times, which, to a person whose time is and must be absorbed during the day by the duties of his station, is wholly impracticable. The application for this purpose was made to Congress some years ago, but it was accompanied by a request that Congress would alter the Charter so as to prevent the universal receivability of the notes."; McGrane (1919, p. 38). Letter to New York Office cited in Smith (1953, p. 52). The branch drafts were accepted by the US Treasury, "thus giving the approval of the government to their use"; Catterall (1902, p. 119). Information on issuance by branch is from 23rd Cong., 2d Sess., S. Doc. 17, pp. 62–4. Biddle quote from his March 3, 1832, letter to H Birney, Cashier of the Washington branch of the Second Bank, Kelsey Burr Papers, Box 2.

50 Dewey (1910a, p. 174, 211–20).

51 S. Doc. 17, 23rd Cong., 2d Session, p. 191. Even after the federal deposits were removed from the Second Bank, prospective federal depositories (state-chartered banks) expressed a preference for explicitly paying interest on federal deposits and charging for funds transfers over relying on interest income to cover their expenses. S. Doc. 17, 23rd Cong., 1st Session, pp. 65–73, 83–4, 190–2.

52 S. Doc. 17, 23rd Cong., 2d Sess., pp. 180–2. The non-income-earning transactions included "notes of Bank U.S. and offices received, Transfers of Treasurer of the U.S., and Transfers of office balances." Another category, "State bank notes received at Bank U.S. and offices out of places where offices are located," earned revenue for the Bank if state-banknotes were received at discounts from par.

53 By contrast, the First Bank of the United States (1791–1811) also performed fiscal services without charge for the federal government, but did not develop a domestic exchange dealing operation as well; the share of assets invested in bills of exchange averaged 0.8 percent between 1792 and 1800, dates for which reasonable balance sheet data are available; J. Wettereau (1985). According to various sources, the government account was a drag on the First Bank's profitability. Taus (1943, p. 19); Holdsworth (1910, pp. 58–62).

54 23rd Cong., 2d Sess., S. Doc. 17, p. 181.

55 Catterall (1902, pp. 463–4).

56 Kelsey Burr Papers, Box 2, June 19, 1825, letter from Biddle to C. West, cashier at New Orleans.

57 15th Cong., 2d Sess., H. Rep. 92, p. 58.

58 Kelsey Burr Papers, Box 2. In late 1829, Secretary Ingham issued a Circular to the customs collectors, "renewing the instructions heretofore given that in those places where

branches of the Bank of the US are established (or where there are so near that they may be conveniently used for the purpose) the collectors will from time to time deposit their Custom House bonds in the branches for collection where there are no branches the Collectors will deposit their Bonds in the State Banks in which they are authorized to deposit the public monies collected by them. But a preference should always be given to the Bank of the US and its branches." Biddle was appreciative, writing to the cashier of the Boston office, "For this prompt corrective of an abuse the Secretary deserves approbation."

59 Quotation from Rush's letter to Biddle, in 23rd Cong., 2d Sess., S. Doc. 17; a Circular from the Post-Office Department, dated September 9, 1829, from Kelsey Burr Papers, Box 2. On monetary arrangements with Receivers, sample is from Rush's Letters to Thomas A. Smith, Receiver at Franklin, MO; 20th Cong., S. Doc. 193, p. 61. The federal officers included the Superintendent of Indian Affairs, the Assistant Quartermaster, the Assistant Commissary of Subsistence, the Surveyor General, the US Army Paymaster, and Superintendent of US Lead Mines.

60 Biddle Papers, September 9, 1829, Biddle to Albert Gallatin. This quote is a good example of the somewhat threatening tone Biddle sometimes took in his advocacy for the Bank, which did not serve the Bank well.

61 Govan (1959, p. 86).

5 The "production" of monetary stability

By many measures, the US monetary system performed well in the 1820s. It was one of the most stable decades in nineteenth-century US monetary history: there were no suspensions of specie payments by the banks, and no banking crises. The nation enjoyed monetary stability despite the scarcity of specie, the asset at the foundation of the monetary system. Specie per banking office fell from $114,000 in 1820 to $72,000 in 1830, and specie per capita fell from $4.30 in 1820 to $2.40 in 1830.[1]

This chapter shows how the Bank "produced" monetary stability in an environment of specie scarcity. The first issue taken up, which is fundamental to the Second Bank's role in the monetary system, is whether the Bank was an issuer of high-powered money or a holder of high-powered money. High-powered money is money that functions as bank reserves and as the ultimate means of settling obligations. It is argued here that, in the 1820s US monetary system, specie was king; the Bank did not issue high-powered money, but it did actively manage it. The Bank was the single largest holder of specie, and it held a much larger specie reserve than any other bank in the system. The balance of the chapter shows how the Bank used its position of "specie strength" or, in Biddle's words, "ascendancy," to manage money. As a result of this work, public confidence in bank money rose during the 1820s and the country enjoyed the "greatest economizing upon the use of specie in the pre-Civil War years."[2]

The Second Bank: issuer of high-powered money?

Modern central banks underpin the money supply by issuing liabilities on themselves that function as high-powered money that the other, commercial, banks use as their ultimate reserve. Such a monetary authority can stabilize the banking system by providing more reserves when bank liquidity is strained, make reserves more expensive when bank credit is growing too rapidly, and so forth. With these modern arrangements in mind, and in light of the superior quality of Second Bank money, some scholars have treated Second Bank notes and deposits as part of the stock of high-powered money. This section evaluates two kinds of evidence on the status of Second Bank notes and comes to the conclusion that they were not generally regarded as high-powered money, fully equivalent to specie, by the state banks.[3]

Evidence from state bank balance sheets

In the 1820s, as today, banks held reserves against the money (notes and deposits) that they created. Banks came into the possession of each other's money on a daily basis, and regularly exchanged it for their own money, with net outstanding debt paid in an agreed-upon superior monetary asset. Banks held reserves to insure their ability to meet current payment obligations that could not be met with new inflows of liquidity (claims on other banks). In modern banking systems, the "superior monetary asset" is central bank money.[4] In the 1820s, final payment between banks (after swapping lower-order claims) was expected to be made in specie or in "specie funds."[5] The high cost of moving specie over any significant distance drove banks toward the use of specie-substitutes (specie funds), instruments with low credit risk, lower shipping costs compared with specie, and broad, if not universal, acceptability, particularly in intercity and interregional settlement. Second Bank notes would seem to have been the ideal instrument for this purpose.

Officer (2002), relying heavily on Rutner (1974), included the notes and deposits issued by the Second Bank in high-powered money in one version of his model of long-run monetary growth, just as the notes and deposits of the Federal Reserve make up the monetary base in contemporary arrangements.[6] In so doing, Second Bank money is treated as a perfect specie-substitute. Rutner reviewed information on state bank balance sheets from Congressional reports between 1835 and 1841 and found 100 instances (out of an unidentified total) in which "(state) banks split up their holdings of notes between the BUS and other state banks." For Rutner (and Officer), this separation of Second Bank notes from state-bank notes was evidence that the state banks regarded Second Bank notes as a reserve asset.[7]

Here, the balance sheets in the primary sources cited by Rutner are examined to understand how state banks represented, named, organized, and listed cash assets generally, and Second Bank notes and deposits in particular, on the balance sheets that they reported to the US government. The listing of cash items conveys information about the hierarchy of money forms as seen by the banks themselves, and also reflects the banks' perception of how those viewing their balance sheets would assess different forms of liquidity (specie, notes and checks of the Second Bank, notes and checks of city banks, notes and checks of local banks, etc.). All individual bank balance sheets from Rutner's sources available for 1834 and 1835 were examined, covering sixty-six banks from six states (Pennsylvania, Maryland, North Carolina, Virginia, Georgia, and Kentucky). These balance sheets were supplemented with nine balance sheets of Washington, DC, banks from year-end 1828 and one balance sheet for the State Bank of Indiana from November 1835, making a total of seventy-five balance sheets dated between late 1828 and late 1835, almost 20 percent of all state banks operating at the time.[8]

A distinct minority of the banks in this data set listed Second Bank notes separately from other kinds of banknotes on their balance sheets (see Table 5.1). Of the seventy-five, there were only fourteen that listed Second Bank notes separately from state-bank notes on their balance sheets. The fourteen banks include two (of thirty-three) Pennsylvania banks, in western cities of Pittsburgh and Brownsville, two of three North Carolina banks, six of twelve Georgia banks (in both coastal and interior locations of Savannah, Augusta, Columbus, and Hawkinsville), two of three Kentucky banks (in Louisville and Frankfort), one (of nine) Washington banks, and one (of one) bank in Indiana. Within the group of fourteen, eight went further than listing Second Bank notes separately from state-bank notes (a somewhat weak test of specie equivalence), to list Second Bank notes *with specie* in a subtotal, titled, for example, "Cash on hand." Only one bank went so far as to add Second Bank notes to specie in a combined total, as if specie and Second Bank notes were perfect substitutes.[9]

Thirteen of the fourteen banks that listed Second Bank notes in a separate category, subtotaled with specie or otherwise, treated *other* forms of bank money in a privileged way as well. For example, a bank in western Pennsylvania, the Monongahela Bank of Brownsville, listed US notes in the same category as eastern and Pittsburg notes, in an intermediate category between its specie (silver and gold) and notes of "Western banks." The Marine and Fire Insurance Bank of Savannah, Georgia listed notes of the Bank of the United States separately from the "notes of specie paying banks in this State," but also in the same category as "foreign"

Table 5.1 Treatment of Second Bank notes on state-bank balance sheets, 1828–1835

	Of 75 state banks in data set			*Of 14 state banks that listed Second Bank notes separately from other banknotes*	
Number that listed Second Bank notes separately from other banknotes	14			Number that also listed other banknotes separately	13
Number that did not	61			Number that did not	1
	Of city banks (n)	*Of country banks (n)*			
	36	39			
Number that listed Second Bank notes separately from other banknotes	3	11		Number in eastern core	1
Number that did not	33	28		Number outside eastern core	13

Source: Author's calculations from 23rd Cong., 2d Sess. H. Doc. 190; 20th Cong., 2d Sess., H. Doc. 86; 24th Cong., 2d Sess., H. Doc. 76.

note holdings and balances due from other banks, the largest of which was from the Bank of America, in New York. The Bank of Augusta combined notes of the Second Bank with notes of "other foreign banks, in good credit."[10]

All but one of the fourteen banks that listed Second Bank liabilities in some fashion as specie funds were located outside the eastern centers, in interior, western, and southern regions (see Map 5.1). In hearings on the Second Bank, its currency was said to be "as safe as silver; more convenient, and more valuable

Map 5.1 Number of state banks that treated Second Bank notes as specie funds in US cities and towns, 1828–1835

than silver, . . . through the whole Western and Southern, and interior parts of the Union," and to be "eagerly sought in exchange for silver; which in those sections, often bears a premium paid in silver; . . . equal to silver in payment to the Government and payments to individuals in business;" at par with silver "in any part of the country." It is "equivalent to silver in all dealings with all of the 9000 agents of the Government . . . in dealings with the interior, it is better than silver; in dealings with the commercial cities, equal to silver." On one occasion, the Louisville branch ran out of banknotes, and it had to pay out silver; this had "the consequence that the notes of the bank went to a premium of 0.5 percent to 1 percent," as Bank notes were in fact better than silver coin for transactions purposes.[11] Based on the Bank's dominant market share in the interior, its $5 notes and branch drafts must have made up a large part of the circulating medium in the interior.

Country banks in eastern and central Pennsylvania did not list Second Bank notes separately on their balance sheets, either because they had Second Bank notes but did not regard them as equivalent to specie, or because they did not come into possession of Second Bank notes in the course of business. Either way, they regarded specie or their balances with Philadelphia banks, not Second Bank notes, as their reserve assets. None of the eight Maryland banks (including a mix of city and country banks), and none of the four Virginia branch banks represented Second Bank notes, if they held them, with specie or separated them out from the notes of other banks. Seventy percent of the banks in smaller cities in this data set did not list treat Second Bank notes separately from state-bank notes or as specie funds.[12]

Only three of the thirty-six city banks in the data set (one each in Louisville, Washington, and Savannah) treated Second Bank notes as nearly specie on their balance sheets. The city banks in Philadelphia and Baltimore represented claims on the Second Bank on their balance sheets in the same way they treated claims on other city banks in Philadelphia and Baltimore, in an aggregated "due from other banks" category. No bank in either Philadelphia or Baltimore listed Second Bank notes or "due froms" separately from those of state banks or with specie. Eight Philadelphia banks and four Baltimore banks listed cash assets in three categories: specie, due from or drafts on other banks, and notes of other banks.[13] Three Philadelphia banks (the Mechanics' Bank, the Bank of Penn Township, and the Manufacturers and Mechanics' Bank of the Northern Liberties) differentiated between "city banks" and "foreign banks," or between "city banks and country banks" in their listing of claims due from other banks, but did not separate out their claims on the Second Bank from those of other city banks. This suggests that Philadelphia banks viewed claims on the Second Bank as equivalent to, not better than, claims on Philadelphia city banks.

The eastern city banks' failure to list Second Bank notes in a separate category as specie funds on their books is a significant social fact. These were "systemically important" financial institutions; large-scale, interregional payments were settled on their books. In contrast, the London private bankers—the British counterparts of the New York and Philadelphia banks—used the notes of the Bank of

England to settle debts among themselves at the London Clearing House. According to Thornton (1802),

> The larger London payments are effected exclusively through the paper of the Bank of England; for the superiority of its credit is such, that, by common agreement among the bankers, whose practice [*sic*], in this respect, almost invariably guides that of other persons, no note of a private house will pass in payment as a paper circulation in London.[14]

Evidence on the currency of large foreign Second Bank notes in eastern financial centers

There was a good reason why eastern city banks did not treat Second Bank notes as if they were equivalent to specie: the Second Bank did not unconditionally accept its own large-denomination notes when they were presented by state banks in interbank note exchanges or to pay net balances due to the Bank. After 1818, the Bank paid specie for its large-denomination notes only at the branch that issued them and did not accept large foreign Second Bank notes in interbank payments, even at a discount, in the major eastern cities.[15]

Congressional testimony of state-chartered banks in New York and Baltimore from 1833 provides evidence of the Bank's treatment of its large foreign notes. The President of the Mechanics' Bank, in New York, reported that the New York Branch Bank

> did, invariably, refuse to receive from most, if not all, our city banks, either in daily exchanges or in payment of balances, the notes of the mother bank, or other branches, with the exception of bills of five dollars. The Mechanics' Bank, and most, if not all, the other State banks here, were nevertheless in the constant practice [*sic*] of receiving such notes (uncurrent as they were termed) in limited amounts from their own dealers; and, notwithstanding such limitations, sums of from fifty to sixty thousand dollars would frequently accumulate in our bank alone, at times, too, when required by the branch to liquidate our balances in specie.

This report was confirmed by the President of the Bank of America, who added that the brokers or dealers, in whose hands "millions of dollars" of "uncurrent" Second Bank notes accumulated, "would seek for the bond-payers, and sell the notes to them at a small discount or other equivalent." The Manhattan Co. also had, at times, to pay its balance due to the New York Second Bank branch in specie even when it had "United States' Bank notes in their possession for more than the amount, and, in some instances, double the amount thus claimed to the credit of the Manhattan Company in the BUS in Philadelphia."[16]

The state banks in Baltimore told the same story. The Cashier of the Union Bank of Baltimore, Maryland, reported that

> The Branch of the Bank of the United States in Baltimore had not been in the habit of receiving the notes of the mother bank, or its branches, before

the early part of October last, in payment of its claims on the State banks. . . . the notes of the Bank of the United States and its branches, other than Baltimore, were always at a discount here. This was the case, notwithstanding the State banks usually received them at their nominal par value, to limited amounts, from some of their customers, whose accounts they deemed to sufficient value to induce the sacrifice, or to promote the general facilities of commerce. These notes, thus received, were held in the vaults of the banks, until an opportunity offered to paying them to persons having debts due to the Government, when they were paid into the Branch Bank to extinguish the Government claims.[17]

The rejection of large foreign Second Bank notes by the New York and Baltimore branches when presented by the state banks in those cities was an understandable point of contention. Gallatin defended the practise in his 1831 treatise, saying that

> It is obvious that no bank which has branches, can have funds at every place sufficient to meet a sudden demand for the payment of *a large amount of notes* payable elsewhere, which may fortuitously *or designedly* have accumulated at some one place [emphasis added].[18]

The New York and Baltimore branches' policy, implicitly or explicitly endorsed by Biddle, was a defensive one: the Bank wanted to limit the state institutions and brokers' ability to present large volumes of its notes for cash credit toward repayment of balances due to the Bank, which would deprive the Bank of claims on the eastern banks and of exchange income. The Bank also wanted to protect its specie from redemption demands whose purpose was to weaken the Bank, or to realize specie arbitrage profits (or both).

 If the eastern branches of the Bank had taken these large foreign notes, it would have been a valuable service to the state banking system, that of taking on the task of clearing intercity claims without compensation. The Bank was not interested in providing such a service for either the banks or its own customers. For large-denomination transfers of value, the Bank steered mercantile customers to their interbranch drafts, on which the Bank charged a premium. In a letter to the cashier of the New York office, Biddle explained why it was in the Bank's interest to direct merchants making long distance payments to the Bank's drafts instead of its large notes:

> The merchants remit our large notes to New York. These are either deposited directly with the office—in which case they operate as drafts without a premium, or else finding that they will not all be taken by you, they are deposited with the State Banks. In these State Banks, therefore, the merchants must keep accounts, and when they receive discounts they take these identical notes to you for duties . . . Now if instead of giving large notes, we give drafts, what would be the effect? The drafts might it is true be deposited in other Banks in New York but more naturally they would be deposited directly

> with you and *you would probably gain in general deposits and business since merchants would not be obliged to keep accounts in other Banks* [emphasis added].[19]

The Philadelphia (but not New York) office came to accept large foreign Bank notes at full face value, but *from merchant customers only.* Through a process of experimentation in Philadelphia, Biddle had figured out that, as he wrote to the New York cashier,

> you do not receive in the course of the week a dollar less of our notes [by refusing them], than you would if they were directly deposited with you in the first instance, and you lose the . . . general business of those merchants who are obliged to keep accounts in other Banks.[20]

Although not its first choice, the Bank was willing to allow merchants—but not banks—to use its large notes as premium-free means of long distance payment, as it was pointless to do otherwise, and it meant the Bank would gain other income-earning business.

Because the state banks in New York and other eastern cities could not present large foreign Second Bank notes to discharge obligations to the Second Bank, they had larger "due to" balances to the local Second Bank branch, on average, than they would otherwise have had. This put the Bank in a better position of control. In the eastern financial centers, the Bank added insult to injury by insisting on getting the weekly balances paid in specie only: other liquid assets, such as good commercial bills, US government debt, or Bank of the United States stock itself, were not accepted. The Bank's insistence on clearing balances in specie had a restraining effect on credit growth by reducing the specie in the vaults of less conservative state banks and increasing specie in the vault of the more conservative federal bank.

The Second Bank: "central holder" of high-powered money

Specie sat at the top of the hierarchy of money in the 1820s' US monetary system. From the beginning of his presidency, Biddle was looking for ways to build the Bank's specie reserve. One idea he had was to capitalize on political instability in Mexico to facilitate specie exports to the US (entering through the Bank). In 1823, he wrote to a US Senator from Massachusetts:

> From all the information we can obtain, there are many persons in Mexico, who in the troubled state of that country are very desirous of placing their property out of the reach of revolutions, and who by thus occasioning a more than ordinary demand for Bills on foreign countries, raise their rate. It is conceived therefore that the Bank might operate advantageously by selling its Bills of Exchange there. Besides the direct profit of such a business, *the possession of the amount of Specie which may be thus acquired, would*

establish and secure the ascendancy of the Bank over all the other monied institutions (emphasis added) while to the country at large, it would be an object of great interest to possess the means of extending the benefits of a sound circulation.[21]

Biddle sought the protection of the US Navy in transporting the specie from Mexican to US ports, the same service provided by the British Navy to the British ships. Although he did not get the naval protection for the ships carrying the Bank's specie, Biddle achieved his goal of "ascendancy." The Second Bank was far and away the largest single holder of specie in the economy. By the end of the 1820s, the Bank held $8.5 m of specie (averaged over 1829–1831). About half of this specie was held in its New York and Philadelphia branches. The New York branch of the Bank of the United States held an average of $1.7 m of specie in 1829–1831 and the head office in Philadelphia, $3 m. The largest Philadelphia bank, the Bank of Pennsylvania, had $.6 m in "cash items" (specie and nonspecie cash) in the early 1830s, and the largest New York City bank, the Bank of America, had $.25 m of specie.[22]

The Bank's share of specie in the banking system rose from a three-year average of 30 percent in 1820–1822, to 37 percent in 1830–1832, and its share of all specie in the US rose from 15 percent in 1820–1822 to 27 percent in 1829–1831.[23] The Bank came to own such a large share of the nation's stock of specie because of its role in financing international trade. Spanish American silver entered the US economy primarily in New Orleans, and secondarily in New York, Philadelphia, and Baltimore, in payment for exports to Latin America.[24] Merchants bought Second Bank drafts with their silver, since drafts were a much less expensive and more secure way to make long-distance payments. An estimated 20 percent - 25 percent of the silver coin imported into the country came into the Bank's possession, based on changes in the Bank's specie reserve, gross national silver imports, and the Bank's specie market transactions between July 1824 and July 1831.[25]

This number makes sense based on what we know about the Bank's market share in major port cities where silver entered the economy. In all of these cities, the Bank shared the market with a number of other state-chartered banks by 1830. If banking services had been divided equally among all banks, and it is assumed that half of the imported specie entered in New Orleans, 30 percent in New York, and 10 percent in Baltimore and Philadelphia, the Bank would have acquired 14 percent of all silver imports. However, the banking business of the larger mercantile firms engaged in intercity and international trade would not have been evenly distributed across all banks. As one of the largest banks in each of these cities, the Second Bank could discount larger bills and notes. In addition, these merchants would have particularly valued the Bank's domestic and foreign exchange services, boosting the Bank's share of silver imports above 14 percent.

The Second Bank had the highest reserve ratio and the most liquid composition of reserves in the banking system. The Bank used this position of "specie strength" to bring greater discipline to interbank payments, to limit the duration of monetary expansions, and to cushion the impact of shifts in net specie imports. These behaviors together maintained continuous convertibility, internally, of bank money into specie at the official rate.

Keeping liquid

The Bank's reserve ratio, a key measure of liquidity, was significantly higher than the state banks' throughout the period (see Figure 5.1). The Bank's decision to hold a large stock of specie was driven by several factors. First, its charter imposed a high penalty on any suspension of specie payments. It held that if the Bank were to

> suspend or refuse payment in gold or silver, . . . the persons . . . entitled to . . . receive such moneys . . . shall be entitled to receive and recover interest on the said bills, notes, obligations, or moneys, until the same shall be fully paid and satisfied, at the rate of 12 percent per year from the time of such demand.[26]

Second, the Bank needed a larger specie reserve than the state banks because it issued significantly more money in the form of notes, rather than deposits, than they did. In the early 1820s, about half of the money issued by the Bank was in the form of notes; by the late 1820s, almost 70 percent. State banks issued

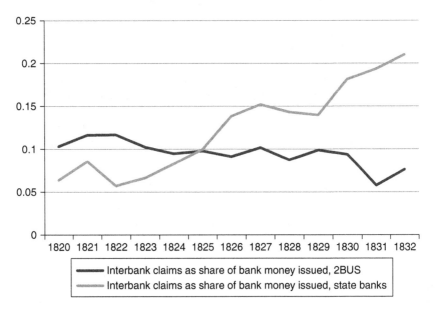

Figure 5.1 Interbank claims held by state banks and the Second Bank as a share of bank money issued, 1820–1832.

Source: Author's calculations from sources described in Appendix F.

60 percent of the money they created as notes in the early 1820s, and slightly less at the end of the decade.[27] Outstanding notes that were not extinguished through the clearing process represented a potential future claim on a bank's specie. The issuing bank had to be prepared to meet these claims, without knowing exactly where those notes were, whether they were held by banks or individuals, or whether large holdings were being accumulated for conversion into specie. In the case of bank deposits, the issuing bank knew how much it owed and to whom. In the 1820s, most bank depositors were also bank borrowers, hoping to continue to borrow from the bank in the future, creating a shared interest in avoiding a call for specie.

Finally, the Bank needed a large specie reserve to execute its duties as fiscal agent to the US government and to manage the cost of providing those services. It was the Bank's job to make sure that US government debt was serviced in specie or its equivalent. The Bank's own notes and deposits were specie-equivalents for this purpose at home, but not abroad. In 1828, one-third of the $58.4 m outstanding stock of national debt was held abroad. In addition, one-fourth of the Second Bank's shares were owned abroad by 1832. Practically speaking, ensuring timely payment abroad in specie-equivalents meant ensuring that all sterling, franc, and guilder drafts drawn on the US government's and the Bank of the United States' accounts with foreign correspondent banks in London, Paris, and Amsterdam were covered with foreign exchange remittances.[28] When things went smoothly, current remittances in paper exchange (sterling, franc, and guilder bills of exchange) were large enough to cover current obligations. The Bank held a large "buffer stock" of specie (silver and gold coin) and foreign exchange for those times when things did not go smoothly. As noted in Chapter Four, by keeping internal and external exchange rates within specie points, the Bank avoided the costs associated with shipping specie to meet the government's payment obligations.

The Bank was more conservative than the state banks in terms of the composition of its reserves and its loans. The state banks' holdings of interbank claims (notes of other banks and balances due to other banks within redemption networks) grew in relation to the money they created over the 1820s, as state banks substituted paper reserves (interbank claims) for specie reserves. In contrast, the Bank of the United States holdings of interbank claims fell in relation to its money creation (see Figure 5.1). Interbank claims were a form of secondary reserve; they were less liquid than specie, particularly during a crisis and in international payments.

The Second Bank's portfolio of private debt was a better source of potential liquidity than the average state bank's portfolio. The Second Bank set high standards for who would receive credit, and it closely monitored credit through its local boards. The Bank geared many of its financial services for the larger, better-established, lower default-risk merchants engaged in mediating interregional and international trade, and strongly preferred to extend credit of shorter duration. Short-term credit was intrinsically less risky than longer-term credit, because it allowed for more frequent confirmation of the borrower's ability to repay and more frequent opportunities to increase the liquidity of the Bank's balance sheet by withholding the renewal of credit.

Bringing discipline to interbank payments

As part of its fiscal role, it was up to the Second Bank to determine which state banks were "specie-paying" banks, and which were not. The US government accepted payment of obligations due to it (whether customs duties, land purchases, or internal taxes) in specie, Second Bank money (by charter), or money issued by specie-paying banks, as determined by the Bank. If a state bank wanted to maintain its reputation as a specie-paying bank, it had to remain current in interbank payments with the Second Bank. The drawing of checks, and the debiting and crediting associated with banknote clearing, gave rise to interbank due-to and due-from entries in bilateral accounts between banks, both within and between cities. The Bank's philosophy of banking was that "every bank should always be ready to provide for its notes."[29] The only way of confirming that a bank could "provide for its notes" was to require it to do so.

The Second Bank brought greater rigor and discipline to the process of settling interbank debt in terms of the frequency of settlement and the form of settlement. Over the course of a week of daily note exchanges, a state bank would accumulate net balances due to (from) the Bank if the Bank presented more (fewer) notes to the state bank than the state bank presented to the Bank. When Biddle assumed the Presidency in 1823, the Bank introduced daily note exchange in cities where it had branches, and weekly settlement of the net balances that accrued during the week *over a certain credit limit*. That is, the Bank did not seek to eliminate all debt due to it from state banks, only that which exceeded a limit.

The "parent bank" in Philadelphia set limits on how much credit the Bank should extend to the state banks in interbank payments. In 1817, the head office instructed the Lexington branch not to allow the notes of any state bank to exceed $20,000. In a similar directive to the office in Savannah, Philadelphia directed that the total balances due from Savannah banks, whether in notes or in balances due to the Bank from the state banks, be kept to $10,000 in the aggregate, divided equally among three banks considered specie-paying. If any bank allowed its debt to exceed that ceiling, the Savannah office was to demand payment in specie. The Board Committee directed the office at Baltimore

> not to suffer the aggregate of balances, due to it by the local Institutions with whom they do business, and the notes of Such Institutions together, to amount, at any one time, to more than $10,000 (exclusive of the Balances due by the city Banks).[30]

The Bank wanted to keep the state banks "uneasily aware that indiscreet credit policies on their part would lead to demands for redemption of balances due [or banknotes] in cash."[31]

In New York, and presumably Philadelphia, Boston, and Baltimore as well, the Bank required balances over the stipulated credit limit to be cleared on a weekly basis with specie.[32] In the south and west, the Bank showed some flexibility and leniency in terms of the mode of final settlement. As Biddle told Congress, the Bank's policy was

> to keep the State banks within proper limits; to make them shape their business according to their means . . . they are called upon to settle; never forced to pay specie, if it can be avoided, but payment is taken in their bills of exchange, or suffered to lie occasionally until the bank can turn round.[33]

In his private correspondence with branch cashiers, Biddle articulated a less-flexible policy on "letting balances lie" than that represented in his claims to Congress. In a letter to the President of the Savannah branch, Biddle wrote:

> In the relations between the Bank of the United States and the State Banks, the fundamental principle is, that when their mutual exchanges are made, the balance should be at once paid. It may not be paid in gold or silver—but it should be paid in their equivalents—in drafts or Stocks or some other property which the creditor is willing to receive and the debtor able to give. There should be an actual discharge and settlement of the debt in some form or other.[34]

After this policy was communicated, the Savannah branch discounted

> approved bills on the North at a .5 percent discount for bills with less than 15 days to maturity, .75 percent for bills running between 15 and 30 days into the future, and 1.25 percent for bills maturing in 30 to 60 days.[35]

The Bank's branch network was used to screen the quality of the bills and to efficiently collect the bills of exchange. On these transactions, the Bank earned interest and a bid-ask spread on the intercity movement of funds. "Good" bills of exchange, made liquid by the Bank itself, were thus converted into a kind of settlement instrument or secondary bank reserve.

The Bank also accepted drafts on money-center state banks in settlement of interbank debt. In another letter to the Savannah branch, Biddle wrote:

> As part of our system of exchanges with the State Banks we have always been willing to take in settlement their drafts on such terms as would make them equivalent to specie . . . . The rate at which these drafts would be equivalent to specie is a matter of easy calculation. If therefore in the progress of your operations with those Banks, you feel that the Office is strong enough to take these drafts on New York, or Philadelphia, and they are offered at fair rates, there would be no objection to your doing so. At the present moment, drafts

in favor of the Bank on the Banks either of N York or Philadelphia would be acceptable, as the Bank is just now in debt to the City Banks of Philadelphia. If then the office is so much at its ease as to take such drafts it will render settlements with the State Banks more easy to them by giving their drafts at proper rates, it would operate very advantageously here.[36]

Similarly, in 1817, the head office instructed the Lexington branch to collect payment from the state banks once they hit their credit limit

either in specie or in such bills of exchange as may enable you to remit to this bank, or any of its offices east of the mountains, or to the office at New Orleans; and if the demand shall not be satisfied, you will cease to receive the notes of any such bank, unless it shall engage to pay interest, and liquidate the balance in a reasonable time.[37]

Biddle gave similar instructions to the Richmond branch when he wanted them to start returning the notes of the state banks for payment instead of receiving them and paying them out again. Richmond was to

Write to the Branches that you have a certain amount of their notes on hand which you desire them to pay—that you wish to make this as convenient and as little burdensome as possible, and that if it be not desireable [*sic*] to pay Specie, you will accept in payment their drafts either on their mother Banks at Richmond, or on the Northern Cities, that you wish the remittances *in two weeks time* (emphasis added) or you may be obliged to send for the Specie.[38]

The Bank's role as the US government's fiscal agent, combined with federal fiscal surpluses, softened the trade-off between profit and duty that the Bank would have otherwise faced.[39] A bank that sought to stay in a net-creditor position vis-a-vis other banks would typically need to expand credit more slowly than the other banks and so to be less profitable. As customs and other revenues were paid to the Treasury, the Bank came into possession of state-bank notes, which put the Bank into a net-creditor position, and when the Bank made disbursements for the Treasury, control over the state banks was relaxed. The US government's fiscal surpluses in the 1820s allowed the Bank to maintain its net-creditor position most of the time without curtailing its own loan growth. In any given city or region, fiscal outlays may have exceeded receipts, potentially putting the Second Bank branch in a net-debtor position vis-a-vis the state banks, but these problems could be, and were, addressed with interbranch liquidity movements orchestrated from Philadelphia.

Stabilizing the monetary system

To be a stabilizer of national income, the central holder of specie should, in principle, reduce its reserve ratio during periods of slow growth and increase it during periods of rapid growth. Figure 5.2a shows that the Bank's reserve ratio

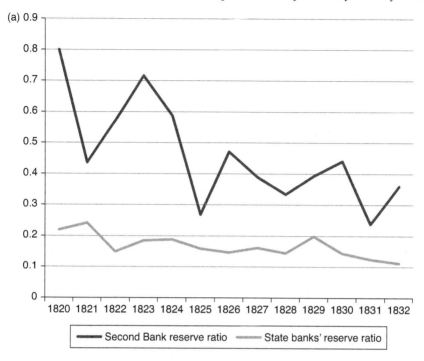

Figure 5.2a Second Bank and state banks' specie reserve ratios, 1820–1832.

Source: Appendix E.

did fluctuate significantly, in sharp contrast to the more or less constant reserve ratio of the state banking sector. But the timing is counterintuitive to modern eyes, as the Bank's reserve ratio fell at the peak of import expansions, a good proxy for aggregate demand growth, and rose as import growth slowed (see Figure 5.2b). The changes in the Bank's reserve ratio were not the result of shifts in the Bank's policy stance, but rather reflect the way the Bank insulated the state banks in the short run from the effects of changes in net specie imports (imports net of exports) during the Biddle presidency.

Before Biddle took office in 1823, the Bank was a destabilizing force: it gained specie at the expense of the rest of the national economy (see Figures 5.3a and 5.3b). Between 1821 and 1823, the state banking system took the brunt of net specie losses. The Bank's specie holdings rose, and it reduced outstanding notes and deposits while the state banking system modestly expanded its liabilities. By 1823, the state banks held 18 cents of specie for each dollar of notes and deposits they issued, while the Second Bank held 72 cents for each dollar of outstanding monetary liabilities.

After 1823, when the Bank started its large-scale operations in domestic exchange, foreign exchange, and specie under Biddle's leadership, the pattern changed. Year-to-year changes in the Bank's specie holdings were almost exactly equal to the net specie imports during the period. In periods of falling and negative

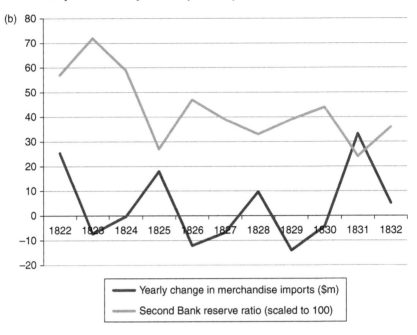

Figure 5.2b Merchandise import cycle and the Second Bank's reserve ratio, 1822–1832.

Sources: Second Bank's reserve ratio, see Appendix E; merchandise imports from Smith 1953, p. 86.

net specie imports (1824–1825, 1826–1828, 1830–1831), the Bank's specie hold-ings fell by very similar amounts. In periods of rising and positive net specie imports (1825–1826, 1828–1830), the Bank's specie holdings rose by the same or similar amounts. In this way, the Bank sterilized the effect of fluctuations in net specie imports on money and credit creation.[40] After 1823, the changes in the Bank's specie holdings account perfectly for swings in the Banks reserve ratio; its reserve ratio fell when its specie reserve fell (1824–1825, 1826–1828, 1830–1831) and rose when its specie reserve rose. The Bank rebuilt its "buffer stock" when its reserve ratio rose, and drew it down when its reserve ratio fell.

By acting as a "sink" for net specie imports and exports, the Bank's vault cush-ioned the state banking system from these changes, as can be seen by comparing Figures 5.3a and 5.3b. After 1823, state banks' specie holdings either change in the opposite direction from that in the economy at large (1826–1828), or in the same direction, but in a smaller amplitude, and more gradually (1824–1825). In 1824–1825, the Bank lost 40 percent of its specie, $2.7 m, in one year; the state banks lost $1.8 m over two years, 13 percent of what they had in 1824.[41]

The Bank's operations in the market for sterling bills of exchange comple-mented the buffer stock pattern in the Bank's specie holdings. In the 1820s, short-run macroeconomic expansions were characterized by growth in imports and growth in state bank credit. Growth in imports (some share of which was paid for, domestically, with specie) ahead of exports (some share of which was also

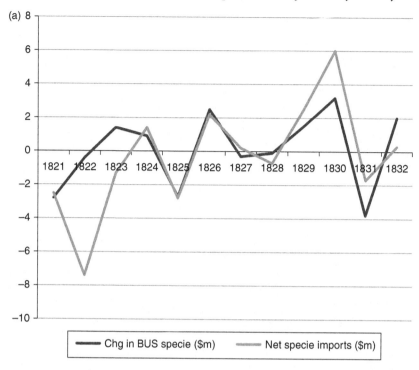

Figure 5.3a Changes in specie holdings of the Second Bank in relation to specie imports, 1821–1832.

paid for, abroad, with specie) would manifest itself as falling net specie imports. At such times, importers bid for foreign exchange to meet obligations abroad, causing sterling exchange to approach or exceed the silver export point.[42] These were peaks in the import cycle. Periods of falling specie imports coincided with tightness in the sterling exchange market, itself a signal of balance-of-payments problems (see Figure 5.4). At such times, in addition to allowing its own stock of specie to be drawn down (and its reserve ratio to fall), the Bank also sold its own sterling drafts, if need be at below-market rates, to bring the price of sterling exchange below the silver export.

The Bank's sales of foreign exchange moderated the increase in the price of sterling bills and, over time, constrained growth in state bank credit by increasing the state banks' net due-to position with the Second Bank (much like Federal Reserve open-market sales of securities today). Once duties on the high level of imported goods came due, their payment would reinforce the shift in interbank payments in favor of the Bank. The pressure on the state banks would eventually reduce their supply of credit and curtail the demand for imports, producing the desired reduction in the demand for foreign exchange and specie.[43] In the absence of Bank intervention, high import demand, high demand for foreign exchange, and specie outflow could have continued unabated, potentially ending

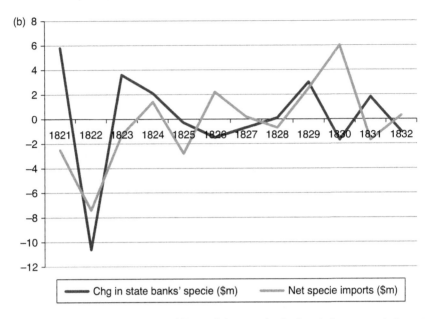

Figure 5.3b Changes in specie holdings of the state banks in relation to specie imports, 1821–1832.

Sources: Annual Report of the Secretary of the Treasury on the State of the Finances, October 24, 1855; and Appendix E.

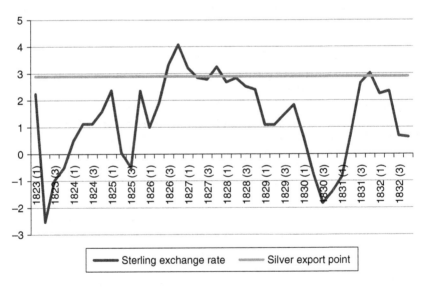

Figure 5.4 Sterling exchange rates and the silver export point in the United States, 1823–1832.

Sources: Officer 1996, Table 6, for sterling exchange rates, and Tables 9.1–3, 9.7, 9.8, 9.16, and p. 141 for data used to calculate silver export point. Sterling exchange rates are percentage premium or discount from true mint.

in the suspension of specie payments. The specie suspensions of the late 1830s and late 1850s, after the demise of the Bank, occurred at the end of periods of rising asset prices and rapid expansion in bank money and credit, which left the banking system more exposed to shocks to confidence that increased demand for the safest asset, specie.[44]

To sum up, the Second Bank accumulated a buffer stock of foreign exchange and specie, and used it to try to bring an earlier end to state bank credit-financed import expansions than there would have been, had the state banking sector been left to its own devices. Biddle was prepared to use the Bank's ample stocks of foreign exchange and specie to prevent a sudden shortage of liquidity, preserve specie convertibility, and give the state banks time to reduce their levels of credit. The driving logic behind the Bank's stabilization operations was to keep exchange rates within specie points. Once exchange rates moved outside the specie points, either internally or externally, there would be an increased demand for specie as a means of payment or instrument of arbitrage. These demands would be centered on the Bank as the "central repository of specie," as Biddle put it. The Bank had to manage money for the nation in order to preserve its own ability to pay specie for its notes and, as noted earlier, to manage the operating costs of serving as the government's fiscal agent.

Meerman (1961) came to the same conclusion:

> The Bank was not a 'lender of last resort' in the way the Federal Reserve is. The Bank rarely lent to its sisters; nor did they keep reserves with it. But with its holdings of foreign exchange as well as specie, . . . in a crisis it was the only institution which could meet heavy calls for foreign exchange or specie with equanimity.

In a letter to Albert Gallatin in 1830, Biddle explained the strategy as follows:

> The Bank . . . by means of its accumulation of bills and its extended credits in Europe is enabled . . . to supply the demand at rates which ward off from the state banks too great a demand for coins . . . to allow them to diminish their issues without ruin to their customers and by the gradual reduction of their business cure the existing disorder.

Govan put it this way:

> Time was the essential factor during every period of strain and pressure, since every merchant, banker, and producer operated on credit. If one of them were suddenly called on to pay the whole of his debts, he would have had to default because his assets were never immediately collectible. What Biddle did during moments of danger was to provide time for individuals to make their own adjustments to changed circumstances by protecting them from the full and immediate force of the financial pressure.[45]

The Second Bank allowed its specie reserve to function as a buffer stock during periods of excess demand for specie and sterling exchange. But the depletion of its reserve could only go so far; at some point, restoration of its specie strength became the top priority, as illustrated in a narrative account of the Bank's management of the monetary crisis of 1825–1826.

The Second Bank and the crisis of 1825–1826

The Second Bank's behavior during the crisis of 1825–1826 exemplifies the Bank's approach to monetary stabilization. This section starts with a brief review of the literature, then provides a narrative of Bank's management of the crisis, focusing on the New York money market. As the nation's importing center, New York was exposed to liquidity shocks originating in international trade and finance; as the center of large redemption networks, New York had the potential to propagate shocks to many other state banks.

The downturn of 1825–1826 started with a break in cotton prices in July 1825, gained steam with a wave of failures of merchant banking houses in England and the US, and culminated in a banking crisis in England, but not in the US, in December 1825. There are a variety of views in the economic history literature about the Bank's conduct during the crisis. On one end of the debate, Redlich (1968), Govan (1959), Catterall (1902), and Hammond (1957) credited the Bank with taking the right step at the right time to forestall a banking crisis, whether it was preventing a shipments of specie out of New York (Redlich), or allowing the New York branch to expand its discounts (Govan, Catterall). Redlich interpreted Biddle's behavior as trying to "avoid a situation where the Bank of the United States and the state banks from mutual dread of each other reduced their discounts and became unable to accommodate the public."[46]

Other authors have been more circumspect. Temin argued that the Bank's first priority was to maintain its net creditor position vis-a-vis the state banks, not to assist the banks as a lender of last resort. Meerman credited the Bank with preventing a specie outflow from New York, and authorizing expansion by the New York branch, but pointed out that this took place after the peak of the pressure on the specie stock. Smith concluded that Biddle's "ideas were correct enough, but the activities of the Bank, viewed in their entirety, did not live up to Biddle's version of this well-conceived policy." Smith gave Biddle credit for careful management of its cotton bills and its accounts with the state banks. The Bank maintained its net-creditor position with the state banks (except, crucially, in New York), a task made more challenging by the large debt retirement disbursed by the Bank in October 1825. Smith applauded the Bank for increasing its discounts, but noted that these were offset, in their effect on the state banks, by the sales of government securities.[47]

A lender of last resort would have been more concerned about the liquidity position of the other banks, than with its own. It is hard to say this of the Second Bank, based on Biddle's correspondence with the cashiers of the branches in New York, Boston, Baltimore, and New Orleans during 1825. As the following chronology of this correspondence will show, Biddle actively managed the Bank's holdings of specie, was particularly concerned about the liquidity of the New York branch, and kept a close eye on the market for the "prime" Spanish dollars that were accepted by Asian trading partners, the Carolus and Ferdinand dollars, so as to maximize the Bank's earnings from specie sales.

During the spring of 1825, Biddle wrote frequently to the Cashier at New York, advising him to protect his foreign coin by "keeping in front always a sufficient force of American coin." This was an important dynamic in the monetary system of the 1820s: the holder of a banknote could demand payment in specie, but could not force the issuer to pay in a certain type of specie if there were more than one type available. At this time, the country was effectively on a silver standard, but there were a variety of silver coins in circulation, ranging from the strongest foreign coins to American dollars and half-dollars, and degraded Spanish American coins. Biddle advised the New York cashier, "If you are likely to lose them [the Carolus and Ferdinands], it will be better to sell them and throw the demand on the State Banks."[48] That is, if New York did not have enough American coins "in front," it was better to sell the strong Spanish dollars at the prevailing premium of 2–3 percent, which would have the added benefit of turning the balances against the state banks and in favor of the Bank. The Bank of the United States specie holdings fell by $2.7 m between year-end 1824 and year end 1825; the Bank sold $1.6 m of specie (silver coin) during the year.[49] These specie sales had a contractionary effect on the state banks, increasing their net due-to position to the Second Bank.

In April, Biddle sent sterling bills to New York, which continued to be under liquidity pressure, directing Robinson to "use only if necessary to relieve you," and only at a certain minimum price (9.5 percent over nominal par). Liquidity was also on the way from Boston and New Orleans, which had been directed to remit drafts to New York. Biddle was very aware of the spatial realities of moving money. He wrote to the Boston cashier that Philadelphia had "parted with much of our Specie for the China Trade" (a demand which typically fell on the New England branches), and

> we are desirous of concentering our resources at some point where they may be disposable so as to protect immediately any quarter which may be exposed. We would prefer therefore that this Special-deposit should be at New York rather than at Boston.[50]

If Boston needed to restore its own liquidity, it was authorized to sell a certain amount of the 4.5 percent Florida loan at whatever price it could get. The same month, Philadelphia sent Baltimore funds and sterling bills to the Baltimore branch, apologizing for their inability to send any American coin. Throughout the summer, the price of bills on London and the good Spanish dollars continued to rise. Biddle told the Cashiers that they should not sell either asset under a certain price and that, if they needed to rebuild their liquidity, they should sell their US debt securities instead.

Throughout the year, Biddle directed the Cashiers of the branches to, initially, keep their discounts "within their income" (that is, to repayments of past discounts) and, later, to reduce their discounts in order to keep out of debt to the State Banks—confirming Temin's critique. In October, Biddle wrote to New York:

> I am surprised that the balances still continue so much against you with the State Banks. On the 15th inst. [of October] you owed them only $35,000 since then you have reduced your discounts, you have had large receipts of revenue, and have sold a very heavy amount of Sterling yet the balances now stands at $150,000.[51]

Finally, at the apex of the crisis, Biddle wrote to a member of the New York board about possible courses of action—none of which included expanding discounts or lending to the state banks: "First, if we could sell our 4.5 percent stock to a considerable amount for cash, and bring out funds lying idle for want of confidence, we might strengthen the office and enable it to discount more." That is, expanding discounts was contingent on improving the liquidity of the office; a modern central bank would not feel constrained in this way. Biddle's concern about liquidity was not misplaced; at the end of December 1825, the New York branch had a net due-to balance with the State Banks of $486,890, which was larger than its specie balance of $419,410.

> Second, It has been suggested that we might sell our 4.5s on credit for undoubted paper . . . [but] the money which would buy these 4.5s is either on deposit with the Banks who are discounting on it, or else it is occupied already in discount out of doors, and would therefore only change hands without bringing new funds into the market, unless indeed, as is said, people are beginning to hoard Specie which would thus be let loose by investments in 4.5s.[52]

A couple of days later, Biddle again wrote to Lenox:

> Before proceeding in further measures of a general nature, I wish you would make negociation [sic] with that cautious Frenchman, and try to get his Specie for four and a halfs [sic]. We want to strengthen the office in Specie, and would be willing to make some sacrifice to do it. There is now one per cent at least due on these, which would be so much gain to him, if he bought them at par. But we would go even lower, and give them to him if you could not make a better bargain even at 99.[53]

The final idea was to lend the 4.5 percent stock

> to some of the Banks who are pressed, and when they are called upon for Specie they might agree to pay interest, on giving Stock as a Security. The value

of this measure depends on the Solvency of the Bank to whom we would lend, and also whether it would in fact be a relief.

In short, Biddle was not prepared to lend liquidity (specie) to a state bank in distress, but he would lend stock (meaning Bank shares or US government securities), in the hope that the bank could convince someone with a specie claim against it to accept deferred payment and interest instead. The Bank's strategy was to stabilize the money market by mobilizing "other people's specie"—not its own.

As liquidity pressure intensified in the Fall of 1825, the Bank of the United States continued to protect its "good" specie, moved specie and other funds from branches with "excess" liquidity to branches with inadequate liquidity, and tried to coax specie out of private hoards. It was not an easy year for the Bank, but it was a profitable one. In January 1826, Biddle wrote to a correspondent that the dividend would remain constant even though "the profits of the Bank would have justified fully an increase." The Bank pulled back from new commitments to cotton early, so commercial losses to the Bank were small, while the Bank's sterling bills increased in value; as Biddle said, they "ought to be worth one per cent more in these times of unmeasured speculation."[54] As others have noted, selling assets (whether government securities, specie, or foreign exchange), as the Bank did throughout 1825, was the opposite of what a central bank should do in a monetary contraction. In 1825, the Bank's safety came first.

The Second Bank as lender of last resort?

Documented cases of lending of last resort by the Second Bank are few and far between. Much of the literature cites Redlich, who supported his case with Biddle's letters from the late 1820s; these are examined more closely here. Redlich did not identify any specific case of the Second Bank lending to another bank. Biddle's correspondence, Congressional documents, and the records of the Baltimore branch of the Second Bank yield five examples, over ten years, of the Bank lending to a specific financial firm in distress: one case in Savannah, one in Baltimore, and three cases in Philadelphia. These examples include two state-chartered banks, one savings bank, and two separate loans to one private (unincorporated, unchartered) bank. Taken together, these cases provide little support for the lender of last resort hypothesis.

The strongest proponent of the view that the Bank was a lender of last resort, often cited by others, is Redlich (1968). In reaching this conclusion, Redlich relies on three letters written by Biddle in 1829, from which Redlich concludes that "it was the accepted practice [*sic*] of the parent bank and of the branches to back state banks which, although sound, were temporarily in distress." Redlich describes Biddle as "exceedingly cautious in lending to country banks, never relying on their assets and good will, but always requiring tangible and convertible security, making loans . . . in the form of rediscount."[55]

Redlich read too much into Biddle's letters, once their context and full content is considered. In the late 1820s, a number of New York bank charters were expiring, and the state legislature adopted laws that made the ownership of bank capital much less attractive. None of the banks that applied for charter renewals in 1828 succeeded.[56] The letters are written on June 4, 11, and 13, 1829, to a Director of the New York branch, to the Secretary of the Treasury, and to A. Davis, of New York, respectively. In the letter to the Treasury Secretary, whose positive regard was of great importance to the Bank, Biddle reported that the Bank had expanded its discounts in New York in order to counteract a contraction of discounts by some of the state banks and to

> prevent further trouble from the conflicts between the State Institutions. . . . As I wish to avoid all interference in State quarrels and am most anxious on the present occasion that the Bank should furnish the relief than seem to be the ostensible agent in producing it.

He enclosed a copy of the letter to A. Davis and invited him to share it with the President as well.[57]

The letter to Davis laid out Biddle's views in regard to requiring "some tangible and convertible security" on any direct loans to the country banks. In the case of "good Country Banks keeping accounts with City Banks remitting their city paper for collection and making their deposits there" that were to find themselves "deprived of their accommodations in other City institutions," they

> could receive at the Office facilities denied elsewhere, [and] might become valuable and habitual dealers with the Office. In this way good might be done. But the best and safest form of relief is the discount of city paper, the indirect effect of which is felt in the Country, *and nothing is farther from our thoughts than any general project of relief to every body* [sic]*which must only end in disappointment to all concerned* [emphasis added].[58]

Finally, in the letter to Robert Lenox, a member of the Board of Directors of the New York branch of the Bank of the United States, Biddle wrote:

> With regard to the Country Banks, I have not a great opinion of them and would not be willing to support for an hour an unsound Bank. But if at the present moment, a well conducted Bank gets into a temporary difficulty *and its friends step forward to relieve it on their own responsibility* [emphasis added], it is well to give our aid whatever may be the result. . . . After all you know the existence of this institution must depend on the opinion entertained of it by those who will before long be asked to continue its charter and although I would sacrifice nothing either of right or of duty . . . to please anybody, still if a proper occasion presents itself of

rendering service to the interior and proving the usefulness of the Bank, so as to convert enemies into friends, we owe it to ourselves and to the Stock-holders not to omit that occasion.[59]

That is: if the Bank were to lend to a bank in difficulty, the purpose would be to demonstrate the value of the Bank and to create friends for the Bank, and it would be conditional on others stepping forward with loans also, before the Bank would come in.

In sum, these letters describe a political situation—not a banking crisis—in which the Bank considered lending to select country banks that maintained redemption accounts in New York, to offset a contraction initiated by the state banks, for the ultimate purpose of deflecting blame for any money market disturbances that may have transpired away from the Bank, at a time when the Bank's approaching need to renew its charter was on Biddle's mind. It was not a "general project of relief," but selective lending with a well-considered political purpose.

The previous year (1828), the Savannah branch of the Second Bank made an emergency loan to one of the state banks. Philadelphia was not happy about this loan; Biddle wrote to the President of the Savannah board clearly stating the Bank's view on lending to state banks:

Undoubtedly there may be occasions where a Bank like an individual meets with some unexpected misfortune which might render it extremely inconvenient to be pressed for immediate payment, and it was we suppose under this view of the subject that the loan in question was given, presuming that another would not be wanted and that the present loan would be certainly paid at maturity. These expectations will not we trust be disappointed, but I am instructed by the Board to express their opinion, that *it is inconsistent with the true policy of the Bank to make loans to other Banks in order to enable them to pay their notes* [emphasis added] and that should the case recur, they wish the office to avoid making similar loans in future.[60]

During the Baltimore banking panic of 1834, the Second Bank did lend to an institution in distress, the Savings Bank of Baltimore, but not to the commercial banks under liquidity pressure. The Savings Bank was a quasi-philanthropic financial institution that did not compete with the Second Bank for prime commercial banking relationships. The panic started on March 24 with the unexpected closure of the Bank of Maryland, which had attracted small deposits by paying high interest rates, and invested the funds in speculative ventures of two of the directors of the Bank. The Bank of Maryland's Board announced that they had ascertained, "with surprise and deep regret . . . that this institution is unable to proceed with its business," and that they would be transferring "all its effects to a trustee, for the equal benefit of the creditors of the bank." The directors urged the creditors "not to sacrifice their claims," notwithstanding which, a run for "small sums in coin" on the Bank of Maryland quickly ensued, and spread to other institutions, especially those that also served small depositors, such as the Savings Bank of Baltimore. The run did not extend to the Second Bank, reflecting the Baltimore office's strong reputation for safety and liquidity by 1834, and also the fact that the Bank did not serve small savers. According to *Niles' Weekly Register*, a Baltimore periodical, the Second Bank Baltimore office was "willing to extend the use of its means . . . for the demand on this bank [the Second Bank] was insignificant."[61]

The Savings Bank of Baltimore was especially vulnerable to a run because, in addition to serving small savers, its cash on hand was down to $500 due to an overdraft of the Franklin Bank. On March 26, two days after the failure of the Bank of Maryland, the Board of the Savings Bank approved a borrowing of $10,000 from the Baltimore Branch Bank of the United States "for the purpose of meeting any sudden calls upon the Savings Bank during the present alarm in the community," and authorized the President and Treasurer of the Savings Bank to increase the loan "or make additional loans elsewhere, whenever in their judgement it may be necessary for the purpose of paying deposits promptly and daily."[62] The loan was secured with a pledge of 200 shares of US Bank stock as collateral security. The Savings Bank also received short-term assistance from Alexander Brown and Sons, whose principal had called a meeting "of merchants and bankers . . . in the early stages of the panic" and declared that "'no firm inherently solvent, would be allowed to fail'."[63] The affirmative, proactive commitment of liquidity support during the panic was provided by Alexander Brown and Sons, not by the Baltimore branch of the Second Bank.

The other three documented examples of the Bank extending a loan and providing liquidity to a financial institution took place in Philadelphia and outside of the context of a banking panic. The Second Bank loaned the Girard Bank, a large private bank in Philadelphia, $50,000 in specie in 1828 when the Girard Bank was unable to meet a sight draft drawn upon it, and another $10, 000 in 1831. In 1833, the Bank rediscounted commercial paper of the Bank of Philadelphia, which was in "some temporary embarrassment."[64]

In sum, an exhaustive review of the secondary literature and primary yields five instances of the Second Bank providing liquidity assistance to a specific financial institution. This is a very thin base of evidence upon which to conclude that the Bank systematically behaved as a lender of last resort lender of last resort to the state-chartered commercial banks. Although Biddle made public pronouncements about the willingness of the Second Bank to assist state banks in need, in his private correspondence he sang a different tune. For example, in 1828, Biddle wrote to John Campbell White, Cashier of the Baltimore branch:

> While the state banks go on in their present career (of overtrading), it is hardly fair to throw on the stockholders of the Bank of the U.S. the burden of protecting them against the effects of their own improvidence—of relieving them at the first moment of difficulty by incurring a heavy debt in Europe bearing an interest of five per cent. It seems more just that the Bank

of the U.S. should reserve its strength—and let the state banks feel the pressure which their thoughtlessness occasions. . . . [The Bank] keeps within its limits—discounting cautiously—and when demands for specie come, turns them over to the state banks.[65]

Biddle seemed to think that the state banks were ultimately on their own. Some of the time, the Bank would cushion the effects of liquidity shocks and give the banks time to adjust; at other times, the Bank would actually divert specie demands onto the state banks. Anticipating the debate between Bagehot and Hankey in England fifty years later, Biddle seems to come down closer to Hankey, with his concerns about moral hazard, than to Bagehot.

Results: growing confidence in bank money, slower monetary growth

During the 1820s, the general public became more willing to use bank money, due to the banknote redemption systems established by the state banks and the monetary stabilization by the Second Bank. Banks "earned" the confidence placed in them, as there were no suspensions of specie payments on the Bank's watch. There was a cost of this monetary stability, though, in the form of slower growth in money and credit. Ironically, within stagnant monetary aggregates, there was one sector that saw impressive growth: the Second Bank itself.

Shift out of specie and into bank money

During this decade, the non-bank public shifted its holding of money, defined as specie, banknotes, and deposits, out of specie and into bank money, banknotes and deposits (see Table 5.2). (See Appendix E for banking aggregates and Appendix F for a discussion of sources and methods.) Specie's share fell from 19 percent of money held by the non-bank public to 7 percent; the share of bank money rose accordingly.[66] Bank money was better than specie, and more available.

Table 5.2 Composition of the stock of money held by the non-bank public, 1820–1831

Period (3-year average)	Share held as specie	Share held as BUS notes	Share held as BUS deposits	Share held as state banknotes	Share held as state bank deposits
1820–22	0.19	0.05	0.05	0.43	0.28
1823–25	0.12	0.07	0.05	0.47	0.30
1826–28	0.12	0.09	0.05	0.43	0.31
1829–31	0.07	0.13	0.05	0.43	0.32
Change in share, 1820–31	−0.12	+0.08	0	0	+0.04

Sources: Appendix E for banking aggregates; Temin (1969), Table 3.3 for national specie; Rockoff (2006) for specie in state banks.

The alternative to bank money as a circulating medium—the coinage—deteriorated in quality compared with banknotes, which made it easier for banknotes to gain broad acceptance.

By the mid-1820s, the coin in circulation was made up of small, worn Spanish silver coins and fragments of coins. These coins made up a large part of the small currency used in wage payments and retail trade, displacing both the fuller-weight, larger-denomination Spanish dollars and the fractional US coins. In 1827, US law granted legal tender status only to Spanish coin that weighed at least 415 grains to the US dollar, but most of the coin in circulation at that time did not meet this standard. As Carothers noted of a similar coinage law in 1792:

> Under a strict interpretation of the law a large proportion of the current coins had no legal standing. The provision was impractical. The impossibility of weighing coins in retail trade meant that the entire mass of Spanish coins would be accepted as legal coins. . . . The Senate Report of 1830 said that the entire coin currency was depreciated from 6 to 20 percent, the smaller coins showing the greater losses. Storekeepers habitually accepted coins in any state of depreciation, protecting themselves against losses from the receipt of hopelessly worn coins by a general increase in prices for their goods.[67]

Wage earners and farmers also accepted coins in "any state of depreciation."

In 1819, Treasury Secretary Crawford reported that "Spanish milled dollars compose the great mass of foreign silver coins which circulate in the United States, and generally command a premium when compared with the dollar of the United States." Twelve years later, a Congressional report on the coinage observed that "The money unit of the United States, or its concurrent tender, the Spanish milled dollar, is rarely, if ever, seen in circulation."[68] Between 1819 and 1832, then, the better silver coins, Spanish milled dollar and the American half-dollar, were culled from the circulating medium and diverted to other uses. The Sanford Report to Congress of 1830 described how merchants, bankers, and money dealers used their superior knowledge of monetary matters to cull "good silver" from the stock:

> In every society where coins are used, they are treated very differently, by two classes of persons. One class comprising far the greater number, pay and receive coins, without regard to their actual weight; and the great circulation of the community takes place, by mere tale. Another class consists of persons who in various ways, deal in the precious metals as merchandize; and this class traffic in coins, according to their actual weight and intrinsic value. While an immense majority of the society are incessantly circulating diminished coins as equivalent to those of full weight, dealers of gold and silver are constantly making the discrimination which is not made by others; and their business is, to derive profits from these disparities. While others circulate by tale, they ascertain the value of coins, by weight. They receive coins of full

weight, and pay those of reduced weight; they exchange diminished coins for coins of full weight; and the constant commerce of the society renders those substitutions easy and endless. When a diminished coin has been used to obtain a coin of full weight for gain, the coin of full weight circulates no more. It is converted into bullion, or treated as bullion; and is exported or used in manufactures.[69]

The rising share of bank money took place in two components: in banknotes issued by the Bank of the United States (the share of which rose from 5 percent to 13 percent), and in deposits issued by state banks (the share of which rose from 28 percent to 32 percent). Over 90 percent of the growth in the stock of bank deposits took place in the state bank sector. The Bank apparently had a comparative advantage in issuing notes, while the state banks' comparative advantage lay in deposits. Second Bank notes were better than specie as a means of long-distance payments; they were equally uniform in value across space, they cost less to move, and they were more secure. The Bank's $5 notes were redeemed for specie at par at all Bank branches, wherever issued, and the Bank's larger notes were often (it is impossible to know how often) redeemed for specie at par *when presented by members of the non-bank public*, but not reliably when presented by state banks or other financial firms.

These shifting shares reflect both supply-side factors (how banks chose to fund their asset growth) and demand-side factors (how households and businesses preferred to hold money). They also reflect the different roles of state banks and the Second Bank in the economy; the state banks, especially those in the better-banked New England and the Middle Atlantic were more involved in financing internal trade, where deposits were a means of payment between merchants, while Second Bank notes were used in the triangle trade between the under-banked upper Mississippi, New Orleans, and New York/Philadelphia. Banknotes were a good form of money in places where there were few banks, and many people did not have bank accounts.[70] As shown in Table 5.2, much of the shift out of specie and into Bank of the United States notes took place at the end of period, a time of rapid growth in the Bank's portfolio of bills of exchange, which was financed with branch drafts injected into circulation in western cities where the Bank had few competitors.

Slow growth in monetary aggregates

Over the 1820s, the capacity of the commercial banking system grew only slightly faster than the US population (see Table 5.3). Bank capital per capita fell 1.6 percent annually, and bank assets per capita grew .33 percent annually, reflecting rising leverage (rising assets per dollar of capital) from 1.54 in 1820 to 1.90 in 1830. Within these aggregates, the state banking sector actually contracted: bank capital per capita fell 1.35 percent annually, and bank assets per capita fell .41 percent annually. State bank capital per capita continued to grow in those regions where the Second Bank had the smallest market share: New England, the Middle

Table 5.3 Change in commercial banking capacity, 1820–1830

	State banks	BUS	All banks
Paid-in bank capital per capita			
1820	11.47	3.70	15.17
1830	9.92	2.80	12.72
Avg. ann. percentage chg., 1820–30	–1.35%	–2.43%	–1.62%
Bank assets per capita	*State banks*	*BUS*	*All banks*
1820	17.89	5.42	23.32
1830	17.17	6.93	24.09
Avg. ann. percentage chg., 1820–1830	–0.41%	2.78%	0.33%

Sources: See notes to Table 5.7.

Table 5.4 Change in paid-in state bank capital (K) per capita, by region, 1820–1830

	1820	*1830*
New England		
Paid in K adjusted	39.09	49.03
Population	1.66	1.95
Per capita K	23.55	25.14
Mid. Atlantic		
Paid in K adjusted	32.95	42.50
Population	3.20	4.10
Per capita K	10.30	10.37
Southeast		
Paid in K adjusted	17.95	24.17
Population	2.40	2.90
Per capita K	7.48	8.33
Southwest		
Paid in K adjusted	17.50	10.00
Population	1.36	2.10
Per capita K	12.87	4.76
Northwest		
Paid in K adjusted	1.75	0.69
Population	0.86	1.60
Per capita K	2.03	0.43

Source: Author's calculations from Van Fenstermaker (1965), Appendix B. Paid-in capital adjusted for percentage of banks reporting from Table 11; national reporting rates assumed to apply to all regions.

Atlantic, and the Southeast. In the Southwest and Northwest, state bank capital per capita fell at rates of 6.3 and 7.9 percent annually. (See Table 5.4.) Financial stability was won in large part through financial suppression in frontier regions, where there was the potential for rapid growth with, invariably, some speculative aspects.

Table 5.5 Changes in monetary aggregates per capita ($), 1820–1830

	Money stock (bank money plus specie) per capita	State Bank money per capita	Second Bank money per capita	Bank money per capita	Specie held by non-bank public per capita
1820	9.54	6.44	1.00	7.44	2.11
1830	9.80	7.24	1.93	9.17	0.63
Avg. ann. percentage chg., 1820–1830	0.27%	1.25%	9.29%	2.33%	–7.01%

Source: Appendix E. Specie holdings of non-bank public equal total specie in country, from Temin's Table 3.3, minus specie holdings of banks, from Appendix E.

Table 5.6 Changes in leverage and liquidity in the commercial banking system, 1820–1830

	State banks		Second Bank		All banks	
	A/K	r	A/K	r	A/K	r
1820	1.56	0.20	1.47	0.60	1.54	0.25
1830	1.73	0.16	2.51	0.36	1.90	0.20

Source: For leverage ratio, see source note to Table 5.7. Reserve ratios are from Appendix E.

The money stock per capita (bank money plus specie held outside banks) grew 0.27 percent annually, but different components of the money stock grew at much different rates. Specie holdings per capita fell 7 percent a year, state bank money per capita grew 1.25 percent annually, and Second Bank money per capita grew 9.3 percent a year(see Table 5.5). Increased holdings of the Bank's notes accounted for two-thirds of the "shift" in the public's holdings from specie to bank money. Only 30 percent of the growth in Second Bank money per capita is explained by the rise in the Bank's share of specie owned by the banking system and by the fall in the Bank's reserve ratio; the rest was due to the rise in the Bank's leverage (assets per dollar of capital) from 1.47 to 2.51 (see Table 5.6). Each dollar of Second Bank capital supported $.47 of monetary liabilities in 1820, and $1.51 in 1830.

Table 5.7 presents the consolidated balance sheet of the state banking system and the Second Bank in 1820 and 1830. The Bank's capital was constant, at $35 m, while its total assets rose from $51.5 m in 1820 to $88 m in 1830, 7 percent a year. About 40 percent of its asset growth was financed with growth in notes and deposits (which increased $14.5 m), and 60 percent was financed with "other monetary liabilities" (which increased $22 m), which included deposits of the federal government, branch notes, and branch drafts created in the course of the Bank's exchange business. In the state bank sector, asset increased by $48 m (2.8 percent annually), $31 m of which was financed by growth in notes and deposits, and the rest by growth in capital (equity).

Table 5.7 Second Bank and state banks' consolidated balance sheets, 1820 and 1830

Second Bank balance sheet, 1820 ($m)

Assets		Liabilities	
Specie	8	Notes and deposits of individuals	10
Earning assets	43.5	Other monetary liabilities	6.5
		Capital	35
Total assets	51.5	Total liabilities	51.5

Second Bank balance sheet, 1830 ($m)

Assets		Liabilities	
Specie	11	Notes and deposits of individuals	24.5
Earning assets	77	Other monetary liabilities	28.5
		Capital	35
Total assets	88	Total liabilities	88

State banks' balance sheet, 1820 ($m)

Assets		Liabilities	
Specie	13	Notes and deposits of individuals	61
Earning assets	157	Capital	109
Total assets	170	Total liabilities	170

State banks' balance sheet, 1830 ($m)

Assets		Liabilities	
Specie	13	Notes and deposits of individuals	92
Earning assets	205	Capital	126
Total assets	218	Total liabilities	218

Sources: Second Bank balance sheet is based on Catterall (1902), Appendix V, amended by substituting Catterall's estimates for annual bills of exchange in Appendix VI for the smaller, bi-annual amounts reported in Appendix V. (Without this substitution, the observed net profits of the Bank cannot be explained.) State bank capital is from Van Fenstermaker (1965), Appendix B, adjusted for percentage of banks reporting from his Table 11. State bank notes and deposits is from Van Fenstermaker (1965), Table 10, again adjusted using Table 11. State bank specie is from Rockoff (2006).

Conclusion

The scarcity of specie could have created a barrier to monetary expansion in the 1820s, but it didn't. It was not that the Second Bank provided high-powered money to the banking system in place of specie, as modern central banks do. Rather, the Bank, as central holder of specie, played a key role in attracting and retaining specie within the banking system, then creating an environment in which banks could safely operate with low reserve ratios. The Bank used its holdings of specie and foreign exchange to, first, bring monetary expansions to an early end, and second, to cushion the state banks from large swings in net specie imports. As a result, the state banking system did not become more leveraged during business-cycle expansions with weak debt on its balance sheet and thin cash reserves.

Over the decade of the 1820s, the capacity of the commercial banking system barely kept up with population growth. However, the Bank's assets grew at a rate that modern banks would envy, to some extent at the expense of the state-chartered banking system. All of the Bank's asset growth was accomplished through rising leverage. This did not create greater financial fragility, however, since the Bank started out with very low leverage in the early 1820s, and maintained a high specie reserve ratio and conservative credit policies throughout the decade.

Gallatin summed up the role of the Second Bank in the monetary system as follows:

> The general complaints on the part of many of the State banks, that they are checked and controlled in their operations by the Bank of the United States, that, to use a common expression, it operates as a screw, is the best evidence that its general operation is such as had been intended. It was for that very purpose that the bank was established. We are not, however, aware that a single solvent bank has been injured by that of the United States, though many have undoubtedly been restrained in the extent of their operations much more than was desirable to them. This is certainly inconvenient to some of the banks, but in its general effects is a public benefit to the community.[71]

Notes

1 Officer (2002) compared the monetary performance of sub-periods in the US between 1792 and 1932, and found that the gold standard period (1879–1913) outperformed the Second Bank period in terms of price stability, per capita income growth, and exchange market pressure. There were several banking crises during the US gold standard period, a criteria not considered in Officer's paper. In addition, the Second Bank period is defined, poorly, as 1817–1838, which includes two years of monetary instability after the Bank's federal charter ended, and it continued business as the Bank of the United States of Pennsylvania. The Second Bank period ended, arguably, in 1833, when the US government started moving its deposits to state-chartered banks and the Bank started winding down its affairs. Per capita specie numbers are from author's calculations from sources in Appendices B and F.

2 Engerman (1970, p. 727).

3 This was also Redlich's view: "with an almost controlling position in the foreign exchange market, and as a strong factor in the specie market, Biddle was able to act as the holder of the ultimate specie and exchange reserve of the country"; Redlich (1968, p. 135).

4 Central bank money is deposits at or notes issued by the central bank. According to Bank for International Settlements (2003, pp. 10–11), "central banks' interest lies primarily in the use of central bank money at the apex of large-value payment systems, as a complement to the use of commercial bank money" in lower tiers. In general, final settlement instruments are those highest-quality, most-liquid assets used in payment systems for final settlement of net debt due from one bank to another.

5 Van Fenstermaker (1965, p. 43) defined "specie funds" as "instruments easily converted into specie." Disagreements among banks arose on which funds qualified as specie funds. For example, in 1835, there was a dispute between the Bank of Kentucky at Louisville and the Bank of the State of Alabama over acceptable funds for restoring the latter's redemption account at the former institution. The latter believed sight drafts on New Orleans would be considered equivalent to specie, to which the Bank of

Kentucky responded, "you surely could not imagine that we would receive in payment of your notes (for which we are daily paying specie) funds that can be bought at any moment in our market at from 3 to 5 per cent [*sic*] discount"; Bank of Kentucky (1836, p. 13).

6   Officer (2002, pp. 116, 119); Rutner (1974, p. 221). Just to show how muddy these waters can become, Officer (2002, p. 119) also acknowledged that the Second Bank "did not generally behave as [a lender] of last resort."

7   Rutner (1974) and Officer (2002) did not differentiate between reserve assets and settlement assets, but the two are typically one and the same. Rutner convincingly shows that the non-bank public preferred Second Bank notes to state banks' notes, based on an analysis of shifts in their holdings during periods of monetary unrest, but this does not automatically extend to liquidity preferences in interbank relations, especially in light of the Bank's asymmetric treatment of its small ($5 notes) notes, used by the general public, and its largest notes, most useful to financial institutions.

8   23rd Cong., 2d Sess., H. Doc. 190, for the balance sheets cited by Rutner (1974). The Washington banks' balance sheets are from 20th Cong., 2d Sess., H. Doc. 86, pp. 2–10; the Indiana balance sheet is from 24th Cong., 2d Sess., H. Doc. 65, p. 171. In interpreting this evidence, it is important to keep in mind that 1834 was the year federal deposits began to be moved out of the Second Bank, into state bank depositories. It is hard to say how much state bank practise, in terms of representing their liquid assets to the US government, was affected by the winding down of the Second Bank, and by the fact that the Second Bank was not in the good graces of the executive branch of the federal government. It may be that some state banks wanted to publicly disassociate themselves from the Second Bank, but still regarded the Second Bank notes as a valuable asset for making long-distance payments or for accessing the Second Bank's liquid assets. Many of Rutner's observations must have come from balance sheets dated after 1836, when Second Bank notes would have been issued by the Bank of the US of Pennsylvania, which maintained a wide ranging national operation and was in serious financial difficulty by the fall of 1839. By 1840, the separate presentation of BUS notes on balance sheets was a list of bad debts, not of near-specie bank money.

9   This was the Bank of Cape Fear, in North Carolina. Another North Carolina bank, the Bank of Newbern, listed United States notes separately from specie, but did add them together in a subtotal.

10 23rd Cong., 2d Sess., H. Doc. 190, various records. This analysis aligns with the findings in Van Fenstermaker (1965), which are based on a review of a number of state bank balance sheets in state governments' banking records. Van Fenstermaker concluded that the assets counted as "specie funds" varied widely from state to state, and included balances with a redemption agent, bills of exchange, Second Bank notes, and Second Bank stock. Redlich defined "specie funds" as the "deposits of country banks with city banks." Van Fenstermaker (1965, pp. 44–5); Redlich (1968, p. 51). Contemporary bank analyst William Gouge came down on the side of Rutner and Officer. Gouge (1833, p. 386) said that just as the country banks of Pennsylvania regarded Philadelphia notes as equivalent to specie, so did "Banks throughout the Union regard United States' Bank notes and drafts." Gouge's claim is not supported by these balance sheets.

11 21st Cong., 1st Sess., S. Doc. 104, p. 4. The speaker was Sen. Smith, Chair of the Banking and Finance Committee, and known to be a strong Bank supporter; 22nd Cong., 2d Sess., H. Doc. 121, pp. 140–3.

12 For example, in Savannah, the Planters' Bank listed "Specie in the vault; Funds at north, equivalent to specie, and City bank notes on hand." Presumably, notes of the Savannah branch of the BUS were included in "City bank notes."

13 The Philadelphia banks were the Girard Bank, the Commercial Bank of Pennsylvania, the Schuylkill Bank, the Bank of North America, the Southwark Bank, the Philadelphia Bank, the Kensington Bank, the Bank of the Northern Liberties, and Bank

of Pennsylvania. The Baltimore banks were the Marine Bank, the Franklin Bank, the Bank of Baltimore, and the Mechanics' Bank.

14 Matthews (1921, p. 34); Thornton (1802, pp. 105,113–14). Curiously, the Bank of England itself was initially not a member of the London Clearing House.

15 Meerman (1961, pp. 19–20), went too far in asserting that the "substitution of BUS notes for state notes, particularly for 'long distance' transactions," produced a par currency, since large BUS notes were not received at par at all BUS offices.

16 23rd Cong., 1st Sess., S. Doc. 24, p. 9. The "bonds" referred to would have been customs bonds, issued by merchants with customs duties to pay. The scenarios described would be the equivalent of Federal Reserve notes issued in Philadelphia passing at a discount in New York. The revised charter of 1832 (which was never put into place) required the bank to receive all of its notes from state banks in payment of debts, a practise the Bank adopted in the Atlantic seaboard cities in 1833 (when it was too late to save the Bank). Catterall (1902, pp. 416–19). The dealers confirmed the reports of the state institutions with which they were allied. These firms included J.D. Beers & Co., Cosler & Carpenter, P.S. Nevins & Co., J.L. & S. Joseph & Co., and John Ward & Co.

17 23rd Cong., 1st Sess., S. Doc. 24, p. 6. The Bank's behavior changed after the bill to recharter the Bank (which was ultimately vetoed) included language requiring the Bank to redeem its notes at par when presented by other banks; Temin (1969, p. 36). The Bank was trying to build support, or at least weaken opposition, to its rechartering.

18 Gallatin (1831, p. 90). At the time of writing, Gallatin was the President of a New York City bank and well informed about current banking practises. The Second Bank's first President made the same point in a letter to Treasury Secretary Crawford in 1817: "It is utterly impracticable so to distribute the resources of the bank as to be prepared at all times, and at all points, to meet the demands in gold and silver, which the operations of commerce, *the policy of other banks, and the subtilty* [*sic*] *of brokers* (emphasis added) may produce." 18th Cong., 1st Sess., Pub. 705, p. 809.

19 Biddle Papers, August 8, 1827, letter to Robinson, Cashier of New York branch. The drafts referred to here were drafts drawn by one Bank branch on another, which served as interregional means of payment. They were sold at a premium. These are not to be confused with branch drafts, introduced in 1827, which were essentially notes issued by the branches in a different form.

20 Ibid. Biddle "examined the matter particularly and I found by actual experiment that by refusing to receive in deposit the notes of the Offices they were carried to the State Banks and immediately reissued to their customers who had duties to pay and found their way back directly into the Bank. So that they all came to us whether we refused them or not . . .By receiving them on deposit from our customers, we found that we did not receive more of them and that our general deposits and business were greatly increased."

21 Biddle Papers; December 21, 1823, letter from Biddle to US Senator James Lloyd.

22 Bank of Pennsylvania and Bank of America cash holdings from Weber (2008).

23 Second Bank specie holding, from Appendix E; total specie in US, from Temin (1969), Table 3.3.

24 According to the Director of the Mint, "a very large proportion of the whole accumulation of the precious metals in the U.S. . . . has been received through [the port at New Orleans]"; 23rd Cong., 2d Sess., H. Doc. 99.

25 During this period, the Bank's holdings of silver increased by $0.86 m annually, on average, and the Bank sold, net of purchases, $.55 m of silver annually (on average). This means the Bank took in $1.41 m of specie each year, on average (selling $0.55 m per year on average and adding the rest to reserves). For it to have done so, the Bank must have secured 20–23 percent of the $6 m to $7 m of silver that entered the national economy between 1824 and 1831. This calculation is based on the following data sources: Second Bank specie, Catterall (1902, pp. 501–5, taken from 25th Cong., 2d Sess., S. Doc. 128); average annual specie imports, upper estimate from Annual Report

of the Secretary of the Treasury on the state of the finances, October 24, 1855, and lower estimate from Temin (1969, p. 81); average annual silver sold by the Second Bank, from 22nd Cong., 1st Sess., H. Report 460, pp. 198–205.

26 Catterall (1902, p. 487).

27 Author's calculations from Appendix E.

28 The US debt was denominated in US dollars, which potentially exposed foreign holders to currency risk, but for, in Sylla's view, the "implicit exchange clause or specie-convertibility guarantee" on the debt. Explicit exchange clauses fix the coupon in terms of specie. Financial historians have found no evidence of explicit exchange clauses on US debt held abroad before the state government debt defaults of the early 1840s. Sylla believed the specie convertibility of the US dollar was guaranteed because "Hamilton and Congress had made the dollar a convertible currency based on gold and silver" in the Coinage Act of 1792; Sylla (2012, p. 5). In any event, the US government worked with foreign bankers to service debt held abroad in creditors' home currencies.

29 21st Cong., 1st Sess., S. Doc. 104, pp. 6–8.

30 15th Cong., 2d Sess., Pub. 547, p. 321; John Campbell White Papers, Folder 16. The exclusion of the balances due by the Baltimore banks may reflect the fact that balances could be immediately collected from the city banks, which were considered liquid and solvent, as opposed to other "local Institutions." In addition, larger balances were customary in Baltimore to accommodate the greater volume and density of payments associated with the wholesale trade there.

31 Catterall (1902, p. 99); Smith (1953, p. 253); Meerman (1961, pp. 17, 19).

32 Biddle Papers; January 6, 1824, letter to Isaac Lawrence, Esq., President of the Office of Discount and Deposit at New York. The letter concerns the effect of quarterly dividend payments on the accounts with New York City banks and refers to the fact that "You do not exchange with the City Banks for Specie more than once a week, but you have a daily exchange of notes etc."

33 21st Cong., 1st Sess., S. Doc. 104, pp. 6–8. Note that this statement runs counter to other evidence that in New York City, the Bank did insist on payment of balances due in specie.

34 McAllister Collection, Box 6, Folder 231, September 1828.

35 McAllister Collection, Box 6, Folder 231, handwritten information dated February 13, 1829, on the October 1, 1828, letter to the branch president from Biddle. This evidence provides support for Bordo's conjecture that, had Second Bank continued, it would have used the two-name market in bills of exchange to provide backstop liquidity to the money market and/or banking system, in the manner of the Bank of England; Bordo (2012).

36 Biddle Papers, February 5, 1830, letter from Biddle to John Cumming, Cashier. By proper rates, Biddle presumably meant rates that provided appropriate income to the Bank.

37 15th Cong., 2d Sess., Pub. 547, p. 321.

38 Biddle Papers; letter to Charles Nicholas, July 16, 1823. The two-week clearing period reflected the realities of the roads and the postal service between Richmond and the smaller cities of Virginia.

39 Parsons (1977, pp. 59–60) pointed out that the fiscal surpluses "enabled the Bank to retain its creditor position with respect to the state banks and thus to control them without unduly sacrificing its own earnings prospects through limitation of its loans and discounts."

40 Willett (1968) noticed the same pattern between 1834 and 1859. He found that specie imports did not immediately trigger money creation, and specie exports did not immediately trigger money destruction.

41 Rutner (1974) developed and analyzed monetary aggregates for 1824–1834 and found that when the state banks lost specie in 1825–1826, they increased their holdings of deposits with the Second Bank deposits, which Rutner saw as evidence that Second

Bank deposits and notes were high-powered money. Presumably, the availability of a good specie-substitute was stabilizing, though in a different way than that described here. Contrary to Rutner's finding, Second Bank balance sheet data in 22nd Cong., 1st Sess., H. Doc. 147 shows state bank deposits at the Second Bank (due to state banks) falling, not rising, in 1825–1826.

42 In March 1828, as sterling exchange approached the silver export point, Biddle wrote to the Baltimore cashier that "the whole of the present difficulty is the result of over-banking which has produced overtrading. As long as the Banks of New York continue to discount freely, as they have done for some months without looking at the danger before them, they furnish, themselves, the means of excessive importation, and keep up the demand for exchange"; Biddle Papers, March 8, 1828, letter from Biddle to John White.

43 The foreign exchange operations were short-term mechanisms, as the Bank could not draw down its own liquid resources indefinitely. Based on an analysis of monthly changes in the Bank's sales of foreign exchange and net claims on/due to the state banks, Parsons (1977, p. 94) concluded that "the sale of foreign exchange by the Bank of the United States brought pressure on the state banks to restrain their discounts and note issues. Since the Bank consistently sold when the price approached or reached the specie export point, the effect was to replace the sudden and severe impact of specie demands with a gentler but stabilizing pressure."

44 Calomiris and Schweikart (1991); Wallis (2001).

45 Meerman (1961, pp. 26, 28–29); Govan (1959, pp. 97–8). Along similar lines, Timberlake (1978, p. 32) called the Bank a "shock absorber."

46 Redlich (1968, pp. 96, 97, 128, 136); Govan (1959); Catterall (1902); Hammond (1957).

47 Temin (1969, pp. 55–6); Smith (1953, p. 140). Meerman (1961, p. 30), also notes that the increased discounts in New York were accompanied by sales of government securities, but he believed that "on balance the effect was probably stimulating." In a November 1828 letter (recipient unknown), Biddle gave himself credit for having "averted the greatest disaster" in November 1825: "I was perfectly satisfied that there was a tremendous squall coming, that there was a scarcity and a dread which unless immediately quieted, would grow into a panic and get beyond our control. I remember well getting into the stage and riding all night to New York to look at the danger which I considered so imminent that the Bank immediately and in the face of the public alarm, increased its discounts."

48 Biddle Papers, February 23, 1825, letter from Biddle to Robinson, Cashier of New York branch.

49 See Table 6.1 for sources on the Bank's specie sales.

50 Biddle Papers, April 11, 1825, letter from Biddle to Gardiner Greene, President Office BUS Boston.

51 Biddle Papers, October 25, 1825, letter from Biddle to Isaac Lawrence President Office BUS New York.

52 22nd Cong., 1st Sess., H. Doc. 147. As Meerman (1961, p. 30), pointed out, Biddle was trying to mobilize "money" (specie) in private holdings "which would otherwise have lain idle."

53 Biddle Papers, December 7 and 11, 1825, letters to R. Lenox.

54 Biddle Papers, January 4, 1826, letter from Biddle to Robert Gilmor, Baltimore.

55 Redlich (1968, p. 142). Redlich's source, cited in his notes 312, 167, and 168, is a letter from N. Biddle to A. Davis of New York, June 13, 1829.

56 Bodenhorn (2003, p. 158).

57 Biddle Papers, June 11, 1829, letter from Biddle to Treasury Secretary Ingham.

58 Biddle Papers, June 13, 1829, letter from Biddle to A. Davis.

59 Biddle Papers, June 4, 1829, letter from Biddle to R. Lenox.

60 McAllister Collection, Box 6, Folder 231, September 1828 letter to R. Campbell, President, Savannah branch.

61 Several months before it failed, the Bank of Maryland had received a loan from the Union Bank (of Baltimore) after being turned down by the Secretary of the Treasury

for assistance; Bryan (1899, pp. 91–4). The Bank of Maryland presumably did not approach the Bank of the US for assistance, as the Baltimore office of the Bank had stopped receiving its notes in interbank exchanges two years earlier; John Campbell White Papers, Box 16; *Niles' Weekly Register*, March 29, 1834. It is not clear, from Niles' account, how this willingness was made known to the banking community and the public. Niles also reported that "at some of the other banks 'Uncle Sam's money' was preferred to coin," indicating the perceived liquidity, safety, and convenience of Second Bank money. Since there were only $6,000 of Treasury bills outstanding in 1834 (of a total US debt of $4.76 m), Uncle Sam's money must have referred to money issued by the Second Bank, even though the Baltimore branch was winding down its affairs at the time; John Campbell White Papers, Box 16.

62 It is not clear whether Baltimore had to get approval from Philadelphia to extend this loan to the Savings Bank. In 1833, one could travel from Philadelphia to Baltimore in a little over eleven hours; Pred (1973, p. 86). With twice-daily mail service (as existed between New York and Philadelphia) or express service, Baltimore could have received a reply on the following day. In a panic, it was crucial to respond quickly.

63 The Savings Bank thanked the Baltimore BUS branch for "saving an infant institution from . . . unkind and ungenerous feeling exhibited toward it by a neighbouring [*sic*] Bank." Records of the Baltimore Branch of the Bank of the United States, Box 4, March 26, 1834; Payne and Davis (1956, pp. 83–4).

64 Catterall (1902, pp. 432–3, 508). Girard's holdings of Second Bank stock fluctuated between $655,000 and $725,000 in the late 1820s, which comprised about 2 percent of all private holdings of Second Bank stock, and 10 percent of that owned in Pennsylvania in 1831. It is possible that the Second Bank assisted Girard in order to prevent the dumping of a large amount of Bank stock onto the Philadelphia market. On the Bank of Philadelphia, 29th Cong., 1st Sess., H. Doc. pp. 226, 506. This is a letter to Rep. Clayton from Nicholas Biddle, dated April 15, 1841, in which Biddle was (still) defending the Bank, in this case against charges of favoritism toward family members. His brother, Mr. Charles Biddle, was a director of the Bank of Philadelphia. Biddle asserted that "the money borrowed was for the use of the bank at a period of public pressure—the Bank of the United States at all time willing to render necessary assistance to any of the *other* State banks" (emphasis added).

65 Smith (1953, p. 143).

66 The data on specie's share is based on estimates in Temin (1969) of specie held outside the banking system in Table 3.3 and the aggregates in Appendix E.

67 Carothers (1967, pp. 67, 77–81).

68 Crawford quote from Rolnick and Weber (1986, p. 187); quote from Congressional Report is quoted in Martin (1968, p. 434). Carothers (1967, p. 76) confirms that "the only considerable coinage was in half-dollars that did not circulate." Rolnick and Weber (1986, p. 187) point to evidence that the Spanish milled dollars did circulate in 1819 to support their point that "bad money" does not always drive out "good money": when it is cost-effective for the good money to circulate at a premium (and not at par against the bad money), it will continue to circulate. But, as noted, very little of the good money (full weight, Spanish milled dollars) was in circulation by 1832, even though it continued to sell at a premium against American silver. By 1832, the banks' demand for a cost-effective reserve asset and private, non-bank demand to hold the safest monetary asset had pulled both Spanish dollars and American half-dollars out of circulation.

69 21st Cong., 1st Sess., S. Doc. 19 (the 1830 Sanford Report), p. 4. The quote obviously assumes that the stock of coins is heterogeneous in quality. Laughlin (1901, p. 26), described the workings of Gresham's Law in a similar way, saying that "The mass of people do not follow the market values of gold and silver bullion, nor calculate arithmetically when a profit can be made by buying up this or that coin. . . . These matters

are relegated by common consent to the money-brokers, a class of men who, above all others, know the value of a small fraction and the gain to be derived from it."

70 Rutner (1974) analyzed short-run shifts in the composition of money and found that Second Bank notes were much a closer substitute for specie than state-bank notes were, which is consistent with the finding here. Rutner pointed out that BUS deposits did not have the same advantage over state bank deposits that BUS notes had, since all deposits were similar in being payable only to local payers.

71 Gallatin (1831, p. 69). Chapter Two of this book disagrees with Gallatin's view, expressed here, that the Bank was created for the purpose of regulating the state banks. Gallatin's conclusion is confirmed by the econometric analysis in Highfield et al. (1991).

6   The Second Bank's specie market operations

As the nation's central "repository of specie," the Second Bank conducted a variety of specie market operations: it bought and sold silver and gold coin, minted foreign coin into American coin, and moved coin from specie-rich to specie-poor branches. The Bank's specie was constantly on the move. It moved in and out of the country, from one branch to the other, and between the Bank and the Mint—all directed and managed from Philadelphia. There were various purposes to these operations: to earn profit; to defend against raids by private dealers; to promote the use of American coin; and to ensure that the federal government's obligations were met on time, in specie—especially its debt obligations held abroad.

Heterogeneity of the specie stock and the market for specie

The stock of specie in the United States in the 1820s was a mixed bag of coin: there was silver coin and gold coin, foreign coin, and domestic coin, all of which (except US silver coin) had different market values that fluctuated over time. Throughout the period the Second Bank operated, the US government failed to invest in a uniform domestic coinage, and instead passed numerous laws which gave currency to foreign coin. By the 1820s, 60 percent of the stock of specie in the US economy consisted of foreign coin, predominantly coin minted in Spain, in one of Spain's colonies, or one of the new Latin American republics.[1] Markets for specie, populated by merchants, brokers, dealers, and bankers, emerged in the major cities, where coins with different metallic content and degrees of "moneyness" were bought and sold.

The United States was nominally on a bimetallic system, with the US dollar pegged to the Spanish peso, or dollar, and its value defined in terms of both gold and silver. Under the system envisioned by the Coinage Act of 1792, the stock of specie would have consisted of gold and silver bullion, and gold and silver US coin. Under the Coinage Act, gold was officially valued at 15 times that of silver at the US Mint, when the commercial ratio was between 15.5 and 15.6 in London and Paris. After 1818, the commercial ratio rose high enough above the US mint ratio to cover the transportation charges of exporting gold; between 1821 and 1833 the commercial ratio hovered around 15.75, 5 percent above the US mint ratio of 15. By early 1821, according to Martin (1968, p. 433), gold was being "heavily exported"; the cashier of the Baltimore branch of the Bank of the United States observed an "extraordinary change thus in our Specie basis, for previously to 1821, Gold was so abundant that I was enabled to transmit to the Parent Bank from the office in 1819 and 1820 upwards of $240,000."[2]

By 1834, "almost all the American gold coin then in existence" was held in the vaults of the Bank of the United States, and the rest was held as other banks' reserves and private savings. Even so, gold made up a small share of banks' metallic money reserves. In August 1830, the specie holdings of Girard's Bank, a large and systemically important private bank in Philadelphia, included eagles ($10 gold coin), mixed silver, dimes, half dimes, Francs, and "Ferds" (Ferdinands). Silver coin made up 82 percent of the Bank's specie reserves. About the same time, silver made up 85 percent of the Bank of the United States specie reserves.[3]

For most of the period that the Second Bank operated, then, the United States was effectively on a silver standard, not a bimetallic one. Silver imports dominated total metallic money imports in 1820s, much of it entering at New Orleans, a major hub of US trade with Latin America. Spanish dollars entered the economy primarily from the West Indies, Cuba, and Mexico. These countries and colonies imported a variety of foodstuffs produced in the upper Mississippi Valley (flour, pork, hemp, whiskey) from New Orleans, as well as foodstuffs, horses, lumber, and manufactured goods from New York, Philadelphia, and Baltimore. The West Indies and Cuba sent produce in turn (sugar, coffee, tobacco) and paid the balance with specie. Because Mexico paid for most of its imported goods (predominantly cloth, flour, and cotton) with specie instead of exported goods, coin minted in Mexico accounted for 60 percent of the coin imported from Spanish America in 1825–1832.[4]

During the 1820s, the stock of specie was made up primarily of a wide variety of silver coin, mainly Spanish, some "strong" and some, very "weak."[5] Well-crafted, high-silver-content Spanish coin occupied the top rung of the silver coin hierarchy. The "best" silver coins were the heavy, or high silver content, Spanish pesos (Ferdinand and Carolus, from mid-eighteenth century), in demand until the late 1820s by merchants who imported goods from China. These were dollars minted in Mexico in the final years of Spanish rule, under Charles III and IV (the so-called "Carolus" coins) and Ferdinand VII (the "Ferdinands").[6] In an 1835 Report to Congress, the Director of the US Mint said that the Spanish dollar, prior to the independence of the "new States of Spanish America," was of such high and uniform quality "that an actual assay thereof had ceased to be regarded as necessary when offered at the mint."[7]

Just below the Ferdinand and Carolus Spanish dollars sat the Spanish dollar coins minted in Mexico, which had somewhat more silver content than the American standard. After independence, the quality of the stock of Spanish silver became more mixed, but, according to the Director of the Mint, "The coinage of the city of Mexico adheres still on an average, very nearly to the fineness of the Spanish dollar, with more irregularity, however, than formerly, in emissions of the same date." Silver dollars produced at the mint of Mexico City also sold at a premium against American silver, but smaller than that of the Carolus and Ferdinand coins.

The coin produced by the provincial mints outside of Mexico City and by other Latin American mints in the new republics was more mixed, and on average of lower quality than the Mexico City coins. As reported by the Director of the Mint:

> During some years after the royal authority had ceased . . . the deviation of their coinage from the Spanish standard was not important. The real standard was evidently aimed at, and on an average maintained. But, within the last 3 or 4 years, very sensible irregularities are becoming apparent. The silver coins of Peru, Central Am., and Chili [*sic*] maintain their value well . . . while the dollar of La Plata, of recent coinage, vibrates between 94 and 97 cents, and the dollar of Colombia . . . scarcely exceeds 75 cents in intrinsic value.[8]

The American silver dollar was the "numeraire" or standard of value in specie markets; it was used to express the value of foreign coin. No silver dollars were minted between 1804 and 1836, so the stock of American silver was almost all half-dollars by 1830. In terms of silver content, American coin occupied a middle ground between the strongest Spanish silver and weak Spanish silver. According to one estimate, the Mint had produced $34 m of American silver coin by 1830, of which $14 m had been retained within the country. The rest was diverted into foreign holdings. The US silver coinage retained domestically was held as bank reserves or by private individuals and businesses as a liquid asset. Half-dollar silver coin was not an ideal form for bank reserves, due to its small denomination and bulk, but it was better than fragments of light Spanish dollar coins.[9]

The lowest-quality Spanish silver were the older, worn, light coins, including Spanish dollar pieces broken into pieces of eight. These coins made up a large part of the small metallic currency used in wage payments and retail trade. It was well understood at the time that the small fractional Spanish silver would not be minted into US coin. As pointed out by the 1830 Sanford Report:

> While these Spanish coins are legal money, they will not be converted into our own coins. The possessor of these coins can gain nothing by their recoinage, when they are equal in weight, to our own coins; and when they are inferior in weight, but still equal in current value, he will certainly not employ the mint to convert his diminished coins into a less number of pieces.[10]

Specie market operations

Buying and selling specie

Soon after taking office, Biddle saw the possibilities and risks in the specie trade. In early 1823, he wrote to the cashier at New Orleans about the specie market there:

> I am desirous of procuring the best information with regard to the Bullion market of N. Orleans. . . . I should wish to know, 1st from what quarter and in what shape bullion is chiefly introduced into New Orleans; 2nd what

amounts could be occasionally purchased there?; 3rd Have you any means of assaying it, or is it always received by weight?; 4th In the latter case might there not be risk in the purchase unless only a certain proportion (say 80 or 90 per cent) of its apparent value were advanced, the remainder being payable after an assay at the Mint here? Our late assays represent Murbide's dollars of 1822 as of full value—those of Colombia (Cundinaruarca) very inferior being worth only 73 or 75 cents. In the present situation of those countries the government may not easily resist the temptation of debasing their coin, and their bars. 5th Could you make profitable operations to any amount in purchasing bullion and sending it here? Your late shipments have been very fortunate and judicious.[11]

The Bank was an active practitioner of intercity specie arbitrage, particularly after 1823. In intercity specie arbitrage, a dealer would buy strong Spanish silver in southern cities where it was in excess supply (those whose merchants traded with the Caribbean and Latin American trade) and sell it in northern cities where it was in excess demand (those whose merchants traded with Asia) whenever the inter-city price differential exceeded shipping costs. The Bank reported to Congress on specie it purchased between March 1824 and December 1831, and specie it sold between January 1820 and November 1831.[12] The data on specie purchased provides information on individual transactions: what was purchased (silver, gold, or gold bullion), when it was purchased, from whom it was purchased, and what premium was paid. The data on specie sold shows how much specie was sold (broken out into Spanish dollars, Crowns, Francs, American gold, British and French gold, and Spanish gold), and the premium paid. Ninety percent of the silver the Bank sold was Spanish dollars; the rest, British or French coined silver. Transactions over the entire period are summarized in Table 6.1.

The Bank's operations in the silver market served its profit mission, while its operations in the gold market were in service to country. In short, it made money

Table 6.1 Sales and purchases of silver and gold coin and bullion by the Second Bank, January 1820 to November 1831

Total over period	Silver	Gold	Total
$ purchased	605,310	463,629	1,068,939
Premium paid (total premia paid/ total purchased)	0.0053	0.0341	
$ sold	5,051,473	133,011	5,184,483
Premia "earned" (total premia received/total sold)	0.0180	0.0450	
Bid-ask spread	0.0127	0.0110	
Spread as percentage of avg. premium paid	2.36	0.32	
$ sold—$ purchased	4,446,163	−330,618	4,115,544

Source: Author's calculations from 22nd Cong., 1st Sess. H. Rep. 460, pp. 198–205.

Table 6.2 Size of Second Bank specie sales by type of coin ($), 1820–1831

	Spanish dollars	Crowns (British silver coin)	Francs (assume silver)	American gold	British and French gold	Spanish gold
Median transaction value	10,000	9,858	13,000	500	284	680
Average transaction value	25,871	12,136	25,145	5,648	1,636	837

Source: Author's calculations from 22nd Cong, 1st Sess., H. Rep. 460, pp. 198–205.

on silver, and it lost money on gold. Its operations in the two markets differed in other ways as well. The Bank was much more active in the market for silver than in the market for gold in terms of total transactions (sales plus purchases). The Bank was a net seller of silver (it sold more than it bought), and a net buyer of gold (it bought more than it sold). Silver sales were significantly larger than gold sales, whether measured by the average or the median; see Table 6.2, showing the median and average value of specie sales by type of specie.

In the silver market, the Bank was more or less a continuous seller, and a sporadic buyer; in the gold market, the Bank was a sporadic seller, and a more or less continuous buyer, at least after 1828. The Bank's dealings in silver were all in the form of coin (Spanish, French, and English). Almost all of the gold that it purchased was in the form of bullion, which was good for shipments of large sums, but all of the gold that the Bank sold was in the form of coin (American, British, French, and Spanish).

Over the entire period, the Bank's bid-ask spread on its silver purchases and sales was 1.26 percent. The spread fluctuated from year to year, driven by movements in the ask price (the selling price); see Figure 6.1. The Bank's bid price (buying price) on silver fluctuated within a small range, usually between 0.25 percent and 0.5 percent of face value, with a handful of transactions as high as 0.8 percent or 0.9 percent, while the ask price ranged between a high of 2.89 percent and a low of 0.75 percent. The spreads shown in Figure 6.1 were not necessarily the actual spreads earned by the Bank in the months shown, since the Bank did not have to buy and sell in the same month, specie being nonperishable, and there were gains to be made from timing purchases and sales. In addition, the Bank did not buy all the silver it sold; almost 90 percent of the silver that the Bank sold came into the Bank through the course of banking business (deposits, loan repayments), instead of being purchased on the specie market. The Bank probably paid a premium of some form (perhaps in the form of foregone premia or interest) on some of the good Spanish dollars that came into the Bank, but there is no way to know how much it paid for specie that came in over the counter.

In the silver market, the Bank timed its purchases and sales so as to increase its bid-ask spread. The Bank tended to sell more silver when the premium was high,

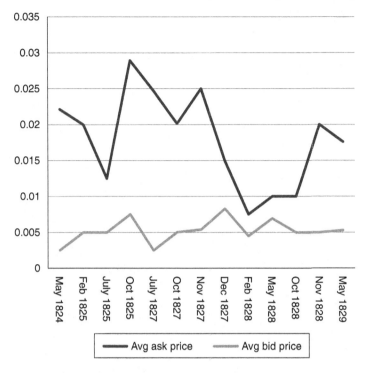

Figure 6.1 Monthly bid-ask spread on Spanish silver coin purchased and sold by the
         Second Bank.

Source: See note to Table 6.1.

Note: Covers only months for which both bid and ask price are available.

and to buy more when the premium was low, a classic case of price-stabilizing speculation that set a ceiling to ask prices, and a floor to bid prices; see Figures 6.2,
6.3, and 6.4b. The bid-ask spread reflected the Bank's earnings from arbitraging
across space (between southern and northern cities) and time (months of lower and
higher supply and demand). The Bank's large specie reserve allowed it to time its
specie sales to the market in this way; it could sell when the market was high and still
have enough in the vault to ensure convertibility of its notes and deposits. The silver
that the Bank purchased and sold included a variety of coin, so the varying premium
on silver sold reflects both changing market conditions and changing composition of
the Spanish silver sold (which cannot be determined from the data source).

The crisis year 1825 was a banner year for the Bank's silver business; in that
year alone, the Bank purchased and sold $2 m of specie, virtually all silver coin,
which made up about 40 percent of the Bank's specie reserve (average value of
January 1825, July 1825, and January 1826), and 40 percent of all silver sold by
the Bank between 1824 and 1831. Although the Bank was concerned about the
decline in its specie holdings, it still opted to sell coins at a premium over having
to possibly redeem notes or deposits for them at par. As noted in Chapter Five,

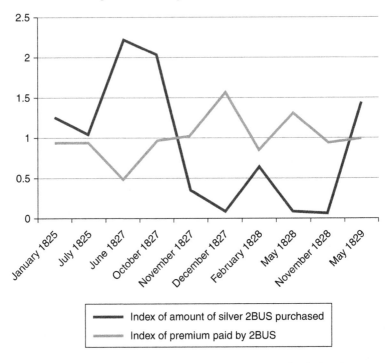

Figure 6.2 Second Bank silver coin purchases and premia paid (indexed to average for 1825–1829).

Source: see note to Table 6.1.

these specie sales had a restraining effect on the state banks. Biddle actively directed the New York branch on the timing of silver sales, writing, for example, in April that "The price of Dollars here is rather rising, and nothing but necessity should make them leave you at less than 3 per cent for Carolus and 2 or 2.5% for Ferdinands necessity however must make its own law."[13] The Bank's ask price reached its maximum value in October of 1825, as the crisis was intensifying— and the Bank's sales increased that month as well.

The Bank's behavior in the gold market was quite different. When it came to gold coin, the Bank's objective was seemingly to hold on to what it had, and to buy more for precautionary purposes as needed. As noted earlier, by the early 1830s, almost all of the American gold coin then in existence was in the vaults of the Second Bank.[14] The Bank sold very little gold throughout the 1820s as the commercial ratio rose; it left potential international arbitrage profits on the table. Further, the Bank tended to buy more gold when there was a higher premium on gold; see Figure 6.4a. Almost all of the Bank's purchases took place between 1829 and 1831, during which time it sold virtually no gold. The sterling exchange rate rose throughout this period of gold buys, and reached the silver export point toward the end of 1831.

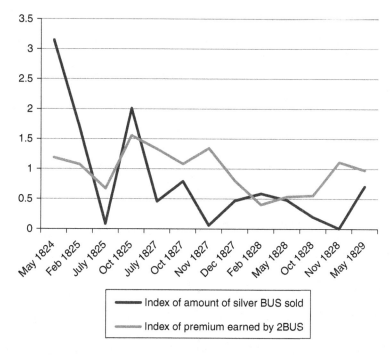

Figure 6.3 Second Bank silver sold and premia received (indexed to average for 1824–1829).

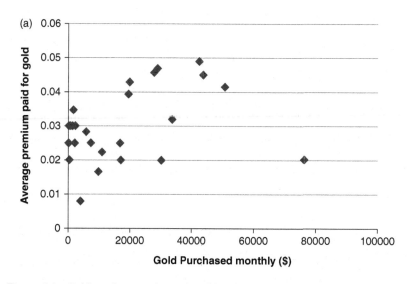

Figure 6.4a Gold purchases and premia paid, July 1828 to December 1831.

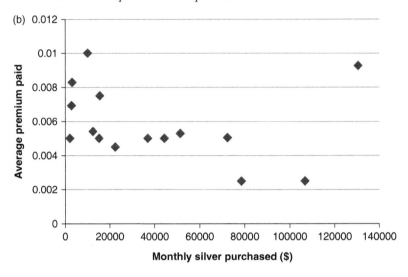

Figure 6.4b Silver purchases and premia paid, January 1825 to May 1829.

Minting American silver coin

US Mint output increased in the mid-1820s, almost all silver coin, largely from Mexican coin deposited by the Second Bank.[15] The Bank minted American (US) silver for two reasons: to defend itself against specie-banknote arbitrage, and to promote a uniform national coinage.

In specie-banknote arbitrage, dealers presented large volumes of banknotes to the bank that issued them, and demanded payment at par in specie, hoping to be paid in some higher-value specie which they could recoin, or sell at a premium to those who needed "good" coin for international trade. Chartered banks were required to pay specie on demand for their notes, but they could elect what form of specie to pay. It made sense to pay out the lower-valued specie first. But once this stock was exhausted, the bank would have to hand over the good coins (and pay as much as $103 in silver for every $100 in notes). For the Second Bank, US silver coin served as a "shield" for the higher-valued coin in its vaults.

The Bank was the target of specie-banknote arbitrageurs throughout its existence. Soon after the Bank started operations in 1817, Second Bank President Jones wrote to Treasury Secretary Crawford that the Boston branch had lost specie as

> certain eastern banks, whose discounting business, being entirely subordinate to their traffic in specie, enables them to collect the notes of and drafts on this institution, and draw the [Spanish] dollars, the sale of which, from 3½ to 4% premium, repeated in quick succession, is far more safe and lucrative than the tardy accumulation by discounts, at the rate of 5% per annum, upon precarious personal security. When the dollars are exhausted, gold is drawn and

sent into Canada, there exchanged for dollars, which pass through the same process, and thus the country is drained of both gold and dollars.[16]

The Second Bank was required to borrow in London to import specie to replace the specie it lost to these arbitrage operations. This was not a sustainable business model.

The Bank's first line of defense was to tell someone who was presenting a batch of large notes for conversion into specie that its notes were payable into only at the branch that issued the notes. Strictly speaking, this practise was consistent with its charter.[17] This practise increased the dealer's cost of collecting enough notes on an individual branch to make the arbitrage operation worthwhile. The dealers soon found a way around this barrier: they bought large drafts on the target branch instead. In February 1823, Biddle wrote to Robert Lenox, Esq., a wealthy New York merchant and regular confidant that "Beers & Bunnell of your City are collecting large drafts on [the Charleston] office with a view, as I understand, of forcing from it its Spanish dollars. We know already of $70,000 drafts between this and Baltimore." When the Bank caught on to the purpose of the drafts, it refused applications for more. Biddle wanted to know if Beers & Bunnell were working in concert with another financial firm, asking Lenox:

> Are Beers & Bunnell strong enough for this? Or are they the agents of others and of whom? If you know, or can learn without exciting remark . . . , you will oblige me by communicating it as soon as convenient.[18]

The other strategy the Bank used to protect its good specie was to accumulate a stock of American coin within its overall specie reserve. In October of 1825, Biddle wrote to the cashier of the New York branch:

> To defend our Spanish Dollars by keeping in front always a sufficient force of American coin, is one of the most delicate of our operations. I have seen in our own vault here reduced at one moment to somewhere about 14,000$ of American Coin yet we managed to protect our foreign coin. You must do the best you can making your American Coin go as far as possible, and if you are prest [*sic*], sell your Spanish Coin for cash.[19]

That is, in lieu of paying Spanish coin worth 3 percent in the market at par when presented with New York Second Bank notes from the exchange dealers or when faced with the necessity of settling net debt to the state banks in specie, New York was to sell its high-value Spanish coin, taking arbitrage profits and turning the interbank balances in New York in favor of the Second Bank. Over time, Philadelphia would need to replenish New York's stock of American coin.

To accumulate such a stock of US coin, the Bank had to mint it. Much of the American silver coin issued by the Mint in the 1820s was done by and for the

Bank, on deposits of Mexican coin. The Bank had three ways to use the Mexican coin that came into its vault: it could keep it as reserves to meet redemption demands; it could sell it to traders at a premium (a smaller premium than the Carolus and Ferdinands); or, it could deposit it at the Mint for recoinage into American half dollars of greater value (because of the higher silver content in the Mexican coins). The first option was inferior to the other two, as the Bank lost potential profit when it paid a Mexican dollar coin for a dollar of its notes. In fact, the Bank was selling and minting Mexican silver at the same time in the late 1820s. It came down to a decision about how much to sell, and how much to recoin. If it had sold all of its coin, it may have spoiled the market and eliminated the premium. By holding a large enough buffer of American coin in its stock of specie, the Bank could better time its sales of Mexican, Ferdinand, and Carolus coins.

The Bank also had nationalist motives for minting US coin, to provide coin for public land purchases, and to reduce reliance on foreign coinage.[20] Biddle criticized the national government's policy on the coinage in a letter to Treasury Secretary Richard Rush in 1827. For Biddle,

> The mint . . . is not, or at least ought not to be a mere empty appendage of sovereignty, its object is to assure the genuiness [*sic*] and the uniformity of the coinage. To accomplish this, it should rate to seek to attract to the mint the coins of other countries, so as gradually to convert them into the national coinage. But if the Government declares that any foreign coinage will be received by its Citizens in payment, it diminishes the motive to a recoinage, and . . . tends to diminish the mass of the national coinage. It tends moreover to introduce multiplicity and confusion in a matter where simplicity and uniformity are most desirable.[21]

The Bank tried to induce others to mint American silver half-dollars as well. In an August 21, 1827, letter to Treasury Secretary Rush, Biddle explained (or complained) that "The Bank endeavors to attract him (the owner of the coin) to the Mint by giving him the money at once, but this is a disadvantageous operation, since the Bank loses the use of the money during this long interval." In light of the delays in coinage, the Mint gave depositors mint certificates which "have uniformly . . . been readily cashed in this city (Philadelphia)" at 0.5%, "generally by some of the city banks, and invariably by the Bank of the United States."[22]

Moving specie

The Bank was continuously moving specie from city to city as part of its operations in specie markets. In intercity arbitrage, the Bank moved specie from southern cities, where specie was in excess supply, to northern cities, where specie was in excess demand. Its minting operations required it to ship Mexican coin that entered, in part, in southern ports, to Philadelphia, where the US Mint was located, and then out to the various branches as needed.

The Bank maintained strict control over interbranch movements of specie from Philadelphia. This policy was spelled out in a September 1823 letter from Biddle to two directors of the Baltimore branch. Biddle explained that

> the Parent Board cannot allow the branches to draw specie from each other without management from Philadelphia . . . as they (the Philadelphia board) alone know the exact situation of the Southern Office, its Specie, its resources, it engagements with other Offices, they ought to be able to regulate in some degree the Specie draft upon it. This seems reasonable, and even necessary for the security of all the Offices none of which can be put to hazard without endangering the credit of the whole establishment.

The Parent Board was "unwilling to part with what they deem a Salutary control over the Specie operations." Further, "Without this concert between the Bank and its offices, they are liable to be played off against each other by the activity of the dealers, and the article is often either sacrificed or sold to disadvantage."[23] Philadelphia wanted to prevent interbranch drawing that may have left branches exposed to a specie drain, and it wanted to place the specie of the Bank in those locations where it was most needed.

Some of the interbranch specie transfers bolstered branches that were potentially exposed to specie withdrawals. In October 1832, Biddle wrote to the cashier of the Louisville, Kentucky, branch that

> We have good reason to believe that a combined effort is meditated by the opponents of the bank, to bring a heavier demand against it at some point than it is supposed it will be able to meet, and so discredit the institution. That office will of course be selected which is deemed weakest, and . . . the office at Lexington seems to have been threatened.

The Philadelphia branch sent $110,000 in gold, and ordered New Orleans, St. Louis, and Louisville to collectively send another $150,000. This would put almost $1 m of specie in the vaults of the upper Mississippi River branches, an amount, Biddle believed,

> which puts us beyond the reach of any combination that we believe it possible to form for the purpose of annoyance. . . . If it were known that more than a million in specie could be concentrated in the course of a week at one of the five offices, it is probable that the attempt of our enemies would be abandoned.[24]

Primary sources contain a wealth of evidence on Biddle's instructions to cashiers to ship specie, especially the cashier at New Orleans, where much of the

Mexican and other Spanish silver entered the country. In April and June 1825, Biddle wrote to West:

> Your statement of the 30th exhibits an account of $501,418.58 of specie. With nearly a million of notes of all denominations which you will have received since that period and a comparatively small demand for specie at N Orleans you would I think be entirely safe with between three and four hundred thousand dollars in your vaults. The very large demand for China and Calcutta this spring, has considerably drained all the Banks in this quarter, and left our specie means comparatively low.

Biddle reminded the cashier that New Orleans had an incentive to ship as much specie as they could "spare with entire safety" since

> your remittances are sold on your own account and . . . your office will have a credit for all the profits, a mode of settlement which is deemed just and proper, as I wish you to feel an interest in this very interesting branch of business.[25]

Another example comes from Baltimore in 1830. In January of that year, the Philadelphia office wrote to the Baltimore branch's cashier:

> Dear Sir, Altho we have here an ample supply of Specie, the Mint works so slowly as to leave us badly prepared with American coin, to meet the heavy demands of the public creditors upon us; *and we run some risk of being obliged to pay away Carolus Dollars unless you can furnish us promptly with half Dollars out of your uncommonly good Stock* [emphasis added]. The weather fortunately continues mild, and I ask you to avail yourself of the open water to give us whatever halves you can Spare, making up with Ferdinands & Mexicans a Sum not exceeding 250/m Dollars. Mexicans would pay their way, but we have nearly half a million of them in the Mint, and Ferdinands would perhaps Serve our purpose better as a Safeguard to the Carolus Dollars. In the assortment however and amount exercise your own discretion, after meeting our wishes, as far as possible, with American coin. Mr Andrews would send you an Officer to assist in the transportation, if he could do so without inconvenience.[26]

The "public creditors" likely referred to US pensioners, many of whom would not have had bank accounts, and whose small payments would have needed to be made with coin.

Philadelphia was the center of the Bank's specie holdings. Over the entire period, the Bank of the United States shipped $34.8 m of specie shipments from one branch to another, 90 percent of which was silver coin. Of all domestic movements of coin (silver and gold), 70 percent was sent to Philadelphia, confirming Philadelphia's role as the central managing point for the Bank's specie. Of the silver coin alone shipped between branches, 60 percent went to Philadelphia, and 28 percent to New York. Two-thirds of the interbranch silver shipments originated in either New Orleans (39 percent of total) or New York (26 percent of total). Seventy percent of all gold that was shipped domestically was shipped to Philadelphia; only 3 percent to New York. During the Biddle years, all interbranch (domestic) gold shipments were directed to Philadelphia. In 1819–1821, 22 percent of the Bank's specie was held in Philadelphia; in 1829–1831, 33 percent.[27]

Between 1817 and 1831, $5.1 m of specie was shipped abroad (to either London or Paris); this sum was split roughly fifty-fifty between silver and gold, and between shipments to London and shipments to Paris. Silver dominated shipments to Paris, and gold dominated shipments to London. Every shipment of specie abroad originated in Philadelphia.

Private and public benefits of the Bank's specie market operations

The Bank made a small net profit from its dealing in silver and gold. Between January 1820 and November 1831, the Bank earned net premium income (premia received minus premia paid) of $87,600 on silver, and –$9,800 on gold. If the cost of transporting silver from southern to northern markets is taken into account, the Bank's net earnings on silver over the period as a whole was around $25,000, or about 0.7 percent of total sales.[28] The Bank's net earnings on its silver dealings covered the losses on gold, and defrayed the cost of interbranch specie movements for other purposes (e.g. bolstering vulnerable branches). Although the Bank's net earnings on specie dealing were thin, it enjoyed other, corollary benefits from these operations.

First, the Bank gained a competitive advantage over the state banks and the private bankers from being a large repository of the good Spanish silver. Being a client of the Bank conferred access to the only acceptable means of payment in the Far East before the Bank introduced its own long-dated bills of exchange into the Asia trade in 1825, which did not fully displace silver.[29] The correspondence of the Bank's Baltimore branch includes many letters from merchants in Baltimore, New York, and Philadelphia applying for discounts from the Second Bank, specifying that they needed the proceeds in Spanish silver.

In October 1821, Leonard Kimball asked for "60000 Spanish Dollars for a good note at 60 days, payable either in Philadelphia or New York and secured by 600 shares of US Bank stock—on my allowing you 50 days interest on the note." In November, Edward Thompson of New York wrote, "I want to send out in a Ship I am just fitting out for China 100000 Dollars (Spanish Dollars). Can you furnish them if I send you Bank drafts at Sight on New York." And in December of that year, a merchant in Philadelphia wrote to the Baltimore cashier:

> I wish to obtain Fifty Thousand Spanish Dollars to ship to Calcutta, and on applying at the Bank of the United States (in Philadelphia) for the sum, I was informed the Bank had no Spanish Dollars in its possession, but that perhaps they might be obtained at the Office of D & D at Baltimore in payment of the proceeds of satisfactory paper if offered there for discount.

Finally, in May 1824, S & J Nevins & Co wrote to the Cashier of the Baltimore branch of the Bank of the United States that they were sending by the bearer of the letter

> our note for Fifty Thousand Dollars and a certificate for Five Hundred Shares US Bk Stock in your name for which you will please to deliver him the Fifty Thousand Spanish Dollars the premium on which and the discount on the Note he will pay you.[30]

As the latter quote indicates, the Bank charged a premium in addition to interest when it extended a loan in Spanish dollars instead of its own, at-par, notes, deposits, and drafts.

The Bank's accumulation of gold was a public good, a form of credit insurance in meeting sterling-denominated debt obligations issued by US borrowers to English creditors. England, the US primary source of imports and trade credit, was nominally on a bimetallic standard, like the United States, but was effectively on gold.[31] In a pinch, to make sure that creditors of the US government were paid on time, gold might have to be shipped to meet US debt repayments, should commodity exports falter and not enough sterling bills be available. For such a purpose, gold was better than silver, and bullion bars (the only form of gold the Bank purchased) were much more useful than coin.

Another public benefit of the Bank's specie operations was that they kept some of the stock of specie out of the hands of private arbitrage firms, whose objective was to make gains on intercity and international disparities in the prices of different coins. Their operations could cause specie outflows that were potentially destabilizing to the commercial banking system. Biddle regularly contrasted the Bank's operations, which served the public interest (and, at times, the Bank's private interests), to the operations of "monied men" who looked only to private profit. The Bank's supporters in Congress, who tended to follow Biddle's lead in their arguments on behalf of the Bank, pointed out that

> the transmission of specie from New Orleans to the northern Atlantic cities, is nothing more than a natural operation of trade . . . . This operation is carried on by the bank instead of being left to individuals, to the undoubted advantage of the community.[32]

By competing directly with the private arbitrage firms, the Bank reduced the size and growth of the private banking sector by denying them the profits they needed to accumulate equity.

At the same time the Bank cast the private bankers in a negative light, it did business with some of them. The Bank obtained 64 percent of all specie that it purchased ($1.07 m) from one of three firms: Lewis Clapier (silver), Hale & Davidson (gold), and Biers, Booth, & St John (gold). Lewis Clapier was based in Philadelphia and was active in the French trade. He had a global network of correspondents in Marseilles, China, East India, Havana, and Vera Cruz. Biers,

Booth, & St John were exchange dealers with offices in New Orleans, Charleston, Augusta. Hale & Davidson was a private banking firm in New York. The Bank had a particularly close relationship with a handful of private bankers in New York and Philadelphia. Biddle had frequent correspondence with Nathanial Prime and Roswell Colt, of New York, and with Thomas Biddle & Co., a Philadelphia private banking firm, requesting and receiving the latest specie and security market information. As seen in Chapter Four, the Bank used its partnership with Biddle & Co.to carry out large-scale stabilization operations in the sterling exchange market.

Conclusion

The Bank's specie operations can be summed up simply as follows. The Bank took in a variety of Spanish silver at New Orleans. It moved as much as possible to Philadelphia and New York. It sorted the stock, reserving the prime Ferdinand and Carolus coins to sell at highest premia to East Asia merchants, earning profits from the difference between the bid price in New Orleans and the ask price in northern markets. The Mexican coin it sold or recoined into American silver, which it shipped out to other branches to protect the Ferdinand and Carolus coins in the Bank's vaults in those locations.

As with the Bank's domestic and foreign exchange operations, the Bank's specie operations provided a public good without sacrificing private profit. By suppressing private arbitrage in specie markets, "undesirable" specie movements, either between cities or abroad, were reduced. By taking arbitrage profits for itself, the Bank limited the growth of private bankers, preserving its own market power in specie and bills of exchange. Profits from the Bank's silver market operations paid for losses on the Bank's accumulation of gold, which served as insurance in international payments.

Specie management worked: there was no suspension of specie payments during the Second Bank period, and currency maintained its par value with American specie throughout this period.[33] The federal government's obligations were met on time, including those payable abroad in specie or its equivalent (sterling, francs, and guilders).

Notes

1 Martin (1968, p. 434); Martin (1977); Redish (2000, p. 231).
2 Redish (2000, p. 227); John Campbell White Papers, Box 21. English banks resumed specie payments in 1821. These shipments are confirmed by 22nd Cong., 1st Sess., S. Doc. 98. Laughlin (1901) stresses the fact that the substitution of gold with silver as a circulating medium was not caused by the increased English demand for gold after resumption, but began "as early as 1810, if not before, and that little of it was in circulation by 1818." Resumption of specie payments in England accelerated the process.
3 Martin (1968, p. 434); Girard Papers Reel 148. At other times, the Girard Bank's silver holdings included Mexican and Carolus dollars.
4 According to the Director of the US Mint, "a very large proportion of the whole accumulation of the precious metals in the U.S., . . . has been received through the port at

New Orleans"; 23rd Cong., 2d Sess., H. Doc. 99; on origin of silver coin imported into the US, see Temin (1969), Table 3.5.

5 Martin (1968, p. 433); Carothers (1967).

6 Banco de Mexico (2013).

7 From 23rd Cong., 2d Sess., H. Doc. 99.

8 23rd Cong., 2d Sess., H. Doc. 99, Communication from the Director of the Mint in relation to the establishment of Branches of that institution, January 23, 1835. See also Irigoin (2009). Biddle observed that "the Banks receive freely these Mexican dollars, because they can be recoined at a small profit", and quoted the Director of the Mint's observation that Mexican coins, while not a legal tender, "are always an acceptable and current tender, the coins of France tho a legal tender form no part of the circulation"; Biddle Papers, August 21, 1827, letter from Biddle to Rush.

9 On denomination of silver coin minted in the US, see Laughlin (1901, p. 31). On estimate of the amount of US silver coin in the US economy in 1830, see 21st Cong., 1st Sess., S. Exec. Doc. 19, p. 11. In her analysis of specie prices, Redish (2000) assumed that the numeraire was American silver dollars before 1834 and notes in support of this assumption that "no prices are given" for American silver dollars.

10 21st Cong., 1st Sess., S. Doc. 19 (1830 Sanford Report), p. 12.

11 Kelsey Burr Papers, Box 1, March 20, 1823, letter from Biddle to Charles S. West.

12 22nd Cong., 1st Sess., H. Rep. 460, pp. 198–205.

13 Biddle Papers, April 6, 1825, letter from Biddle to Robinson, Cashier at New York.

14 Martin (1968), p. 434.

15 In calendar year 1827, $2.87 m of silver coins were minted, the highest level in the history of the Mint up to that time; Laughlin 1901, p. 338. According to the January 1, 1828, Report of Mint of the US, 20th Cong., 1st Sess., H. Doc. 70, "The supply of silver, under various forms of unwrought bullion, and in foreign coins, has been unusually abundant, especially during the first three-quarters of the year. The heavier deposites [*sic*] have been received, generally, through the Bank of the United States. Of the amount of silver coined within the last year, more than $2 m consisted of deposites [*sic*] received from that institution."

16 18th Cong., 1st Sess., H. Doc. 705, p. 830.

17 Catterall (1902), p. 415; American State Papers, Finance, Vol. 3, p. 367. This "Circular" dated 1818 from the Cashier of the Second Bank in Philadelphia to "City banks" announced that "the notes of this bank which are made payable at its several offices of discount and deposite [*sic*] will not be received at this bank after this day, except in payment of debts due to the United States. Such notes, however, of the offices as your bank may have received during this day, will be received in exchange to-morrow [*sic*] morning."

18 Biddle told Lenox that they " . . .have . . . warned the whole establishment against these drafts." Biddle Papers, February 20, 1823, letter from Biddle to Robert Lenox of New York. A day earlier, Biddle wrote to John White, the cashier in Baltimore, on the same topic: "Applications similar to those you mention had already been made to us, and were granted to some amount. The repetition of them however caused us to examine the nature of a transaction *so contrary to the natural course of things*, and we have traced them to the house of Beers & Bunnell brokers of N. York, whose object we believe to be to obtain Spanish Dollars from this Office. As however the operation may be inconvenient to the Office, we have ceased to draw and have directed the Office at N York to do the same. You will also forbear to repeat your drafts."; Biddle Papers, February 19, 1823, letter from Biddle to White. By the "natural course of things", Biddle is presumably referring to transactions grounded in seasonal trade flows.

19 Biddle Papers, letter to Robinson, February 23, 1825.

20 In a letter to one of the branch cashiers, Biddle wrote, "In a circular to the receivers of public monies issued by the Treasury Department under date of the 22nd of Feby [*sic*] 1826 . . . one of the rules is, that, 'No Bank note of a less amount than five dollars is to

be received.' I do not know whether this rule has been applied to any Officers except those who are technically called receivers—that is those who collect the revenue from the sales of land. It was the wish of the Government that the prohibition should be general and certainly the general policy of discouraging the small notes and making the circulation more metallic is an object of great interest to the Government." Kelsey Burr Papers, Box 2. The charter set the $5 note as the smallest note the Bank could issue.

21 Biddle Papers, August 21, 1827, letter from Biddle to Treasury Secretary Rush.
22 Biddle Papers, August 21, 1827, letter from Biddle to Treasury Secretary Rush; 23rd Cong., 2d Sess., H. Doc. 99.
23 Biddle Papers, September 23, 1823, letter from Biddle to Wm Patterson & Robert Gilmor, Esquires, Baltimore, and April 19, 1825, letter to John White, Cashier, Baltimore office.
24 22nd Cong., 2d Sess., H. Rep. 121; Biddle Papers, October 3, 1832, letter from Biddle to Edward Shippen, Esq.
25 Kelsey Burr Papers, Box 2, April 5, 1825 and June 19, 1825, from N. Biddle to C. West.
26 Baltimore Second Bank Branch Records, Box 4, January 4, 1830, letter from Cashier of Philadelphia Second Bank office to John White, Cashier, Office of the Bank of the United States, Baltimore. "Half dollars" referred to US silver coin.
27 22nd Cong., 1st Sess., Sen. Doc. 98; 22nd Cong., 1st Sess., H. Doc. 147. The Bank reported on "the amount of Silver, Gold, and Mixed Bullion, annually remitted by each Branch Bank to the Parent Bank, or to any other place, by order of the Parent Bank" from 1817 through 1831.
28 Estimate based on information from and 1835 communication from the Director of the Mint to Congress (23rd Cong., 2d Sess., H. Doc. 99) stating that the freight and insurance cost of 1–1.25 percent to moving specie from New Orleans to Philadelphia was 1–1.25 percent; the estimate applies 1.25 percent to $5 m, the total amount sold.
29 Catterall (1902, p. 112); Temin (1969, p. 82); Smith (1953, p. 89). According to Smith, the bills were a "partial substitute" for silver coin.
30 Records of the Baltimore branch of the Bank of the United States, Boxes 2 and 3.
31 Redish (2000, p. 229); Cameron (1967, p. 18).
32 22nd Cong., 1st Sess., H. Rep. 460, p. 308.
33 Officer (1996, p. 78) presented data showing that there was no premium of specie (presumably American silver although it is not specified), over currency in Baltimore, New York, or Philadelphia between 1817 and 1837. For the period after 1837, the specie standard is identified as American gold.

7 Conclusion

This book has argued, as the title indicates, that the Second Bank was a "central" bank in an era of nation-building. The title refers to the Second Bank as a "central" bank to convey the view that the Second Bank was not a central bank in the sense that is commonly understood today. The book stands apart from that strand of the economic history literature of the Bank that sees the Bank, more or less, as a central bank in the manner of the US Federal Reserve. It returns to a historically grounded interpretation of the Bank as a different kind of central banking institution, one that would meet the needs of a young, geographically expanding nation-state in the early nineteenth century while keeping its stockholders happy.

Capie et al. (1994) conducted an exhaustive study of the development of central banking since the late seventeenth century. Many central banking institutions in their study started out, like the Second Bank, as hybrids, commercial banks that were also public banks, or the central government's banker. This work identified two key turning points in the lives of these banks, moments when their fundamental character shifted. One turning point was when public banks became lenders of last resort for the banking system. The other, closely related, turning point was reached when the public bank withdrew from competition with the commercial banks.

Where public banks evolved into central banks, there was a "largely uncodified concordat, whereby, in return for the central bank's withdrawal from commercial banking, the commercial banks voluntarily accepted the central bank's leadership" (Capie et al. 1994, p. 3). Once the central bank withdrew from competition, it no longer faced a fundamental conflict of interest in carrying out its role as the lender of last resort, in which it could potentially fail to lend, when it should have lent, because it stood to benefit from the failure of a rival bank. A marker of the commercial banks' acceptance of the central bank's leadership is their use of the central bank's liabilities to clear debt among themselves. This amounts to an acknowledgment that the money issued by the central bank is superior to the money issued by the commercial banks, another key turning point in the evolution of central banking.

This book has presented a variety of evidence showing that the Second Bank reached neither of these turning points during its tenure. State banks' balance sheets were analyzed to understand whether state banks listed Second Bank notes and deposits as specie equivalents. This test failed, even using the relatively weak test of the literature, whether Second Bank money was listed separately from state bank money. A minority of banks did treat Second Bank money as a "superior" monetary assets; thirteen of the fourteen banks that did were located outside of the northeastern core. City banks presented Second Bank money on their balance sheets in the same way they presented other city banks' money. Testimony from city banks in Congressional documents revealed that these city banks could not use central bank money issued elsewhere in clearing debt *to the Second Bank itself!* The New York banks held foreign Second Bank notes until they could sell them, at a discount, to note brokers. Second Bank money was not unequivocally "as good as gold" (or silver) to the state banks in the country's financial core.

The Second Bank did not act like a lender of last resort during the monetary stress of 1825–1826. As the price of silver coin reached its decadal peak of 3 percent premium in the Fall of 1825, the Bank sold $200,000 of its Spanish dollars, the single largest sale of silver between 1824 and 1831. The Bank sold the silver at a premium in order to avoid having to provide it over the counter at face value. This released silver from the Bank's vaults, while at the same time shifting inter-bank balances in favor of the Second Bank—strengthening the Bank's position vis-a-vis the other banks in the system. In modern arrangements, during stressful times, the central bank becomes less liquid so that the other banks can become more liquid.

Neither did the Bank act like a lender of last resort when it designed its branch network. The transportation infrastructure of the 1820s United States was relatively undeveloped, being limited to overland transport on improved roads in the most densely populated sections of the country, and water transport on the coasts and some rivers. It took four days to travel between New York and the South Atlantic cities, ten days between New York and the Ohio River, and thirteen days between New York and the Gulf Coast. To be an effective lender of last resort, the Second Bank needed to locate branches where it would have immediate access to the maximum number of state-chartered banks. This it did not do.

Instead, the Second Bank designed a branch network to maximize its effectiveness as the central manager of the domestic and foreign exchanges, particularly after Nicholas Biddle became President of the Bank. The cities that received new branches after 1823 were cities that would eventually become significant producers of bills of exchange drawn against commodities being shipped to market. In every case except one (Portland, Maine), these cities had either no banks or only one bank. The Second Bank managed the domestic and foreign exchanges with the needs of merchants, commodity producers (including, perhaps particularly, planters), and the US government in mind, not the state banks. Even before Biddle, the Second Bank was quite clear about its competitive relationship with the state banks. In 1817, President Jones instructed the board of the New York branch not to transfer funds between cities for the state banks for free: "it has never been the contemplation of this board to furnish to the state banks all the facilities of exchange, . . . while the bank and its offices should undertake the invidious task of collecting the debts."[1]

Nicholas Biddle, who spoke authoritatively for and on behalf of the Second Bank, was philosophically opposed to the idea of a lender of last resort. He didn't think it was right for the state banks to "overtrade," then for the Bank's stockholders to take losses from assisting the state banks that were overextended. He was willing to use the Second Bank's ample stock of specie to give the state banks time to contract their balance sheets in an orderly manner, but the day of reckoning would come. When the Savannah branch lent to a local state bank with a liquidity problem, it got its hands slapped by Philadelphia. This kind of lending is what modern central banks do: they make loans to solvent banks so that the banks can "pay their notes," or, more generally, avoid defaulting on immediate payment obligations.

While not a central bank in the modern sense, the Second Bank was a central bank for its times, a central banker to an emerging nation. The term "central" has several meanings in this context. The Bank was the single largest holder of high-powered money (specie) in the US economy. From its central headquarters in Philadelphia, the President and his staff managed the branch network's extensive operations in domestic and foreign exchange; shipments of banknotes, exchange instruments, and specie between branches; and receipts and payments for the US government. Biddle quickly understood the need for operations of the branches to be coordinated, especially when it came to specie. Seven months after being installed as President, Biddle wrote to members of the Baltimore board that the Parent Board is "unwilling to part with what they deem a Salutary control over the Specie operations."[2] The importance of a "higher authority" within a central bank with branches was a lesson that took twenty years, and a Great Depression, for the US Federal Reserve to learn.

The Second Bank held a significantly larger stock of specie reserves in relation to its notes and deposits than the state-chartered banks did, with an average reserve ratio of 41 percent over 1823–1832 compared with the state banks' 16 percent. The Second Bank managed this large buffer stock for the benefit of the US government, monetary stability, and its own self-defense. Its stock of gold was a form of credit insurance for the US government. In case of shortages of sterling exchange, the Bank could draw down its stock of gold to meet the government's payment obligations in London. During the Biddle years, the Second Bank did concern itself with the stability of the entire system. The Second Bank stabilized the monetary system by allowing its vault to absorb changes in net specie imports that could have otherwise destabilized credit conditions in the state banking sector. Finally, the large stock of specie protected the Second Bank against potential "raids" from arbitrageurs seeking to profit from intercity differences in the prices of different types of coin.

In many ways, the Second Bank was neither fish nor fowl: neither a "pure" profit-maximizing private bank, nor a pure national bank, devoted to the public good. Through its operations in domestic exchange, foreign exchange, and specie markets, the Second Bank promoted the economic integration of the west, kept the US dollar at par with silver and gold, and strengthened the federal government's international fiscal reputation as a borrower that paid on time and in full. The Second Bank blended the public and private aspects of its mission and identity into a successful business model. Its domestic and foreign exchange business generated revenue that covered the cost of fiscal transfers and attracted the most credit-worthy merchants to do all their banking business with the Second Bank. Profits from dealing in silver coin covered the cost of buying and holding gold coin and bullion, a form of credit insurance for US debt obligations abroad. The Second Bank's very high profitability in the early 1830s was a direct result of its engagement in the nation-building project of "settling the West" (which, of course, was already populated).

The Second Bank was a complex financial institution, and its successful management required an acute understanding of the Atlantic economy, credit analysis, balance sheets, state banking, and the federal government. Biddle mastered all of these subjects (and more). He was a hands-on manager, directly involved with coordination of the branches and management of flows of notes, bills, and specie between branches, all accomplished through a voluminous correspondence with the branch cashiers and board presidents. Like other great central bankers, Biddle consumed good information voraciously. He was, by turns, witty, sarcastic, and diplomatic in his letters with colleagues. Take, for example, a letter he wrote to Thomas Perkins, at the Boston branch, in December 1825:

> I live, as you know, in a kind of whispering gallery, where every columny [*sic*] and every idle piece of gossip, that is spoken in an under tone at any point between Portland and New Orleans is borne full and distinct upon my ear. In this scene of windy exaggeration, it is refreshing occasionally to meet with a fact, and I was really glad to know the particulars stated in your letters.[3]

Biddle could also be sarcastic in his testimony before Congress. During extensive hearings during the debate on rechartering the Bank, Biddle responded to a question as follows:

> Now, if there was a demand for money, and the bank had the means of supplying it, why should it not? The object of its creation was precisely that; . . . it seems a singular objection to a bank, that, finding a demand for money, and having the means of supplying it, did supply it.

During the same hearings, Biddle answered a series of questions by pointing out the errors in the questions, and noted that certain problems at the Louisville and Cincinnati branches were caused by "the rise of the river Ohio, over which the bank has no control."[4] Clearly, Biddle did not suffer fools gladly, and did not manage the politics of charter renewal very well.

The Bank was a success, measured against the purposes for which it was created. There were no banking crises or suspensions of the specie payments; the country enjoyed monetary stability. The federal government built a reputation in international capital markets for timely payment in specie or its equivalent from the creditor's point of view. The Bank "opened" the west for commercial agriculture by providing an affordable means of financing trade between the interior, New Orleans, and the eastern seaboard, which had the desired effect of binding the west to the nation and, over the long run, stimulating national economic growth. The Bank was a commercial success, particularly after Biddle took charge, and paid a competitive and stable dividend to its shareholders.

In closing, one can reflect on the lessons of the Second Bank for central banking in the twenty-first century. The Second Bank secured some of its success as a stabilizer by reducing the rate of growth of the financial sector. The overall pace of monetary expansion was relatively slow in the 1820s, which reduced the profitability of state banking and the formation of new banks, especially on the frontier. The Second Bank dominated the region that had the highest growth potential, the frontier, and adopted a monetary regime that tied the growth in bank assets to the growth in commodity production, not land sales. The Second Bank deliberately closed off private capital's arbitrage opportunities in specie markets and the foreign exchange market when they were deemed not in the public interest.

After the demise of the Second Bank, the state-chartered commercial banking system grew rapidly in the 1830s, particularly in the frontier areas formerly dominated by the Bank.[5] In retrospect, finance expanded too rapidly, resulting in the accumulation of bad debt on balance sheets at home and abroad, a financial crisis, and a long financial recession. In an era of financialization and an expanding public safety net for finance, using the central bank to suppress "excessive" growth of finance may be one useful lesson for the present from this history of the Second Bank.

Notes

1 H. Rep. 92, 15th Cong., 2d Sess., pp. 46–9.
2 Biddle Papers, September 23, 1823, letter to Wm Patterson & Robert Gilmor.
3 Biddle Papers, December 14, 1825, letter to T. Perkins.
4 22nd Cong., 1st Sess., H. Doc. 460, pp. 336, 338.
5 Knodell (2006).

Appendix A

Table A.1 City database, 1820

Cities (pop. > 2,500) (largest to smallest)	1820 Population	State bank offices (n)	Center of a customs district?	Index of relative customs receipts, 1823[1]	Had a Second Bank branch?
New York City inc. suburbs	130,881	9	Y[2]	10.16	Y
Philadelphia inc. suburbs	108,809	8	Y	3.67	Y
Baltimore	62,739	8	Y	1.28	Y
Boston inc. suburbs	54,024	6	Y	4.68	Y
New Orleans	27,176	3	Y	0.92	Y
Charleston	24,780	4	Y	0.80	Y
Washington DC	28,825	12	Y	0.10	Y
Salem MA	12,731	3	Y	0.48	
Albany	12,630	3			
Richmond VA	12,067	2	Y	0.08	Y
Providence RI	11,767	7	Y	0.37	Y
Cincinnati	9,642	3			Y
Portland ME	8,581	2	Y	0.19	
Norfolk, VA	8,478	2	Y	0.15	Y
Savannah	7,523	2	Y	0.29	Y
Portsmouth NH	7,327	4	Y	0.15	Y
Newport RI	7,319	4	Y	0.08	
Nantucket	7,266	2	Y	0.00	
Pittsburg	7,248	2			Y
New Haven CT	7,147	2	Y	0.17	
Newburyport MA	6,852	2	Y	0.05	
Petersburg VA	6,690	2			
Lancaster PA	6,633	3			
Gloucester MA	6,384	1	Y	0.03	
Marblehead MA	5,630	1	Y	0.04	
Hudson City NY	5,310	1			
Lexington KY	5,279	0			Y
Troy, NY	5,264	2			
Hartford CT	4,726	2			

(*Continued*)

Table A.1 (Continued)

Cities (pop. > 2,500) (largest to smallest)	1820 Population	State bank offices (n)	Center of a customs district?	Index of relative customs receipts, 1823[1]	Had a Second Bank branch?
Middleborough MA	4,687	0			
Taunton MA	4,520	1			
Lynn, MA	4,515	0			
Plymouth, MA	4,348	1			
Reading, PA	4,332	1			
Beverly, MA	4,283	1			
Louisville KY	4,012	1			Y
New Bedford MA	3,947	1	Y	0.03	
Trenton NJ	3,942	2			
Schenectady NY	3,939	1			
New Bern, NC	3,663	2	Y	0.03	
Frederick MD	3,640	1			
York, PA	3,545	1			
Fayetteville NC	3,532	2			Y
Elizabeth NJ	3,515	1			
New London CT	3,330	2			
Harrisburg PA	2,990	1			
Norwich CT	2,983	1			
Utica NY	2,972	1			
Carlisle PA	2,908	1			
Raleigh NC	2,674	3			
Wilmington NC	2,633	2	Y	0.08	
Middletown CT	2,618	1	Y	0.16	Y
Chillicothe OH[3]		3			Y

[1] Index = the customs duties for the city divided by the average of customs duties for all cities with customs districts.

[2] Y = yes.

[3] Chillicothe was not large enough to be a city, but it did have a Second Bank branch.

Sources: Cities and their population, Gibson (1998); cities with Second Bank branches, Catterall (1902, p. 376); Customs districts and their duties, 18th Cong., 1st Sess., Sen. Doc. 5, Dec. 3, 1823; number of state banks, Appendix B, Master list of state bank offices.

Table A.2 City database, 1830

Cities in 1830 (pop. > 2,500) (largest to smallest; italicized cities = cities not on 1820 list)	1830 population	State bank offices (n)	Center of a customs district?	Index of relative customs receipts, 1828[1]	Had a Second Bank branch?
New York City	202,589	18	Y[2]	10.99	Y
Baltimore	80,620	7	Y	1.24	Y
Philadelphia	80,462	11	Y	4.06	Y
Boston	61,392	16	Y	3.68	Y
New Orleans	46,082	4	Y	1.14	Y
Charleston	30,289	5	Y	0.36	Y
Cincinnati	24,821	0			Y
Albany	24,209	4			
Washington DC	35,508	8	Y	0.06	Y
Providence RI	16,833	10	Y	0.16	Y
Richmond VA	16,060	2	Y	0.05	Y
Salem MA	13,895	6	Y	0.26	
Portland ME	12,598	4	Y	0.26	Y
Pittsburg	12,568	1			Y
Troy, NY	11,556	4			
Newark, NJ	10,953	1			
Louisville KY	10,341	0			Y
New Haven CT	10,180	2	Y	0.07	
Norfolk, VA	9,814	2	Y	0.04	Y
Rochester, NY	9,207	1			
Buffalo, NY	8,668	0	Y		Y
Utica NY	8,323	1			Y
Petersburg VA	8,322	2	Y	0.02	
Portsmouth NH	8,026	6	Y	0.11	Y
Newport RI	8,010	4			
Lancaster PA	7,704	2			
New Bedford MA	7,592	1	Y	0.06	
Gloucester MA	7,510	1	Y	0.10	
Savannah	7,303	3	Y	0.12	Y
Nantucket	7,202	3	Y		
Hartford CT	7,074	3	Y		Y
Springfield, MA	6,784	1			
Augusta, GA	6,710	5			
Lowell, MA	6,474	1			
Newburyport MA	6,375	2	Y	0.07	
Lynn, MA	6,138	0			
Taunton MA	6,042	1			
Lexington KY	6,026	0			Y
Reading, PA	5,856	1			
Nashville, TN	5,566	1			Y
Warwich town, RI	5,529	3			
Dover town, NH	5,449				
Hudson City NY	5,392	0			

(*Continued*)

Table A.2 (Continued)

Cities in 1830 (pop. > 2,500) (largest to smallest; italicized cities = cities not on 1820 list)	1830 population	State bank offices (n)	Center of a customs district?	Index of relative customs receipts, 1828[1]	Had a Second Bank branch?
Marblehead MA	5,149	1	Y		
Middleborough MA	5,008	0			
St Louis, MO	4,977	0			Y
Plymouth, MA	4,758	1			
Lynchburg town, VA	4,630	2			
Andover town, MA	4,530	1			
Frederick town, MD	4,427	2			
New London CT	4,335	2	Y	0.01	
Harrisburg PA	4,312	1			
Schenectady NY	4,268	1			
Danvers town, MA	4,228	2			
York, PA	4,216	1			
Worcester town, MA	4,173	2			
Fall River town, MA	4,158	0			
Beverly, MA	4,073	1			
Trenton NJ	3,925	1			
New Bern, NC	3,796	2	Y	0.03	
Wilmington NC	3,791	2	Y	0.04	
Carlisle PA	3,707	1			
Easton borough	3,529	1			
Elizabeth NJ	3,455	1			
Hagerstown, MD	3,371	1			
Mobile, AL	3,194	1	Y		Y
Norwich CT	3,135	1			
Middletown CT	3,123	1	Y	0.10	
Zanesville, OH	3,094	0			
Dayton, OH	2,950	1			
Steubenville, OH	2,937	1			
Fayetteville NC	2,868	2			Y
Chillicothe, OH	2,546	1			
Allegheny, PA	2,801	0			
Natchez, MS	2,789	1			Y
Annapolis, MD	2,623	1	Y	0.00	

[1] Index = the customs duties for the city divided by the average of customs duties for all cities with customs districts.

[2] Y = yes.

Sources: As for Table A.1.

Appendix B

Master list of state bank offices in the United States in 1820 and 1830

This appendix provides a discussion of the sources and methods used to construct the master list of state banking offices used in this study. This master list is the basis for the banking-system tables and maps in Chapter 3.

As a measure of the size of a banking system, a headcount of banking offices is imperfect for several reasons. For one, state banks were not all the same size; a state with fewer banking offices than another state may have had greater bank capacity if its banks were, on average, larger. There is bank-specific information on authorized bank capital in 1820 and 1830 from Van Fenstermaker, but not on paid-in capital, which could be significantly less than the authorized amount. Weber (2008) has some bank-specific data on assets and liabilities for the 1820s, but not for all banks. Another shortcoming of the headcount measure is that it omits private bankers, insurance companies, savings banks, and scrip-issuing transportation companies. Its compensating virtue is that data on the number of chartered banks in operation over time and across space is reasonably consistent and available; data on paid-in capital of operating banks or the number of non-bank financial institutions is not.

The benchmark years of 1820 and 1830 are not ideal in the sense that they are not located at comparable moments in the business cycle. While 1830 was located in the middle of a moderate expansion, 1820 followed the Panic of 1819 and marked the beginning of the financial recession of 1820–1823. They are used because of the availability of population data at decadal intervals.

The primary source is Weber (2011). This file is an update of the data used in Weber (2006). Weber (2011) provides a list of all state chartered banks that existed in the United States before 1861, along with their beginning and ending dates. This data set supersedes that in Van Fenstermaker (1965). Weber used published bank-balance sheets and banknote reporters to determine opening and closing dates, in contrast to Van Fenstermaker, who dated a bank's existence from the date it was chartered. There could be significant lags in time between the chartering of a bank by the legislature and the opening of that bank; and there were some banks that were chartered, but never capitalized and opened.

Weber (2011) was used to produce a Master list of state bank offices and their locations in the United States in 1820 and 1830. Weber's data set was refined in several ways. A variety of primary and secondary sources were consulted to improve the count, particularly for the western states and for the number of branches of state-chartered banks. The Master list used in this study includes 80 branches in 1820 compared with Weber's 69, and 60 in 1830, roughly the same as Weber's 56. Most of the discrepancy in 1820 comes from North Carolina.[1] In addition to refining the headcount of branch offices, the master list identifies the town location of most of the branches (52 of 80 in 1820, and 35 of 56 in 1830). Weber (2011) provides only the location of the head office of a state bank branch, not its branches, and Weber (2006) provides data on the number of branches in each state by year, but not their town location. The Master list is available from the author upon request.

Table B.1 compares the Master list's headcount of the number of state banks in 1820 and 1830 with Weber (2006), which, unlike Weber (2011), included the number of branches in each state. There is a 6 percent variance in both years. The difference is due to several factors, including: the updating of Weber's underlying data between the publication of the article in 2006 and the 2011 version of the underlying data; revisions to Weber's 2011 data based on information gathered from a variety of supplemental sources identified below; and different counting rules (how to treat banks that opened or closed in 1820 and 1830). If a bank operated during any part of 1820 or 1830, it was included in my count for those years.

The following sources were used to update Weber's database.

Secondary literature

Duke, BW 1980, *History of the Bank of Kentucky, 1792–1895*, Arno Press, New York.
Esarey, LE 1912, "State Banking in Indiana, 1814–1873," *Indiana University Bulletin*, vol. 1, no. 15.
Golembe, C 1952, *State Banks and the Economic Development of the West, 1830–1844*, Ph.D. thesis, Columbia University.
Knox, JJ 1900, *A History of Banking in the United States*, B. Rhodes & Co., New York.
Starnes, GT 1928, "Branch banking in Virginia," *Journal of Political Economy*, vol. 36, no. 4, pp. 480–500. www.historync.org.

Primary source documents

Niles' Register, 1818
13th Cong., 3d Sess., American State Papers, Pub. 453
15th Cong., 2d Sess., Pub. 547, Special deposits received on account of the Treasurer of the United States
18th Cong., 1st Sess., H. Doc. 170, pp. 615–16, designation of state banks for collection of internal revenue
18th Cong., 1st Sess., Pub. 705 p. 970, list of banks indebted to or creditors with the Bank of the United States, November 1818

18th Cong., 1st Sess., Pub. 705, p. 949, statement of the Bank of Kentucky and its branches, January 1821

Louisiana State Bank Records, *General Digest of the Acts of the Legislature of Louisiana*, Vol. 1, Louisiana State University, accessed January 5, 2014.

Biographical note for the Records of the Bank of the State of Mississippi, University of Texas at Austin, accessed January 5, 2014.

Note

1 Weber counted seven branches; the Master list constructed for this book counts fourteen: six branches of the State Bank of North Carolina, four branches of the Bank of Cape Fear, four for the Bank of Newbern.

Table B.1 Differences in banking-office headcount between Knodell's Master list and Census in Weber (2006)

1820	Knodell count	Weber count Banks (n)	Weber count Branches (n)	Weber count Total	Knodell count minus Weber count	1830	Knodell count	Weber count Banks (n)	Weber count Branches (n)	Weber count Total	Knodell count minus Weber count
Alabama	6	2		2	4	Alabama	4	2		2	2
Arkansas		0		0	0	Arkansas		0		0	0
Connecticut	11	9	1	10	1	Connecticut	17	15	2	17	0
Delaware	9	5	4	9	0	Delaware	10	5	5	10	0
DC	12	12		12	0	DC	9	9		9	0
Florida	0	0		0	0	Florida	2	2		2	0
Georgia	10	4	5	9	1	Georgia	17	6	5	11	6
Illinois	3	2		2	1	Illinois	0	0		0	0
Indiana	7	2		2	5	Indiana	0	0		0	0
Kentucky	16	1	13	14	2	Kentucky	1	1	12	13	−12
Louisiana	3	3		3	0	Louisiana	4	3		3	1
Maine	13	15		15	−2	Maine	20	13		13	7
Maryland	23	20	3	23	0	Maryland	17	14	3	17	0
Massachusetts	26	28		28	−2	Massachusetts	63	63		63	0
Michigan		1		1	−1	Michigan	3	2	1	3	0
Mississippi	3	1		1	2	Mississippi	3	1		1	2
Missouri	2	2		2	0	Missouri	0	0		0	0
New Hampshire	10	9		9	1	New Hampshire	20	18		18	2
New Jersey	14	14		14	0	New Jersey	18	17		17	1
New York	34	31	3	34	0	New York	49	37	2	39	10
North Carolina	17	3	7	10	7	North Carolina	16	3	7	10	6
Ohio	21	21		21	0	Ohio	11	11		11	0

Pennsylvania	37	36	3		39	−2
Rhode Island	30	30			30	0
South Carolina	6	4	2		6	0
Tennessee	8	2	5		7	1
Vermont	2	2			2	0
Virginia	18	4	13		17	1
Total national	341				322	19
% discrepancy	5.6%					

Pennsylvania	36	31	2		33	3
Rhode Island	43	47			47	−4
South Carolina	8	5	3		8	0
Tennessee	2	1	1		2	0
Vermont	10	10			10	0
Virginia	18	4	13		17	1
Total national	401				376	25
% discrepancy	6.2%					

Appendix C

Table C.1 Bank density by region, 1820

1820	Population of the states in 1820 (thousands)	2BUS branches (n)	State bank offices (n)	2BUS branches per 10,000 pop. (n)	State banks per 10,000 pop. (n)	Total no. banks per 10,000 pop.	Index of no. 2BUS branches per 10,000 pop.	Index of no. state banks per 10,000 pop.	Index of total no. banks per 10,000 pop.
New England									
Connecticut	275	1	11	0.36	4.00	4.36	1.82	1.12	1.15
Maine	298		13	0.00	4.36	4.36	0.00	1.22	1.15
Massachusetts	523	1	26	0.19	4.97	5.16	0.96	1.39	1.36
New Hampshire	244	1	10	0.41	4.10	4.51	2.05	1.14	1.19
Vermont	236		2	0.00	0.85	0.85	0.00	0.24	0.22
Rhode Island	83	1	30	1.20	36.14	37.35	6.03	10.08	9.86
Total	1,659	4	92	0.24	5.55	5.79	1.21	1.55	1.53
2BUS share of banking offices			0.042						
Middle Atlantic									
Delaware	77		9	0.00	11.69	11.69	0.00	3.26	3.09
DC	28	1	12	3.57	42.86	46.43	17.87	11.95	12.26
Maryland	407	1	23	0.25	5.65	5.90	1.23	1.58	1.56
New Jersey	278		14	0.00	5.04	5.04	0.00	1.40	1.33
New York	1,373	1	34	0.07	2.48	2.55	0.36	0.69	0.67
Pennsylvania	1,049	2	37	0.19	3.53	3.72	0.95	0.98	0.98
Total	3,212	5	129	0.16	4.02	4.17	0.78	1.12	1.10
2BUS share of banking offices			0.037						

Southeast									
Georgia	341	1	10	0.29	2.93	3.23	1.47	0.82	0.85
North Carolina	639	1	17	0.16	2.66	2.82	0.78	0.74	0.74
South Carolina	503	1	6	0.20	1.19	1.39	0.99	0.33	0.37
Virginia	938	2	18	0.21	1.92	2.13	1.07	0.53	0.56
Florida							0.00	0.00	0.00
Total	2,421	5	51	0.21	2.11	2.31	1.03	0.59	0.61
2BUS share of banking offices			0.089						
Southwest									
Louisiana	153	1	3	0.65	1.96	2.61	3.27	0.55	0.69
Alabama	128		6	0.00	4.69	4.69	0.00	1.31	1.24
Mississippi	75		3	0.00	4.00	4.00	0.00	1.12	1.06
Tennessee	423		8	0.00	1.89	1.89	0.00	0.53	0.50
Kentucky	564	2	16	0.35	2.84	3.19	1.77	0.79	0.84
Arkansas	14			0.00	0.00	0.00	0.00	0.00	0.00
Total	1,357	3	36	0.22	2.65	2.87	1.11	0.74	0.76
2BUS share of banking offices			0.077						
Northwest									
Illinois	55		3	0.00	5.45	5.45	0.00	1.52	1.44
Indiana	147		7	0.00	4.76	4.76	0.00	1.33	1.26
Ohio	581	2	21	0.34	3.61	3.96	1.72	1.01	1.05
Missouri	67		2	0.00	2.99	2.99	0.00	0.83	0.79
Michigan	7			0.00	0.00	0.00	0.00	0.00	0.00
Total	857	2	33	0.23	3.85	4.08	1.17	1.07	1.08
2BUS share of banking offices			0.057						
National	9,506	19	341	0.20	3.59	3.79			

Note: 2BUS, Second Bank of the United States.

Sources: US Census (1960); Appendix B, Master list of banking offices.

Table C.2 Bank density by region, 1830

1830	Population of the states in 1830 (thousands)	2BUS branches (n)	State bank offices (n)	2BUS branches per 10,000 pop. (n)	State banks per 10,000 pop. (n)	Total no. banks per 10,000 pop.	Index of no. 2BUS branches per 10,000 pop.	Index of no. state banks per 10,000 pop.	Index of total no. banks per 10,000 pop.
New England
Connecticut	298	1	17	0.34	5.70	6.04	1.64	1.80	1.79
Maine	399	1	20	0.25	5.01	5.26	1.22	1.58	1.56
Massachusetts	610	1	63	0.16	10.33	10.49	0.80	3.25	3.10
New Hampshire	269	1	20	0.37	7.43	7.81	1.81	2.34	2.31
Vermont	281	1	10	0.36	3.56	3.91	1.74	1.12	1.16
Rhode Island	97	1	43	1.03	44.33	45.36	5.03	13.95	13.41
Total	1,954	6	173	0.31	8.85	9.16	1.50	2.79	2.71
2BUS share of banking offices			0.034
Middle Atlantic
Delaware	77		10	0.00	12.99	12.99	0.00	4.09	3.84
DC	30	1	9	3.33	30.00	33.33	16.26	9.44	9.86
Maryland	447	1	17	0.22	3.80	4.03	1.09	1.20	1.19
New Jersey	321		18	0.00	5.61	5.61	0.00	1.76	1.66
New York	1,919	3	49	0.16	2.55	2.71	0.76	0.80	0.80
Pennsylvania	1,348	2	36	0.15	2.67	2.82	0.72	0.84	0.83
Total	4,142	7	139	0.17	3.36	3.52	0.82	1.06	1.04
2BUS share of banking offices			0.048
Southeast
Georgia	517	1	17	0.19	3.29	3.48	0.94	1.03	1.03
North Carolina	738	1	16	0.14	2.17	2.30	0.66	0.68	0.68
South Carolina	581	1	8	0.17	1.38	1.55	0.84	0.43	0.46
Virginia	1,044	2	18	0.19	1.72	1.92	0.93	0.54	0.57

Florida	35	5	2	0.00	5.71	5.71	0.00	1.80	1.69
Total	2,915		61	0.17	2.09	2.26	0.84	0.66	0.67
2BUS share of banking offices			0.076						
Southwest									
Louisiana	216	1	4	0.46	1.85	2.31	2.26	0.58	0.68
Alabama	310	1	4	0.32	1.29	1.61	1.57	0.41	0.48
Mississippi	137	1	3	0.73	2.19	2.92	3.56	0.69	0.86
Tennessee	682	1	2	0.15	0.29	0.44	0.72	0.09	0.13
Kentucky	688	2	1	0.29	0.15	0.44	1.42	0.05	0.13
Arkansas	30				0.00	0.00	0.00	0.00	0.00
Total	2,063	6	14	0.29	0.68	0.97	1.42	0.21	0.29
2BUS share of banking offices			0.300						
Northwest									
Illinois	157		0	0.00	0.00	0.00	0.00	0.00	0.00
Indiana	343		0	0.00	0.00	0.00	0.00	0.00	0.00
Ohio	938	1	13	0.11	1.39	1.49	0.52	0.44	0.44
Missouri	140	1	0	0.71	0.00	0.71	3.48	0.00	0.21
Michigan	32		3	0.00	9.38	9.38	0.00	2.95	2.77
Total	1,610	2	16	0.12	0.99	1.12	0.61	0.31	0.33
2BUS share of banking offices			0.111						
National	12,684	26	403	0.20	3.18	3.38			
2BUS share of banking offices			0.06						

Sources: US Census (1960); Appendix B, Master list of banking offices.

Appendix D

Exchange rates: sources and definitions

The source for the exchange rate data is H. Rep. 358, 21st Cong., 1st Sess., Appendix 2, dated April 13, 1830. The table in Appendix 2 is the most heavily used source of comprehensive information on intercity exchange rates charged at the Second Bank and its branches, and was partially reproduced in Catterall (1902).

The table is a matrix, listing the Bank of the United States (at Philadelphia) and 22 of the Bank's branches across the columns and down the rows (the three branches created in 1830, Utica, Burlington, and Natchez, were omitted). Each cell of the matrix lists two prices, the price at which drafts were sold *on* the column city *at* the row city, and the price at which bills payable *at* the column city were collected *by* the row city. Due to an ambiguity in the reproduction of the table in Catterall, some users of the table have inverted the columns and rows, interpreting each cell as showing prices of drafts sold and bills purchased *at* the city in the column *on* the city in the row.[1] However, it is clear from the original table, and a similar table from a Senate Document in which the row cities are clearly labelled "At" and the column cities "On," that this reading is in error.[2]

The prices of drafts are quoted as par or a percentage premium over par; the prices of bills as par or a percentage discount from par. For example, a draft price of .5% at Louisville on Philadelphia means that to purchase a $1,000 draft on the main office of the Second Bank at Philadelphia, one paid $1005 in Louisville funds; a bill price of .5% at Louisville on Philadelphia means that to convert a bill representing $1,000 of Philadelphia funds to Louisville funds, one accepted $995 in exchange. In this example, the bid-ask spread at Louisville on Philadelphia was 1.0%.

For any pair of cities, for example New Orleans and New York, there were four possible exchange rates, depending on the direction and the instrument (bills or drafts). Although it might seem that all of these rates should be the same, since they are different prices quoted for the same service of transferring funds between two points, they were not. This poses the problem of which exchange rate to use in empirical work.

This problem was addressed by simply averaging all four intercity prices into a single measure, referred to as the "intercity cost of funds" in Figures 4.2 and 4.5, and displayed in Table D.1. This measure uses the most information and potentially allows the different kinds of asymmetry in rates to cancel each other out.

Notes

1 See, for example, Bodenhorn (2000), Table 5.3, which, instead of showing rates of exchange (discounts on bills) *on* selected cities *in* New York, shows the actual rates of exchange *on* New York *in* selected cities.
2 See Sen. Doc. 104, 21st Cong. 1st Sess., p. 8.

Table D.1 Intercity cost of funds at the Second Bank, 1830 (cost per $1,000 of funds transferred)

City pairs	Intercity cost of funds	City pairs	Intercity cost of funds
Philadelphia–Boston	1,000.3	Charleston–Richmond	1001.9
Baltimore–Boston	1,000	Charleston–Mobile	1001.9
New York–Philadelphia	1,000.2	Richmond–Mobile	1,000
New York–Baltimore	1,000	Richmond–Norfolk	1,000
Philadelphia–Baltimore	1,000	New Orleans–Norfolk	1,000
New York–New Orleans	1,007.5	Mobile–Norfolk	1,002.5
New York–Mobile	1,008.1	New Orleans–Richmond	1010
New York–Charleston	1,002.2	Richmond–Savannah	1,002.5
New York–Savannah	1,006.3	New Orleans–Mobile	1,005
New York–Richmond	1,003.1	Charleston–Savannah	1,001.3
New York–Norfolk	1,002.5	Savannah–Norfolk	1,002.5
Philadelphia–New Orleans	1,008.1	New Orleans–Charleston	1,007.8
Philadelphia–Mobile	1,006.9	Charleston–Norfolk	1,001.9
Philadelphia–Charleston	1,003.4	Cincinnati–St. Louis	1,005
Philadelphia–Savannah	1,008.1	Cincinnati–Pittsburgh	1,003.1
Philadelphia–Richmond	1,001.9	Cincinnati–Buffalo	1,005
Philadelphia–Norfolk	1,001.9	Pittsburgh–St. Louis	1,005.3
Philadelphia–St. Louis	1,005.6	Pittsburgh–Buffalo	1,000.6
Philadelphia–Louisville	1,003.8	Louisville–Pittsburgh	1,004.4
Philadelphia–Cincinnati	1,004.4	Louisville–Buffalo	1,001.3
Philadelphia–Pittsburgh	1,002.5	Louisville–Cincinnati	1,004.7
Philadelphia–Buffalo	1,002.5		

Source: H. Rep. 358, 21st Cong., 1st Sess., Appendix 2.

Appendix E

Table E.1 Banking aggregates, 1820–1832 ($m)

	Second Bank			State Banks			Specie reserve ratios					
	Notes in circulation	Deposits of individuals	Specie	Notes in circulation	Deposits of individuals	Specie	Second Bank	3-year averages	State banks	3-year averages	All banks	3-year averages
1820	4.5	5	7.6	35.0	26.1	13.4	0.80		0.22		0.30	
1821	5.6	5.4	4.8	48.8	30.7	19.2	0.44		0.24		0.27	
1822	4.4	3.3	4.4	35.9	21.8	8.6	0.57	0.60	0.15	0.20	0.20	0.25
1823	4.6	3.5	5.8	41.0	25.2	12.2	0.72		0.18		0.24	
1824	6.1	5.3	6.7	46.7	29.3	14.3	0.59		0.19		0.24	
1825	9.5	5.4	4	53.0	35.2	14	0.27	0.52	0.16	0.18	0.17	0.22
1826	8.5	5.3	6.5	50.5	34.8	12.5	0.47		0.15		0.19	
1827	9.8	6.1	6.2	42.7	30.3	11.8	0.39		0.16		0.20	
1828	11.9	6.4	6.1	46.9	35.5	11.9	0.33	0.40	0.14	0.15	0.18	0.19
1829	12.9	6.4	7.6	42.6	32.6	14.9	0.39		0.20		0.24	
1830	16.3	8.2	10.8	53.3	38.6	13.2	0.44		0.14		0.21	
1831	21.3	8.1	7	68.9	52.0	15	0.24	0.36	0.12	0.16	0.15	0.20
1832	17.5	7.5	9	67.1	58.0	14	0.36		0.11		0.15	

Notes: Observations are for year-end: 1820 = January 1821 data point, 1821 = January 1822 data point, etc. State bank data: notes and deposits from Van Fenstermaker (1965), Table 10, adjusted for percentage of banks reporting; specie from Rockoff (2006). Second Bank data: S. Doc. 128, pp. 25–2; "due to other banks" data from 22nd Cong., 1st Sess., H. Doc. 147.

Sources: See Appendix F for a discussion of sources and methods.

Appendix F

Sources and methods for banking aggregates

In the secondary literature on antebellum monetary aggregates, Temin (1969), Van Fenstermaker (1965), and Rockoff (2006) use an approach to basic definitions similar to that used in this study. Each author has constructed estimates of the stock of money (or bank money alone) and its component parts, but they differ in the level of aggregation, definitions of the reserve ratio, and data sources, as summarized in Table F.1.

Discussion of choices

Definition of ultimate reserve as specie: I define the ultimate reserve asset (sometimes called the monetary base or outside money) as specie (coined silver and gold). I do not include Second Bank liabilities in the monetary base, as Officer (2002) and Rutner (1970) did.[i] There are several reasons for this. First, as shown in Chapter 5, Second Bank notes were sometimes, but not universally, held as "specie funds," and deposits with major banks were also held as specie funds. If specie funds are to be included in high-powered money, they should be included in all of their forms, not just some of their forms. Finally, Second Bank "due to state banks" (analogous to bank deposits with the Fed) were only 3 percent of all state banks' "due to" balances by the end of the period.

Level of aggregation: I chose to disaggregate the banking system into the state banks and the US Bank to identify whether the behavior of the two sectors was different.

Definition of reserve ratio: My approach is the same as Temin's (1969) except that I exclude deposits of the US Treasury and public officers. By the early 1820s, the Bank and the Treasury had a set of working rules and agreed-upon lead times for transfers, deposits, and disbursements of Treasury funds that eliminated the need for the Bank to keep a specie reserve against unanticipated shifts in fiscal operations. This explains the discrepancy between the aggregate specie reserve ratios in Appendix E and those in Temin, Table 3.3.

In principle, interbank liabilities should be included in the denominator of the specie reserve ratio, as in Van Fenstermaker (1965), since these all represented

Table F.1 Sources for banking aggregates

	Temin (1969)	Van Fenstermaker (1965)	Rockoff (2006)	Knodell (Appendix E)
Definition of monetary base	Specie	Not applicable	Specie	Specie
Definition of banks' reserve ratio	Specie held by banks divided by banknotes plus bank deposits, including deposits held by the US Treasury (for an individual bank, reserve ratio = specie divided by net liabilities, including net "due to" other banks)	Defined monetary ratio of expansion as ratio of all monetary liabilities to all monetary assets, broadly defined.[1]	Provides only aggregates. Measures money stock as banknotes plus bank deposits plus specie in hands of non-bank public, not including the US Treasury (but estimates of this aggregate start in 1833)	Specie held by state banks/ the Second Bank divided by banknotes plus bank deposits held by non-bank public, not including US Treasury (annual estimates provided)
State and federal sectors separated?	No	Yes	Yes (but state bank data provided only for 1819 and 1829)	Yes
BUS data source	25th Cong., 2d Sess., S. Doc. 128	25th Cong., 2d Sess., S. Doc. 128	Cites Friedman and Schwartz, who used Gallatin, Historical Statistics (1960), and Dewey. The resulting series is very close to 25th Cong., 2d Sess., S. Doc. 128	25th Cong., 2d Sess., S. Doc. 128; 22nd Cong., 1st Sess., H. Doc. 147 (for Second Bank "due to other banks")
State bank data source	Van Fenstermaker (for 1820s)	Generated data set from state-level sources	Cites Friedman and Schwartz, who used Gallatin[2]	Van Fenstermaker, adjusted for percentage of banks reporting
National specie stock source	Developed own estimate	NA	Temin	Temin

[1] See Van Fenstermaker (1965), p. 68. Temin (1969), p 185, pointed out that Van Fenstermaker used data for Second Bank notes that included Bank notes held within the Bank, that were not held by either other banks or the non-bank public. Van Fenstermaker's data show that the Bank had a higher ratio of monetary expansion (lower reserve ratio) during some years of the 1820s, while my measure and data show that the Bank had a lower rate of monetary expansion (higher reserve ratio) than the state banks in all years, and significantly so.

[2] Gallatin compiled state bank statistics for his Considerations on the currency and banking system of the United States (1831), specifically outstanding notes, deposits, capital, and specie holdings, for two years, year end 1819 and 1829. There are a number of letters from Biddle to Gallatin in 1830 conveying state-level bank statistics, which Biddle collected on Gallatin's behalf, and were presumably used to generate the data in Gallatin's work.

potential claims on specie. Temin argued that notes and deposits held within the banking system were a wash for the system as a whole (a liability to one was an asset to another). However, "due to's" and "due from's" were not necessarily a wash for an individual sector in a two-sector system (state banks and US Bank). In addition, not all of an individual bank's claims on other banks could be used to meet other banks' claims on it, since not all bank claims were created equal. A Philadelphia bank would not have been able to clear a debt to a New York bank with a note of a Lancaster, Pennsylvania bank, for example, and the Second Bank was more rigorous in its interbank payment demands than the state banks were with each other.

Using Van Fenstermaker's approach, the Second Bank's reserve ratio would be: its specie holdings/(Bank of the United States notes held by NBP plus Bank of the United States notes held by state banks plus Bank of the United States deposits held by NBP plus Bank of the United States deposits held by state banks). The state banking sector's reserve ratio would be: its specie holdings/(state-bank notes held by NBP plus state-bank notes held by Bank of the United States or state banks plus state bank deposits held by NBP plus state bank deposits held by the Second Bank). However, these reserve ratios cannot be measured, as the data source does not break out the banknotes held by state banks into notes issued by the Bank of the United States and notes issued by state banks. As a default, I have reverted to the standard way of defining the reserve ratio.

Definition of bank-issued money: I have followed the literature by not including the Bank's long-distance interbranch drafts and its branch drafts in the definition of "money", due to data limitations; but, from a conceptual point of view, they should be. Interbranch drafts were interregional means of payment, sold at a premium and issued when the Bank purchased commercial bills of exchange; branch drafts were essentially notes issued by the branches in a different form. Gallatin (1831, pp. 29, 49) observed:

> Five dollar (branch) drafts, drawn by the branches on the Bank of the US, circulate at this moment in common with the usual five dollar notes. Similar (interbranch) drafts, varying in amount to suit the convenience of purchasers, are daily drawn by the bank on its offices, and by those offices on each other, or on the bank. Many of those drafts pass through several hands, and circulate several months, in distant parts of the country, before they are presented for payment. . . . the drafts from the bank on offices, and from these on the bank and on each other in actual circulation, should, as has been observed, be considered as making part of it (the "actual circulation"). The total annual amount of those drafts is about $24 m, and they are on an average paid within fifteen days after being issued. The amount always in circulation may therefore be estimated at $1 m, which, added to the $13 m of (nett) [*sic*] bank notes, gives $14 m for actual circulation of the bank.

At the time he wrote this, Gallatin was the president of a New York City bank, so he was very familiar with actual banking practices. The exclusion of the branch drafts means that the Second Bank reserve ratio was actually slightly lower than the estimates presented here (in 1830, for example, the Bank's reserve ratio was 44 percent without these liabilities included, and 42 percent with them, compared with the state banks' reserve ratio of 14 percent).

Data sources: All authors use the same source for the Second Bank. For the state bank data, the choice is between Van Fenstermaker and Gallatin. The Gallatin figures are 15 percent higher than the Van Fenstermaker figures for 1819, and 20 percent higher for 1829, although Van Fenstermaker's state bank headcount is much larger than Gallatin's. I use Van Fenstermaker's state bank data (adjusted for the percentage of reporting banks) because it is available on an annual basis, but I check my results against Gallatin's (from which I subtract federal deposits) in assessing trends over the decade. Gallatin's data show the same broad trends.

My specie sources are from Temin (1969, p 71). Other sources confirm the broad trends in Temin's data, namely that the specie stock was constant between 1822 and 1832. According to a Report of the Secretary of the Treasury on the State of the Finances for the year ending June 30, 1854, the national specie stock fell by \$3.5 m between 1821 and 1831; see 33rd Cong., 2d Sess. H. Rep., Ex. Doc. 3, p. 282m cited in Martin (1968, Appendix 2). Redish (2000, p. 231) cites a contemporary source that roughly equal (\$90 m) amounts of specie and bullion were imported and exported between 1820 and 1834.

Note

1 Officer's and Rutner's aggregates are not included in this literature review as they are based on a fundamentally different approach to the position of the Second Bank in the banking system. Rutner produced two versions of monetary aggregates, one in which Second Bank money was high-powered money, and one in which it was not. His aggregates cover only part of the Second Bank period, so were not discussed here for that reason.

References

Adams, DR (1978), *Finance and Enterprise in Early America*, University of Pennsylvania Press, Philadelphia.

Albion, RG (1965), *Square-Riggers on Schedule: The New York Sailing Packets to England, France, and the Cotton Ports*, Princeton University Press, Princeton.

Authors unknown (1832), "The Bank question," *The American Quarterly Review*, vol. 11.

Balogh, B (2009), *A Government Out of Sight*, Cambridge University Press, New York.

Banco de Mexico (2013), "The history of coins and banknotes in Mexico." Available online at www.banxico.org.mx/billetes-y-monedas/material-educativo/basico/%7B2FF1527B-0B07-AC7F-25B8-4950866E166A%7D.pdf (accessed December 1, 2015).

Bank for International Settlements Committee on Payment and Settlement Systems (2003), *The Role of Central Bank Money in Payment Systems*, Bank for International Settlements, Basel.

Bank of Kentucky (1836), *Letters of Correspondence Between the Bank of Kentucky and the Branch of the Bank of the State of Alabama at Decatur, Relative to the Reception and Final Rejection of Bank-Notes of the State of Alabama, at the Bank of Kentucky, in Louisville*, I. Van Nortwick, Decatur, Alabama.

Bodenhorn, H (2000), *A History of Banking in Antebellum America: Financial Markets and Economic Development in an Era of Nation-Building*, Cambridge University Press, Cambridge.

Bodenhorn, H (2003), *State Banking in Early America: A New Economic History*, Oxford University Press, Oxford.

Bordo, MD (2012), "Could the United States have had a better central bank? An historical counterfactual speculation," *Journal of Macroeconomics*, vol. 34, no. 3, pp. 597–607.

Brown, K (1942), "Stephen Girard, promoter of the Second Bank of the United States," *The Journal of Economic History*, vol. 11, no. 2, pp. 125–48.

Broz, J (1997), *International Origins of the Federal Reserve*, Cornell University Press, Ithaca.

Broz, J (1999), "Origins of the Federal Reserve System: International incentives and the domestic free-rider problem," *International Organization*, vol. 53, no. 1, pp. 39–70.

Bryan, AC (1899), *History of State Banking in Maryland*, Johns Hopkins University University Studies in Historical and Political Science, Johns Hopkins University Press, Baltimore.

Bureau of the Census (1960), *Historical Statistics of the U.S.*, US Bureau of the Census, Washington, DC.

Calomiris, CW and Schweikart, L (1991), "The Panic of 1857: Origins, transmission, and containment," *The Journal of Economic History*, vol. 51, no. 4, pp. 807–34.

Cameron, R (1967), *Banking in the Early Stages of Industrialization*, Oxford University Press, New York.

Capie, F, Goodhart, G, and Schnadt, N (1994), "The development of central banking," in *The Future of Central Banking: The Tercentenary Symposium of the Bank of England*, by F Capie, S Fischer, C Goodhart, and N Schnadt (eds.), Cambridge University Press, Cambridge, pp. 1–261.

Carothers, N (1967), *Fractional Money: A History of the Small Coins and Fractional Paper Currency of the United States*, Augustus M. Kelly, New York.

Carstenen, V (1963), *The Public Lands: Studies in the History of the Public Domain*, University of Wisconsin Press, Madison.

Carter, S, Gartner, S, Haines, M, Olmstead, A, Sutch, R, and Wright, G (eds.) (2006), *Historical Statistics of the United States Millennial Edition Online*, Cambridge University Press, Cambridge.

Catterall, R (1902), *The Second Bank of the United States*, University of Chicago Press, Chicago.

Dallas, G (1871), *Life and Writings of Alexander James Dallas*, JB Lippincott & Co., Philadelphia.

Dewey, DR (1903), *Financial History of the United States*, Longmans, Green, and Co., London.

Dewey, DR (1910a), *The Second United States Bank*, Government Printing Office, Washington, DC.

Dewey, DR (1910b), *State Banking before the Civil War*, Government Printing Office, Washington, DC.

Ellis, RE (2007), *Aggressive Nationalism:* McCulloch v. Maryland *and the Foundation of Federal Authority in the Young Republic*, Oxford University Press, Oxford.

Engerman, SL (1970), "A note on the economic consequences of the Second Bank of the United States," *Journal of Political Economy*, vol. 78, no. 4, pp. 725–8.

Freyer, T (1976), "Negotiable instruments and the federal courts in Antebellum American Business," *Business History Review*, vol. 50, pp. 435–55.

Gallatin, A (1831), *Considerations on the Currency and Banking System*, Carey and Lea, Philadelphia.

Gibson, C (1998), *Population of the 100 Largest Cities and other Urban Places in the United States, 1790–1990*, U.S. Bureau of the Census, Washington, DC.

Gouge, WM (1833/1968), *A Short History of Paper Money and Banking in the United States*, Augustus M. Kelley, New York.

Govan, TP (1959), *Nicholas Biddle: Nationalist and Public Banker, 1786–1844*, University of Chicago Press, Chicago.

Gudmestad, R (2011), *Steamboats and the Rise of the Cotton Kingdom*, Louisiana State University Press, Baton Rouge.

Hammond, B (1957), *Banks and Politics in America from the Revolution to the Civil War*, Princeton University Press, Princeton.

Hidy, R (1944), "The House of Baring and the Second Bank of the United States, 1826–1836," *The Pennsylvania Magazine of History and Biography*, vol. 68, pp. 269–85.

Highfield, RA, O'Hara, M, and Wood, JH (1991), "Public ends, private means: Central banking and the profit motive, 1823–1832," *Journal of Monetary Economics*, vol. 28, pp. 287–322.

Holdsworth, J (1910), *The First Bank of the United States*, Government Printing Office, Washington, DC.

Homer, S and Sylla, R (1991), *A History of Interest Rates*, Rutgers University Press, New Brunswick.

Hunter, LC (1949), *Steamboats on the Western Rivers: An Economic and Technological History*, Harvard University Press, Cambridge, MA.

Irigoin, A (2009), "The end of a Silver Era: The consequences of the breakdown of the Spanish peso standard in China and the United States, 1780s–1850s," *Journal of World History*, vol. 20, no. 2, pp. 207–44.

Kagin, DH (1984), "Monetary aspects of the Treasury notes of the War of 1812," *Journal of Economic History*, vol. 44, no. 1, pp. 69–88.

Knodell, J (1998), "The demise of central banking and the domestic exchanges: Evidence from Antebellum Ohio," *Journal of Economic History*, vol. 58, no. 3, pp. 714–31.

Knodell, J (2003), "Profit and duty in the Second Bank of the United States' exchange operations," *Financial History Review*, vol. 10, pp. 5–30.

Knodell, J (2006), "Rethinking the Jacksonian Economy: The impact of the 1832 bank veto on commercial banking," *Journal of Economic History*, vol. 66, no. 3, pp. 541–74.

Krooss, H (1967), "Financial institutions," in David T Gilchrist (ed.) *The Growth of the Seaport Cities, 1790–1825*, University of Virginia, Charlottesville, pp. 104–38.

Laughlin, JL (1901), *The History of Bimetallism in the United States*, D Appleton and Co., New York.

McGrane, RG (1919), *The Correspondence of Nicholas Biddle Dealing with National Affairs, 1807–1844*, Houghton Mifflin Co., Boston.

Martin, DA (1968), "Bimetallism in the United States before 1850," *Journal of Political Economy*, vol. 76, no. 3, pp. 428–42.

Martin, DA (1977), "The changing role of foreign money in the United States, 1782–1857," *Journal of Economic History*, vol. 37, no. 4, pp. 1009–27.

Martin, J (1969), *Martin's History of the Boston Stock and Money Markets*, Greenwood Press, New York.

Matthews, PW (1921), *The Bankers' Clearing House: What It Is and What It Does*, Sir Isaac Pitman & Sons, London.

Meerman, J (1961), *Nicholas Biddle on Central Banking*. Ph.D. thesis, University of Chicago.

Meyer, DR (2003), *The Roots of American Industrialization*, Johns Hopkins University Press, Baltimore.

Miller, CA (1991), *The United States Army Logistics Complex, 1818–1845: A Case Study of the Northern Frontier*. Ph.D. thesis, Syracuse University.

Mooney, CC (1974), *William H. Crawford, 1772–1834*, University Press of Kentucky, Lexington.

Officer, L (1996), *Between the Dollar-Sterling Gold Points: Exchange Rates, Parity, and Market Behavior*, Cambridge University Press, Cambridge.

Officer, LH (2002), "The U.S. Specie Standard, 1792–1932: Some monetarist arithmetic," *Explorations in Economic History*, vol. 39, pp. 113–53.

Parsons, B (1977), *British Trade Credit and American Bank Credit: Some Aspects of Economic Fluctuations in the United States, 1815–1840*, Arno Press, New York.

Payne, PL and Davis, LE (1956), *Savings Bank of Baltimore, 1818–1866: A Historical and Analytical Study*, Johns Hopkins University Press, Baltimore.

Perkins, EJ (1975), *Financing Anglo-American Trade: The House of Brown, 1800–1880*, Harvard University Press, Cambridge, MA.

Perkins, EJ (1994), *American Public Finance and Financial Services, 1700–1815*, Ohio State University Press, Columbus.

Phillips, JB (1900), *Methods of Keeping the Public Money of the United States*, The Inland Press, Ann Arbor.

Phillips, RJ (ed.) (2013), *U.S. Credit and Payments, 1800–1935, Vol. 4, Domestic Exchanges,* Pickering & Chatto, London.

Phillips, RJ (2013), *US Credit and Payments, 1800–1935*, Pickering & Chatto, London.

Pred, AR (1973), *Urban Growth and the Circulation of Information: The United States System of Cities, 1790–1840*, Harvard University Press, Cambridge, MA.

Prucha, FP (1953), *Broadax and Bayonet: The Role of the United States Army in the Development of the Northwest, 1815–1860*, The State Historical Society of Wisconsin, Madison.

Prucha, FP (1969), *The Sword of the Republic: The United States Army on the Frontier, 1783–1846*, The Macmillan Co., London.

Redish, A (2000), *Bimetallism: An Economic and Historical Analysis*, Cambridge University Press, Cambridge.

Redlich, F (1951/1968), *The Molding of American Banking: Men and Ideas*, Johnson Reprint Corporation, New York.

Rockoff, H (2006), "Monetary statistics before the National Banking Era" and Table Cj7-21, in Carter, S, Gartner, S, Haines, M, Olmstead, A, Sutch, R, and Wright, G (eds.), *Historical Statistics of the United States, Millennial Edition Online*, Cambridge University Press, Cambridge, pp. 3-598–3-600.

Rohrbough, M (1990), *The Land Office Business: The Settlement and Administration of American Public Lands, 1789–1837*, Wadworth Publishing, Belmont, California.

Rolnick, AJ and Weber, WE (1986), "Gresham's Law or Gresham's Fallacy?," *Journal of Political Economy*, vol. 94, no. 1, pp. 185–99.

Rothman, S (2005), *Slave Country: American Expansion and the Origins of the Deep South*, Harvard University Press, Cambridge, MA.

Rutner, JL (1974), *Money in the Antebellum Economy: Its Composition, Relation to Income, and Its Determinants.* Ph.D. thesis, University of Chicago.

Smith, WB (1953), *Economic Aspects of The Second Bank of the United States*, Harvard University Press, Cambridge, MA.

Sylla, R (2012), "U.S. debt Has always Been different!," in *Is U.S. Government Debt Different?*, Allen, F, Gelpern, A, Mooney, C, and Skeel, D (eds.), FIC Press, Philadelphia, pp. 1–11.

Sylla, R, Legler, J, and Wallis, J (1987), "Banks and state public finance in the new republic: The United States, 1790–1860," *Journal of Economic History*, vol. 47, no. 2, pp. 391–403.

Taus, E (1943), *Central Banking Functions of the U.S. Treasury, 1789–1941*, Columbia University Press, New York.

Temin, P (1969), *The Jacksonian Economy*, WW Norton, New York.

Thornton, H (1802/1965), *An Enquiry into the Nature and Effects of the Paper Credit of Great Britain*, Augustus M. Kelley, New York.

Timberlake, RH (1961), "The Specie Standard and central banking in the United States before 1860," *Journal of Economic History*, vol. 21, September, pp. 318–41.

Timberlake, RH (1978), *The Origins of Central Banking in the United States*, Harvard University Press, MA.

Van Fenstermaker, J (1965), *The Development of American Commercial Banking, 1782–1837*, Bureau of Economic and Business Research, Kent State University, Kent, OH.

Wallis, JJ (2001), "What caused the Crisis of 1839?," *NBER Working Paper Series on Historical Factors in Long Run Growth*, National Bureau of Economic Research, Cambridge, UK.

Walters, R (1945), "The origins of the Second Bank of the United States," *Journal of Political Economy*, vol. 53, pp. 115–31.

Weber, WE (2006), "Early state banks in the United States: How many were there and when did they exist?," *Journal of Economic History*, vol. 66, no. 2, pp. 433–55.

Weber, WE (2008), *Balance sheets for U.S. Antebellum State Banks*, Research Department, Federal Reserve Bank of Minneapolis. Available online at http://cdm16030.contentdm. oclc.org/cdm/about/collection/p16030coll5 (accessed October 14, 2013).

Weber, WE (2011), "Census of state banks." Available online at www.minneapolisfed.org/ research/economists/wewproj.cfm#censusstate (accessed October 8, 2013).

Wettereau, JO (1942), "Branches of the First Bank of the United States," *Journal of Economic History*, vol. 2, pp. 66–100.

Wettereau, J (1985), *Statistical Records of the First Bank of the U.S.*, Garland Publishing, New York.

White, LD (1951), *The Jeffersonians: A Study in Administrative History, 1801–1829*, The Macmillan Co., New York.

Wilburn, JA (1967), *Biddle's Bank: The Crucial Years*, Columbia University Press, New York.

Willett, TD (1968), "International specie flows and American monetary stability," *Journal of Economic History*, vol. 28, no. 1, pp. 28–49.

Wooster, R (2009), *The American Military Frontiers: The United States Army in the West, 1783–1900*, University of New Mexico Press, Albuquerque.

Index

Page number in italics refer to figures and tables

aggregates *see* banking aggregates
Albany (New York state) 31, 65–6
Alexander Brown and Sons 124
Anglo-American trade 84
Astor, John Jacob 10
Augusta (Georgia) 30, 65

Balogh, B 4, 25
Baltimore banking panic (1834) 123–5
Baltimore branch 73, 90, 96, 104–5, 110,
  119, 121, 124, 136, 139, 150,
  151–2, 158
Bank for International Settlements 131
Bank of America 102, 104, 107
Bank of Augusta 102
Bank of Cape Fear 167
Bank of Kentucky 131–2
Bank of Maryland 123–4, 135–6
Bank of Newbern 132, 167
Bank of Pennsylvania 107
Bank of Philadelphia 124, 136
Bank of Steubenville (Ohio) 23
Bank of the State of Alabama 131
Bank of the State of Georgia 22, 65
Bank of the United States *see* Second Bank
  of the United States
Bank of the United States of Pennsylvania
  131
Bank of the United States v. Smith (1817) 94
Bank of the United States v. Weisiger
  (1829) 94
banking aggregates *176*, 177–80
banknotes 56–64, 101–6
Baring Brothers 84, 85, 86, 87
Beers & Bunnell 154

Biddle, Charles 136
Biddle, Nicholas 1, 2, 3, 4–5, 29, 64, 65,
  66, 69, 72, 74, 85, 86, 89–90, 92, 93,
  95, 96–7, 99, 105–7, 110, 111, 113, 117,
  118–23, 133, 136, 140–1, 147, 148,
  149–50, 154–5, 157–8, 159
Biers, Booth, & St John 152–3
bills of exchange 70–1, 87–8, 93
bimetallic system 138
Bordo, MD 3, 5, 134
Boston branch 31–2, 85, 90, 119, 146, 159
Brown, Alexander 86
Brown Brothers (House of Brown) 83–4,
  85, 86, 88, 95, 96

Calhoun, John 6, 12
Capie, F 156
Carothers, N 126, 136
Cass, Lewis 23–4
Catterall, R 1–2, 28
central banks 1, 2–3, 5–6, 49, 99, 120, 121,
  131, 156, 158
Charleston branch 14, 71
Cheves, Langdon 14, 71
Chillicothe branch (Ohio) 20, 23–4
Cincinnati branch 20, 27, 73, 79, 94, 159
Clay, Henry 10
Coinage Act (1792) 138
Commercial and Farmers Bank of
  Baltimore 7
Crawford, William 12, 15, 18, 19, 21–2,
  27, 29–30, 65, 126
crisis of 1825–1826 84, 118–21, 125,
  143–4, 157
customs revenue 17

Dallas, Alexander James 7–10
Department of Indian Affairs 17
Dewey, DR 6, 28
discounting 94
District of Columbia *see* Washington
domestic exchange operations 72–82, 90–2
dual system *see* state banks

exchange operations *see* domestic exchange
   operations, foreign exchange operations
exchange rates 174–5

Fayetteville branch (North Carolina) 27,
   31, 90
Federal Reserve 1, 2, 3, 65
Federalists 24
financial crisis (2007–2008) 1
First Bank of the United States 5, 34, 39, 97
foreign exchange operations 82–8, 92, 135

Gallatin, Albert 11, 25, 94, 105, 131, 133,
   137, 179, 180
General Land Office 17
Girard, Stephen 10
Girard Bank 10, 124, 136, 139, 153
gold market 144, *145*
Gouge, William 9
Govan, TP 96, 117

Hale & Davidson 152, 153
Highfield, RA 3
House of Brown *see* Brown Brothers
Hunter, LC 93

Ingham, Samuel D 91, 92, 97

Jackson, Andrew 1, 65
Jefferson administration 6
Jones, William 12, 14, 18–19, 25, 29, 30,
   72, 146–7

Kimball, Leonard 151

"lender of last resort" role 1, 3, 5, 49–56,
   117, 118, 121–5, 156, 157
Lenox, Robert 85, 122, 147
Lewis Clapier 152
Lexington branch (Kentucky) 53, 90, 110,
   112
Lloyd, James 32
London Clearing House 104
Louisville branch (Kentucky) 26, 30, 53,
   63–4, 79, 103, 149, 159, 174

Madison, James 10
Madison administration 64
Manhattan Company 104
Marine and Fire Insurance Bank of
   Savannah 101
McCulloch v. Maryland (1819) 38
Mechanics' Bank of New York 62, *63*,
   104
Meerman, J 2–3, 117, 118, 133
Mobile branch 90
Monongahela Bank of Brownsville 101

Nashville branch 30–1, 34, 74, 90
Natchez branch 90
New England 7
New Orleans branch 32, 69, 88–90, 92,
   140, 149–50, 151
New York City branch 26, 72, 73, 90, 104,
   105, 107, 118, 119, 120, 151
Niles' Weekly Register 67, 68, 124, 136
Norfolk branch (Virginia) 53

Officer, LH 5, 100, 131, 132, 155, 180

Panic of 1819 42, 47, 67, 165
Panic of 1907 1
Parish, David 10
Patterson, William 86, 96
Perkins, EJ 24, 84, 95, 96
Perkins, Thomas 159
Philadelphia branch 73, 81, 90, 91, 106,
   107
Philadelphia head office 14, 73, 89, 107,
   110, 149–51, 158
Pittsburgh branch 20, 21, 67
Planters' Bank 22, 132
Post Office Department 92
Providence branch (Rhode Island) 95
Prucha, FP 25–6

Quartermaster General Department 17

Redlich, F 2, 121–2, 131
Richmond branch (Virginia) 90, 112
Rolnick, AJ 136
Rush, Richard 29, 32, 33, 91, 92
Rutner, JL 100, 132, 134–5, 137, 180

S & J Nevins & Co 152
Sanford Report (1830) 126–7
Savannah branch 22, 65, 71, 90, 110, 111,
   123, 132, 158
Savings Bank of Baltimore 123, 124, 136

Second Bank of the United States:
    branches 29–65; charter 9–12; reforms
    12–15
silver market 141–4, *145*, *146*
Smith, WB 2, 5
Spanish coins 126, 139–40
specie market 138–53
St. Louis branch 32, 66, 73 149
St. Stephen's Bank (Tombeckbe, Alabama) 22
State Bank of North Carolina 21, 167
state banks 20, 35–64, 65; balance sheets
    100–4, *130*; banking offices 165–9
sterling 83–9, 92, 95, 96, 114–15, *116*,
    135, 152

Temin, Peter 3, 118, 135, 179, 180
Thomas Biddle & Co. 87, 88, 153

Thompson, Edward 151
Thornton, H 104
Timberlake, RH 3

Union Bank of Baltimore 104, 135
US Mint 138, 146, 149
Utica branch (New York state) 31, 48,
    65–6

Van Fenstermaker, J 3, 67, 131, 132, 165,
    179, 180

War of 1812 9, 12, 15, *16*, 25
Washington (DC) branch 29, 90, 91
Weber, WE 136, 165, 166, 167
West, Charles S 97
White, John Campbell 124

Printed in the United States
by Baker & Taylor Publisher Services